ALSO BY GINGER STRAND

Flight: A Novel

INVENTING NIAGARA

GINGER STRAND

Beauty,
POWER,
AND Lies

Simon & Schuster Paperbacks

New York   London   Toronto   Sydney

Simon & Schuster Paperbacks
A Division of Simon & Schuster, Inc.
1230 Avenue of the Americas
New York, NY 10020

First Simon & Schuster trade paperback edition May 2009

SIMON & SCHUSTER PAPERBACKS and colophon are registered trademarks
of Simon & Schuster, Inc.

For information about special discounts for bulk purchases,
please contact Simon & Schuster Special Sales at
1-866-506-1949 or business@simonandschuster.com

The Simon & Schuster Speakers Bureau can bring authors
to your live event. For more information or to book an event
contact the Simon & Schuster Speakers Bureau at
1-866-248-3049 or visit our website at www.simonspeakers.com.

Designed by Nancy Singer

Manufactured in the United States of America

10 9 8 7 6 5 4 3 2 1

The Library of Congress has cataloged the hardcover edition as follows:
Strand, Ginger Gail.
    Inventing Niagara: beauty, power, and lies/by Ginger Strand.
        p.   cm.
    1. Niagara Falls (N.Y. and Ont.)—Social life and customs.   2. Niagara Falls
(N.Y. and Ont.)—History.   3. Niagara Falls (N.Y. and Ont.)—Description and
travel.   4. Tourism—Niagara Falls (N.Y. and Ont.)—History.   5. Strand, Ginger
Gail—Travel—Niagara Falls (N.Y. and Ont.).   I. Title.
F127.N8S825   2008
304.209713'39—dc22   2007040290
ISBN-13:   978-1-4165-4656-6
ISBN-10:   1-4165-4656-1
ISBN-13:   978-1-4165-4657-3 (pbk)
ISBN-10:   1-4165-4657-X (pbk)

Material in this book has appeared previously in *The Believer, Orion,* and the anthology
The Future of Nature.

Art Credits: Images in title *Niagara* from left to right: © Lester Lefkowitz/Corbis; ©
Johansen Krause/Archivo Iconografico, SA/Corbis; © Galen Rowell/Corbis; © iStock-
Photo.com/Dra Schwartz; © Bettmann/Corbis; Courtesy Library of Congress; © Reu-
ters/Corbis. Front cover photograph of the *Maid of the Mist* © Photodisc Photography/
Veer. Full panoramic photograph of Niagara Falls © L. Clarke/Corbis.

*For the people of the Niagara region.
Their stories are the voice of the landscape;
I was privileged to share them.*

Contents

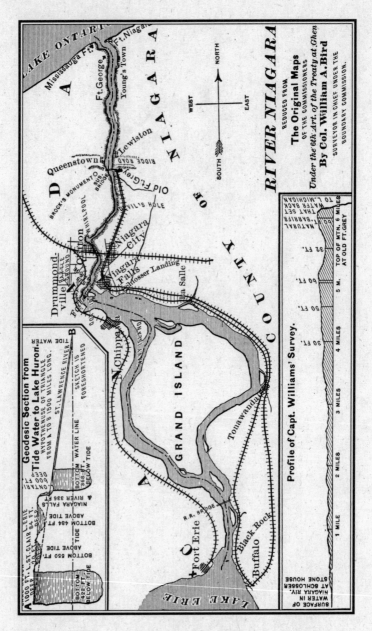

The Niagara region. From George Holley, *The Falls of Niagara with Supplementary Chapters on Other Famous Cataracts of the World* (A. C. Armstrong, 1883). Courtesy of the Niagara Falls Public Library, Niagara Falls, N.Y.

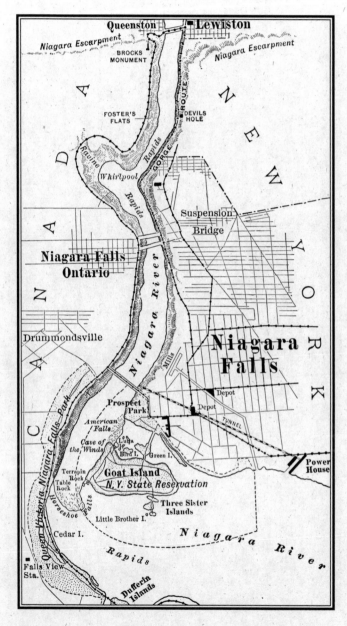

"Scenic Niagara." From Peter A. Porter, *Guide, Niagara* (The Matthews-Northrup Works, c. 1901). Courtesy of the Niagara Falls Public Library, Niagara Falls, N.Y.

DOWN THE MEMORY HOLE

I WENT TO NIAGARA because I wanted to laugh at it. I was a college student, and I considered the Falls no more than a kitschy spectacle, a chance to soak in a heart-shaped Jacuzzi and get some really awful souvenirs for my irony-adoring pals. My college boyfriend and I pulled into the parking lot of the tackiest motel we could find and prepared our world-weary smirks. We had quarters for the vibrating bed, a cheap camera to document our glee. And then we got out of the car. To this day, I remember the stationary blast of sound that filled the air, even though the Falls were nowhere in sight. In spite of myself, I was impressed.

Years later, I went back. I had moved from the Midwest to the East Coast, moved on from the college boyfriend and cycled through a series of jobs—proofreader, box-office manager, teacher, copywriter—to see which might leave me time to finish the novel that was slinking around in my head. I found myself with two weeks open in my calendar, and I suggested to my boyfriend, Bob, that we rent a car and take a road trip around New York looking at hydroinfrastructure.

I love hydroinfrastructure—water tunnels, reservoirs, canals, sewers, aqueducts—I find all of it inspiring, a testament to humanity's ability to come together in the interest of higher ideals like cold drinks and hot showers. Luckily, Bob doesn't mind indulging my arcane obsessions—he's a bit of a hydrogeek himself, so off we went, using a road map to pinpoint hydro hotspots. We started off in the Catskills, visiting New York City's water supply. Then we drove north to the Erie Canal—still, I am happy to report, open for business, though it's largely tourist cruises and pleasure boats today. Following the Erie Canal, we wound up, as did its earliest passengers, at Niagara Falls. And there we visited the Adam Beck Power Plant, on the Canadian side. The Beck plant offers a tour. They take you inside through a tunnel that smells of ozone and let you look through glass windows at giant, whirring generators while the guide unfurls the mysteries of turbines and transformers for the rapt crowd. It was on this tour that I first heard about the waterfall's hours of operation—it gets turned up during the days in summer for the tourists, and turned down at night so it can generate more power. Go at 7 A.M., the guide suggested, and watch the water being dialed up. In other words, Niagara Falls, if not turned off and on like a faucet, is turned up and down like a fancy massaging showerhead. I was taking notes—I always take notes on vacation; otherwise, how do you remember stuff?—but at that point I stopped scribbling and just grinned like a maniacal toddler.

Every American feels something for Niagara Falls, but from that point on, I was obsessed. I began to visit Niagara whenever I had an opportunity. I stayed in hotels on both sides, from Ontario's shiny new Radisson to New York's decrepit Travelodge. I got up on cold mornings to run along the riverfront and stayed up on warm nights to lose at blackjack. I interviewed local historians and park workers and engineers. I got the phone number of a Canadian Mountie. I traced the path of the explorer La Salle as he and his band of idiots toiled up the Niagara Escarpment and built the first European ship on the upper Great Lakes, guarding the work site at night because angry Indians were trying to burn "the big canoe." I bought gas and cigarettes from Smokin Joes Trading Post on the Tuscarora Reservation. I don't smoke, but they were a dollar a pack.

I hung around the public library bugging the librarians, until, exasperated, they left me locked in for the evening. I stayed in a trailer campground in Canada and tromped all over Brock's Monument, searching for the cenotaph of the war hero's horse. I was self-appointed inspector of wax museums, halls of fame, haunted houses, historical societies, scenic tunnels, and the Evel Knievel Museum and Pawn Shop, surveyor of aquariums, water parks and boat rides. And of course, I spent hours gazing at falling water, following the sheets of liquid that hold their shape and then disintegrate, the hypnotic contortions of the mist, the bubbling, gymnastic upper rapids and the frothy race of the lower, all of it creating a fuzzy, wraithlike picture, because Niagara, like Mount Everest or the Mississippi River, is one of those places with so many meanings layered onto it, it's almost hard to see. The Greeks had a god named Proteus, who, if you grabbed him, started endlessly changing shape—a serpent, an eagle, a lion—in the hope you would startle and let go. That's Niagara, always in motion, always transforming, and never just what it seems. A seal. A salmon. A buffalo. A two-headed calf, a two-legged dog. A baby with three ears.

Case in point: Niagara Falls. Three entities go by that name. Two are towns, one in New York State, one in Ontario. Niagara Falls, New York, is by general agreement a mess. The river above the Falls is lined with factories, many of them shuttered. Almost half the population and more than half the jobs have decamped since 1950, and it shows. Housing stock is crumbling, and the center city is a study in urban decay: empty lots, boarded-up businesses, foreclosure signs. The roads are potholed, the sidewalks cracked. Someone's usually pushing a shopping cart down the street. The area around the Falls is a jumble of failed attempts at urban renewal—a bankrupt mall, a foreclosed Native American museum, a shoddy row of cheap attractions, handmade signs and pushcarts selling samosas and souvenir sweatshirts. If you can figure out which way the riverfront is, you'll notice the view is blocked by a giant parking ramp and a smattering of hotels, not fancy ones, but the kind that try to temper their bland mediocrity with the word "inn." Days Inn. Comfort Inn. Quality Inn.

The vast majority of American tourists, faced with this national embarrassment, head straight for the border. Things are different in Niagara Falls, Ontario. Along their riverfront, the Canadians have made parkland: a strip of violently landscaped formal gardens offering access to Canada's classic panoramas and regularly spaced snack stands. Above the park, perched on a steep ridge, is an area about ten blocks square, packed solid with hotels, casinos, souvenir shops, observation towers and franchise restaurants. There, on Clifton Hill—"Niagara's street of FUN!"—you're hit with a loud, lurid onslaught of over forty attractions. You have the IMAX Theatre, the Guinness World Records Museum, Ripley's Believe It or Not! Museum, the Movieland Wax Museum, the Niagara SkyWheel, Dinosaur Park Mini Putt Golf and Ghostblasters, a haunted house merged with a laser tag game. The ghosts spook you and you shoot them.

The two Niagaras wink at one another across the gorge, the contrapuntal faces of globalism: on the Canadian side, the monotony of our worldwide monoculture, the proliferation of malls and brands and franchises proclaiming globalism's intent to make every town look the same, from Benares to Boise. The soul-sapping boredom of it all is reflected in its urgent spawning of ever-more-extreme cheap thrills. Meanwhile, across the river in America, you see globalism's economic underbelly: crumbling row houses, unemployment offices, and defunct factories parked on EPA-designated brownfields, the sediment of a century's toxic runoff. Rising up from the desolation is the one shiny thing on the New York side's skyline, the new Seneca Niagara Casino, a hopeful mirage where grannies, suburbanites and cash-strapped locals—two-thirds of whom subsist on public assistance—unload lives of quiet desperation, quarter by quarter, into the slots.

Poised between these two worlds, oblivious, inexorable, is the third Niagara Falls: the waterfall. Hundreds of millions of gallons plunge every minute over a 176-foot ledge, as Lakes Superior, Michigan, Huron and Erie—one-fifth of the world's freshwater—drain into Lake Ontario and out to sea. It roars, day in, day out, untouchable and untouched by the incursions around it. Nothing—not the tacky plastic fun park of Canada's family heaven nor the hard-at-the-heels squalor of New York's economic hell—can ruin one of the world's prime natural wonders. Or so we're told.

Guidebooks today are quick to deride Niagaras one and two, but they are unanimous in declaring the waterfall splendid. "Nearly everyone who sees Niagara Falls is struck by the wonder of it," proclaims Fodor's. The authors describe the tawdry surroundings, but assure the reader that "the astounding beauty of the Falls remains undiminished, and unending." Undiminished indeed: the waterfall is diminished by anywhere from one-half to three-quarters, depending on the season and time of day. Some guidebooks admit this, but they tell you not to worry. The Lonely Planet guide cites the stats on diversion, but assures us "the falls themselves are amazing." Nature, it seems, can't be harmed by a few miles of kitsch, or the diversion of a little water.

This situation is not new. A hundred and fifty years ago, guidebooks also assured visitors that the tacky tourist carnival flanking the Falls did not impinge on their glory. The great wonder, it's true, was surrounded by Chinese pagodas, dancing pavilions, camera obscuras, Indian bazaars, and sideshows featuring counting pigs and a man named Jo-Jo the Dog-Faced Boy. This carnival, every guidebook assured you, would ruin your experience of the Falls. But if you ignored it, if you went instead to the correct places and gave yourself up to the contemplation of canonized vistas, your experience of Niagara would be sublime. Writers, artists and intellectuals joined guidebook authors in directing visitors' steps and sentiments away from the tacky and toward the transcendent. Ever since its debut as America's tourist icon, Niagara has built a reputation that depends on separating its natural wonder from the artificial accretions around it.

But here's what I learned at Niagara: the distinction is false. Niagara Falls as a natural wonder does not exist anymore. Manicured, repaired, landscaped and artificially lit, dangerous overhangs dynamited off and water flow managed to suit the tourist schedule, the Falls are more a monument to man's meddling than to nature's strength. In fact, they are a study in self-delusion: we visit them to encounter something real, then observe them through fake Indian tales, audio tours and IMAX films. We consider them a symbol of

American manifest destiny, yet we share them politely with Canada. We hold them up as an example of unconquerable nature even as we applaud the daredevils and power-brokers who conquer them. And we congratulate ourselves for preserving nature's beauty in an ecosystem that, beneath its shimmering emerald surface, reflects our own ugly ability to destroy. On every level, Niagara Falls is a monument to the ways America falsifies its relationship to nature, reshaping its contours, redirecting its force, claiming to submit to its will while imposing our own upon it.

My purpose in going to Niagara was to think about nature, and I ended up obsessed with human things. The suicide hotline phones dotting the rapids. The senior housing complex with views of Love Canal. The diner across from the public library called The Why. The wax museum with a room dedicated to the three women who embody the ideal feminine: Mother Teresa, Princess Di and Julia Roberts. The Cave of the Winds—not a cave, but a tunnel blasted out of the rock and a boardwalk taking you into the waterfall's spray. The giant power tunnel intakes, gleaming like outsized radiators, guarding the underwater voids where two scuba divers were sucked to the grating by water entering the tunnels and held there until they drowned.

    And the landfills. Niagara's landfills are spectacular: mountains of made land, rising out of the earth, gently breathing their methane, almost beautiful in their grassy silence. One of them is so large it looms in the distance from the highway exit, and as you drive from Wal-Mart to the outlet mall, the landfill hulks along in the background, a constant companion. The people of Niagara Falls must unconsciously look for it, the way the Swiss glance up at the Matterhorn, or the citizens of Portland, Oregon, locate Mount Hood: *Where's the mountain? There it is. I'm home.*

    There's a standard set of stories about Niagara, recounted in tourist guidebooks and scholarly tomes, and trotted out every few years in an educational documentary that begins and ends with sweeping helicopter shots of falling water. Meanwhile, much of the real story of America's best-known landscape goes untold, and as I began to trace it, I often felt like I was entering Bizzaro World. From a French fur trader with an iron hand to the Army Corps of Engineers reshaping the riverbed, Indian casinos built on brownfields to 280,000 radioactive mice buried at the Falls, many of Niagara's stories are like the drums secreted in its landfills: shoved out of sight, covered over to look presentable, and driven by with glazed eyes, a quick flick of the radio volume. *Oh that—just drive around it.* Once, when I was asking too many unanswerable questions in the Local History section of the Niagara Falls Public Library, librarian Maureen Fennie held up a hand to stop me. "They've put it all down the memory hole," she told me, "and they're not letting it out."

This book documents an obsession. An obsession with the things Niagara has been made to mean throughout the relatively short time it has lived with people—nature, America, power, beauty, death. An obsession with the ways in which the history of Niagara Falls is a history of falsification, prevarication and omission. An obsession with going down the memory hole and retrieving what's buried there.

Why did I become obsessed with Niagara Falls? People ask me that all the time. Niagara has a lot to tell us about nature, but while I care deeply about the environment, I have never been what you call a nature-lover. I never know what kind of tree or bird I'm looking at, woods and their denizens make me nervous, and I don't like being cold, damp, tired or too far from a person with a cocktail shaker. Given a choice between an exhibit of German Expressionist paintings and a hike up some soul-stirring hill, I'll take the thick brush strokes and green faces every time. My college boyfriend—the same one who took me to Niagara—once refused to speak to me for a full day because I declined to hike in the Rockies with him and instead read a Russian novel in the car. "There are things you can't read in books," he fumed, and I remember really meaning it when I said, "Like what?"

But I learned a lot at Niagara, about the natural world and about that human-made idea, "nature." My interest was piqued at first, I think, because I grew up in Michigan, another once-storied, now-shabby corner of the Rust Belt where nature was both monarch and slave. Since 1999, I have lived in Lower Manhattan, and that resonates with Niagara too; often as I walk from my home to the nearest bookstore in search of some account of canal building or the fur trade, I pass the carnivalesque strip of souvenir stands, camera-toting tourists and information booths along the edge of what they now call Ground Zero and I think about how meaning gets layered onto a place.

Mostly I became obsessed with Niagara because I am an American, and although it sits mainly in Canada, Niagara Falls has a lot to tell us about America. Its story is a primer of American history—Indian treaties, conflicts with Britain, the Civil War, the industrial age, the ad age, two world wars, one cold war, environmentalism, globalism. For many years, Niagara was nature, and America was nature's nation. And then the Falls came to stand for power, just as America began discovering its own. It was industry during the rise of industrial America and capital of kitsch when American culture doubled over on itself and turned pop quotation into art. It was America to the European, freedom to the enslaved, opportunity to the impoverished and downfall to the ambitious and proud. Niagara is constantly reinvented, and if nations can be said to have national talents, America's is self-invention. It's what makes people like W. E. B. Du Bois and Marilyn Monroe—two Niagara fans—possible, and it's also what gave us slavery, the Bomb and Love Canal—all things that unfolded, in part, at the Falls. It's all too easy, history reminds us, for self-invention to slip into self-delusion. Put on an act for long enough and it's hard to remember what's real.

Rather than love, than money, than fame, give me truth. When General Leslie Groves, manager of the Manhattan Project, witnessed the explosion of the world's first atomic bomb at Alamogordo, he thought of Blondin crossing the Falls on a tightrope. Why did he think of America's most famous natural wonder as he experienced humanity's violent mastery of nature? Niagara overflows with meaning. The waterfall is the landscape. But the waterfall is also the Bomb. The waterfall is Marilyn, both siren and machine. The waterfall is the light, but at the Cave of the Winds, to see it you pass through darkness. The memory hole feels like a dark cavern, but light that makes us close our eyes is darkness to us. I went into the waterfall and the spray made me blind. I went to the waterfall because I wished, deliberately, to see.

One

WHITE MAN'S FANCY,
RED MAN'S FACT

MOST NIAGARA BOOKS BEGIN in the clear light of geology: sunlight glinting off glaciers, water chiseling a gorge. We'll start in the half-light of myth.

A long time ago, the Indians who lived at Niagara Falls were suffering a devastating plague. People were dying in droves. Hoping to end the carnage, they made sacrifices to the gods. They began with fruits, flowers, the choicest morsels from the harvest. They sent meats and tobacco in canoes over the Falls. Nothing appeased the angry gods. Finally, they decided to sacrifice the most beautiful young maiden in the village. The girl, Lelawala, was packed into a white canoe with a cornucopia of other tasty treats and sent crashing down to her doom. But wait! Instead of hitting the water below, she was caught by the powerful Thunder Beings who live behind the waterfall. There, she learned the cause of the deadly plague that was killing her kinsfolk: a noxious-breathed serpent was poisoning the water. She returned to her village with the news that they must vacate the toxic town. They packed up and left, but the giant snake pursued them, so village warriors—with some help from the Thunder God—killed it. Its body, squirming in its death throes, formed the brink of the Horseshoe Fall.

This "legend" used to be told by the recorded audio on the *Maid of the Mist* tour boats as they nosed their way into the spray below the Falls. It appeared in guidebooks, picture books and regional histories. It found its way into movies about the Falls and was depicted on T-shirts, coffee mugs and shot glasses. To this day it's plastered all over the Web, and postcards showing the Maid are still a staple of Niagara souvenir stands. They usually show a well-formed Indian maiden, often topless, standing up in a canoe as it plunges over the brink. She looks noble and nubile at the same time. In some early versions, the Indian maiden forms a diptych with a naked water sprite writhing in the misty water, apparently meant to personify the Falls. The pair is labeled "White man's fancy; red man's fact."

By 1996, Native Americans had had enough of white man's fancy passing for red man's fact. The region's Senecas, they pointed out, had never practiced human sacrifice. Nor had any of the Iroquois Confederacy's six nations, who call themselves the Haudenosaunee, nor any other Native American people known to have lived in western New York. So why would they have included it in their folktales? The story was clearly a fake. And it was not just inauthentic; it was offensive.

"We're portrayed as savages," Bill "Grandpa Bear" Swanson, executive director of the state American Indian Movement, told the *Buffalo News*. "This has got to stop." Allan Jamieson, director of Nento, a native arts and culture group, called the story "racist propaganda," and Richard Hill, an artist and American studies professor, declared it "a racial stereotype." A group of Indians announced they would begin picketing the Maid of the Mist tour boats unless the fake legend was dropped.

The Maid of the Mist Corporation objected. "To accuse us of racism is outrageous," said Christopher Glynn, a vice president. He explained why the corporation didn't want to drop the story: "We are not real anxious to change what we've been doing for a hundred years."

The protesters held their line. If the tour boat operator would not ax the fake myth, they would picket the boat launch in two weeks. Their timing was perfect. It was September, and Regis and Kathie Lee were headed to town, scheduled to shoot their popular morning talk show at the Falls. Faced with the vision of a flood of bad press swamping their boats, the Maid of the Mist Corporation decided to jettison the Maid. James Glynn, company president, was dispatched four days later to announce the corporate change of heart.

"We are very sensitive to the concerns of Native American people and want to ensure that we do not portray their heritage in an inappropriate manner," he told reporters. The legend was struck from the recorded audio.

All myths are in some sense fictions, of course, but this one is a fake even as myth. The history of Niagara is a history of elisions, artifice and outright deception, so it seems appropriate that its originary myth would be made-up. As the poet Wallace Stevens wrote, a mythology reflects its region. And yet, the more I think about the Maid of the Mist, the more I begin to feel that somehow this odd, obnoxious, prurient fake legend gets something about Niagara exactly right. It has much of Niagara's story in it: the community in crisis, the displaced Indians, the power in the Falls, the poisoned water, even the sacrificial victim for a dying town—these may not be Indian themes, but they are some of the deepest and most continuous Niagara themes. Could there be—despite Indians' protest to the contrary—a Native American kernel in this spurious tale? At some point, I become convinced that if I can untangle the threads of the fake myth, I'll have a key that will unlock a storehouse of hidden history.

I should stop here and admit that I have a bit of a problem dropping things. In the course of looking into, say, the history of a museum at Niagara, I will hear from a librarian that the museum's collection has been bought by a Toronto art dealer. I will start calling and emailing that art dealer until he agrees to let me come and visit his collection, at which point I will drive the nine hours to Toronto and spend two days at his house—

to his great surprise—reading all of the letters he's written and received about the collection. And while I'm there he will show me an electric chair he believes was looted from the Auburn State Prison, though the Auburn Prison electric chair is said to have been destroyed in a 1929 riot, and I will drive nine hours home and the very next day crash my computer downloading newspaper articles off LexisNexis that have accounts of the riots at Auburn Prison with maps that might potentially show the extent of the damage and whether the chair could have been salvaged.

I haven't yet figured out the truth of the chair, but the New York State Archives has some prison account books I'm planning on taking a look at the next time I happen to be passing through Albany.

In any case, this is what happens with the Maid of the Mist story. I keep digging deeper into the fake myth, and I keep finding further levels of fakery. Which means that I have to keep going. Eventually, I find myself at the American Antiquarian Society, looking into Native American history at Niagara.

The American Antiquarian Society is an institution as adorably uptight as it sounds. Founded by Isaiah Thomas, Revolutionary printer of the *Massachusetts Spy*, it's a private library incorporated to "encourage the collection and preservation of the antiquities of our country, and of curious and valuable productions in Art and Nature that have a tendency to enlarge the sphere of human knowledge." I love the "art and nature" bit—in addition to books and papers, the Antiquarian Society used to have a natural history collection: rocks, minerals, shells, butterflies, taxidermied animals. They offloaded it years ago, when it became no longer correct to conflate the works of man with the works of the natural world. This is something that happened at Niagara too, but I'll get to that later.

A Palladian brick building on a hill in Worcester, Massachusetts, the Antiquarian Society's collection comprises miles of rare books, diaries, letters, sheet music, postcards, prints and other assorted detritus (they call it "ephemera") of everyday life in America from Columbus through 1876. They have handbills, advertisements, school certificates and even a paper-doll collection. Best of all, there's a bevy of librarians who actually know about all these things and love to tell you about them. When I was there, another reader asked to see some items in the board game collection, and there was much excitement and joy among the librarians upon delivering them up. Not many people, it seems, take the time to appreciate the board games.

On the down side of being a reader at the American Antiquarian Society is their draconian list of rules. Every day upon arrival, you sign in with a frock-coated attendant (I mean it—a frock coat!) and then hand over everything that to my mind makes historical research fun or even possible—cups of coffee, salty snacks, iPods, cell phones, candy, almonds, pens. You put all those things into a locker and go into a high-ceilinged, octagonal rotunda topped with an oculus and ornamented with the usual portraits of sternly disapproving founders. You fill out little slips in duplicate requesting the materials you want to see, which are then brought to you on carts along with white gloves for handling them and foam cushions for the books to lounge on while you read them. You, I might note, are sitting on a very hard chair, and if you squirm around too much, the portraits glare at you harder.

At the American Antiquarian Society, I start reading the earliest print accounts of the Falls, keeping an eye out for serpents and nubile maidens. The oldest print mention of the Falls is by French explorer Samuel de Champlain; he heard about the big waterfall around 1615 but didn't bother to go see it, though he noted it on his maps. The first European to see and then describe the Falls in print was Louis Hennepin, a Flemish Recollect priest who accompanied the explorer La Salle there in 1678. Hennepin describes the Falls in his 1683 account of that visit, *Description de la Louisiane*. (The whole New World, or at least their part of it, was Louisiana to the French at that point.) Fourteen years later, Hennepin published a revised and expanded version of his report on the New World, this one called *A New Discovery of a Vast Country in America*.

Hennepin, like other early travelers, notes that the area is heavily populated by Native Americans, but makes no mention of myths or stories attached to the place. Priests were too focused on Christianizing the Indians to be interested in hearing their heathen tales—in fact, they did very little asking about the native culture. They seem to have walked into Indian villages already in mid-sermon. The poor Indians probably couldn't get a word in edgewise.

Hennepin does say that the area is rife with snakes, even though on his first trip he tromps the entire length of the Niagara River without ever seeing a single one. He describes the dry space behind the Falls' sheet of water, and claims it is where "the Rattle-Snakes retire, by certain Passages which they find underground." Since he didn't see a single snake or go behind the Falls himself, it's reasonable to suppose his native guides may have told him this. But the local Indians don't live at the waterfall. " 'Tis reasonable to presume," Hennepin concludes, "that the horrid noise of the Fall, and the fear of these poisonous Serpents, might oblige the Savages to seek out a more commodious Habitation."

In Hennepin's second volume, there's an interesting note about waterfalls and sacrifice. "Some have taken notice," he tells us of Indians, "that when they meet with any Cascade or fall of Waters, which is difficult to cross, and apprehend any danger, they throw a Beaver's Skin, Tobaco, Porcelain, or some such matter into it by way of Sacrifice, to gain the Favour of the Spirit that presides there." It's a rare attempt on the part of the self-important priest to understand where the locals are coming from, and it doesn't last long. For the most part, his descriptions of Indians are limited to graphic and probably exaggerated accounts of their supposed barbarity. The Iroquois, for instance, he declares to have exterminated "more than Two million of Souls" in their extended territory. The New York Public Library has George Bancroft's personal copy of Hennepin's book in their Rare Book Room, and the eminent nineteenth-century historian has underlined "Two million" and made a marginal note: "Absurd exaggeration." He isn't alone in doubting the priest. Among the French, Hennepin garnered a reputation as "Un Grand Menteur," a Big Liar.

Not that other writers of the period are much better; few early accounts of exploration give us a real sense of the native inhabitants of the so-called New World. We don't even really get a very strong sense of who the people living in the region were, let alone their feelings about Niagara. From Champlain, we learn that the inhabitants of the Niagara frontier around 1600 were Indians called Onguiaronon, or People of Thundering Waters ("Niagara" is a mispronunciation of Onguiara), which suggests they held the Falls in high esteem. Early historians claim the Onguiaronon venerated the Falls enough to bury their most respected chiefs there, but it's unclear if that's true. Only a few bodies have been found.

The French called the Onguiaronon the "Neutrals," because they remained neutral in the wars between Algonquian Indians of the Great Lakes region and the powerful Iroquois Confederacy of New York. Apparently, this neutrality didn't help them much; in fact, their role in Niagara history is to give the place its name and then be exterminated. Sometime around 1650, Senecas are said to have killed the last of their men and adopted the remaining women and children, as was customary. No doubt the Onguiaronon, like all northeastern native peoples at this time, had already lost much of their population to European-introduced diseases such as measles, smallpox and influenza. The fact that no separate Onguiaronon identity remained in Seneca culture suggests they may have been closely related to the Senecas in the first place.

When the last of the Onguiaronon became Senecas, they also became members of the Iroquois Confederacy, or Haudenosaunee, most often translated as "People of the Longhouse." This political alliance, the oldest continuously operating form of government on the continent, was centered then, as now, on the council fire at Onondaga, New York. There, the Grand Council of Chiefs meets yearly, as decreed by the Haudenosaunee law of governance, the Great Law of Peace. In the days of the earliest European explorers, the Haudenosaunee comprised Senecas, Cayugas, Onondagas, Oneidas and Mohawks, hence the alternate name Five Nations. (In 1720, the Tuscaroras would be added to the alliance, after being driven out of their North Carolina home by colonists, and the confederacy would come to be known as the Six Nations.)

"The whole reason the Senecas were placed in this area was to be guardian of the waterways," Darwin John tells me by phone.

I'm in Niagara Falls on a brief jailbreak from the American Antiquarian Society, enjoying dangerous vices like eating and talking on the phone. Darwin and I were supposed to meet on Goat
Island, because Darwin is in the Falls on business—he is energy
planner for the Seneca Nation of Indians. But he lives 90 miles
away, on the Cattaraugus Reservation, and when he arrived in
Niagara Falls, he realized he had forgotten my cell phone number,
so he simply took the walk around Goat Island himself. He seems
perfectly cheerful about it when I call him later, back in Cattaraugus. The Seneca Nation has recently been involved in relicensing
talks for the Niagara Power Project (about which more later) and
Darwin wants me to understand the Senecas' longstanding connection to the region.

"If you look on our emblem, it says Keeper of the Western
Door," he explains. "That, within the Six Nations, is a very important role, because the Western Door was back then the transportation route for other tribes to come into the area, and for us to
move out of the area. Senecas were known throughout the Midwest, the South and the East for trading with other tribes out west.
Niagara was the doorway to our area and our exploration going as
far west as the Mississippi delta and points in between."

The Western Door, he explains, does not just mean the Niagara
River. "There are actually a couple of doors," he says, "the seaway
trail coming from points west on Lake Erie and into the Niagara
region. It was a transportation route. Ellicott Creek, Tonawanda
Creek: all of these were areas the Senecas had lived in since time
immemorial. All these waterways and trails and transportation
routes were well used and well known and that's why we protected
them. They were an important gift given to the people by the
Creator."

I ask Darwin John about Seneca stories associated with the
region, and he tells me a version of the serpent story that doesn't
involve maids or sacrifice.

"According to our creation story," he says, "Thunder Beings
were trying to remove a serpent that had been terrorizing the area,
and during the struggle they threw down the huge snake and that
carved out the horseshoe shape of the Canadian Falls. He was

placed in the underworld, and the route to the underworld was through Devil's Hole State Park. There's a cave there and that's where the snake passed on his way to the underworld."

The benevolent Thunder Beings behind the Falls are a popular part of Niagara lore for Indians and non-Indians alike. Standard histories, guidebooks, IMAX films and souvenir shop fripperies often feature them. For the Indians, it's a concise way of talking about their ancient spiritual connection to the area. But as I listen to Darwin, I find myself wondering what the locals really thought of Niagara before the French arrived eager for beavers. Their view of the place may have been more similar to the European one than is commonly thought. Even the story as Darwin tells it—the brink of the Falls being formed by an evil serpent—suggests that although the Senecas may have valued waterways, they didn't much like waterfalls.

In this, they would have been in agreement with the Europeans. When Indians first brought the Europeans to Niagara, the newcomers considered the waterfall frankly hideous. Louis Hennepin fills his account with a sense of awestruck terror. The journey is treacherous and the cataract itself terrifying. The precipice he calls "horrible," the water in the Falls he sees foaming and boiling "in the most hideous manner imaginable," the noise of it all is "outrageous, more terrible than that of Thunder." In short, he declares, "when one stands near the Fall, and looks down into this most dreadful Gulph, one is seized with Horror, and the Head turns round, so that one cannot look long or stedfastly upon it." In the engraving made to illustrate his account, this effect on viewers is shown. The waterfall—heightened by the priest's famous imagination—plunges viciously downward in the middle ground, while four figures occupy the foreground. One sits with arms outspread, as if trying to gauge its breadth; one clasps his arms across his breast as if in awe; a third stands with arms raised high in what looks like worship, while the fourth turns his back on the scene, covering his ears in a pose of sick despair, as if he can't bear to look or listen for one second more.

Did the early Senecas like this monster of nature? In a creation story found in most credible collections of Seneca mythology, the earth is created by two brothers, sometimes called Inigorio, or Good Mind, and Inigorhatea, or Bad Mind. Good Mind creates the sun, the moon, stars, plains, rivers, lakes, useful animals and people. Bad Mind creates everything that gives us grief: snakes, reptiles, ravines and of course, waterfalls. The early explorers found the whole Niagara region to be rife with Bad Mind's handiwork: they complained bitterly of the rattlesnakes, the insects, the impossible gorge and its difficult terrain. The Senecas no doubt traveled more easily, and they weren't freaked out by rattlesnakes, but for them too the Falls must have been a pain to get around. All of the waterways Darwin mentions to me—the seaway trail, Tonawanda Creek, Ellicott Creek—are routes used to bypass Niagara Falls.

What's certain is that the Senecas understood how important Niagara was to controlling the area around it. In fact, that's one thing the Maid of the Mist story seems to tell us: that getting control of whatever power, good or evil, lives in the waterfall could easily be the key to survival. The Europeans understood this as soon as they arrived at the Falls; pretty much the first thing they did was try to wrest control of the area from the Senecas. Hennepin's explorer boss La Salle saw the Falls and decided they were just the place to build a fort and a ship. The Senecas were decidedly unhappy about that; they saw the scheme for what it was. He was planning to sail right through the Western Door without knocking.

René-Robert Cavelier, Sieur de La Salle, is one of those guys who has left his name plastered all over our nation. Anyone who's taken LaSalle Street to Chinatown in Chicago, or visited La Salle, Minnesota; La Salle, Michigan; La Salle County, Texas; or La Salle, New York, now incorporated into Niagara Falls, knows his name. If they know little more than that, it's not their fault: when I start reading up on La Salle, I quickly realize that he's one of history's most perplexing characters. Considered a brilliant pathfinder by some and a bumbling idiot by others, La Salle is painted as either hero or villain, depending on the writer's personal view. Born in Rouen to a wealthy, middle-class family, he was ordained as a priest, but quickly decided to leave his order, citing "moral weakness." La

Salle fans say he made that up just to escape a dull monkish life; La Salle critics say it's one of the few times he ever told the truth.

La Salle arrived in Montreal in 1667 and made his first trip to Niagara in 1669, on his way to find the Ohio River, which he thought might lead to the fabled Northwest Passage to China, or maybe offer up a better route to the Great Lakes region than the icy, rapids-filled St. Lawrence River. Detractors and fans agree that this journey didn't go well. La Salle claimed to speak the Iroquois language, but according to his priest on that trip, René Brehant de Galinée, he was lying and furthermore had no idea where he was going. For this reason, he and most of his party ended up cooling their heels about 80 miles east of Niagara, waiting for a nonexistent guide.

French and English history texts never specify the Indian town La Salle visited, but the Seneca oral tradition names it as Ganondagan. The main Seneca village of the time, Ganondagan was a hilltop town near the northwestern shore of Lake Canandaigua, one of New York's Finger Lakes. It held 150 longhouses and an estimated 4,500 people, at that time about four times the population of a small town to the southeast recently renamed New York. La Salle arrived at this thriving metropolis with gifts and, of course, a demand. He required a guide who knew the Ohio territory. The Senecas agreed to provide one—they had captives from the region on hand—then showed no inclination to follow through on the offer. La Salle and some of his men spent four weeks as guest-prisoners of the Indians, during which Galinée gives no account of maidens being sacrificed or Thunder Beings in the Falls, though he does describe his horror when their Seneca hosts decide to honor the Frenchmen by torturing and eating a prisoner. This little spectacle—if indeed it happened—would have been part of the highly codified rituals of Haudenosaunee warfare, a point missed by the self-righteous priest. Nor did he and La Salle pick up on what was no doubt meant to be a less-than-subtle message: don't mess with Senecas.

Ganondagan is a New York State historic site today, a stunning spot perched on a still-bucolic hill. Its reconstructed longhouse, surrounded by acres of milkweed dotted with butterflies, looks as if it were dropped there by a time-traveling UFO. Interpretive trails tell the story of the town's 1687 destruction by the French. Visiting there one morning on my way home from Niagara Falls, I ask the Native American guide about La Salle's visit.

"La Salle was a very pompous person," he tells me, shaking his head, as if the French explorer only left town last week. "The Seneca sachems didn't like that kind of attitude."

La Salle never adjusted his attitude, though eventually he got the hint at Ganondagan. He announced he was giving up the mission to explore the Ohio River valley, at which point the Senecas let him and his men go. Once out of their sight, La Salle faked illness for the benefit of his own crew. Promising to make his own way home, he encouraged them to proceed with the mission. Thus freed of his bothersome train of priests and helpers, he disappeared into the North American wilderness for a year. Historians believe he wintered at the mouth of the Niagara River, building a small fort there, which the Senecas promptly burned when he left. He later claimed to have discovered the Mississippi River during that time—beating rival explorer Louis Joliet to the punch—but this has never been verified. Joliet gets credit for "discovering" a river the Indians had known about for centuries.

(In one of my favorite stories from this time period, La Salle actually *ran into* Joliet in the woods one day. I find this image hysterical: it's as if the forests of North America were so crawling with fur-hungry explorers you couldn't throw a rock without some *voyageur* yelling "Merde!" As soon as that image popped into my head, I laughed out loud. I actually got into trouble at the American Antiquarian Society for giggling too much: the exasperated historian at the desk next to mine finally threw down his pencil and cried, "Fine, you win. *Tell* me what's so funny." History is full of horrors, but it has a lot of hilarious moments too, and I'm convinced you have to laugh at them—but I'm digressing.)

La Salle turned up at Niagara next after taking a trip back to France, during which either through eloquence (fans insist) or bribery (critics counter), he received letters of nobility and a charter to explore the land between Florida and Mexico and build forts for the French king. This time, he brought with him a new crew: a posse of raw recruits fresh from France and even more bumbling than he was. But he also had one able lieutenant who would become his loyal companion: Chevalier Henri de Tonti.

I adore Henri de Tonti. An Italian by birth, he had signed on as a soldier in the French army, where he lost a hand to a grenade (legend holds that it got mangled in the explosion and he sawed it off himself). Tonti's icy bravery quickly earned him a fearsome reputation among the Indians. At one point, he walked through a haze of arrows and bullets into an Iroquois camp only to be stabbed in the chest, and he barely blinked—just began haranguing them for breaking the peace. They were so impressed by his fortitude they immediately ran and got someone to fix him up.

Besides fearlessness, Tonti's claim to fame was his prosthetic appendage and his penchant for using it as a weapon. Some historians describe the prosthesis as a metal hand clad in a glove; others say it was a hook. One intriguingly calls it an "appliance" and assures readers Tonti was handy with it. Indians called him "the man with the iron hand," and an early French historian declares that Indians feared Tonti because he "often knocked their heads and teeth with a blow from the fist" of his metal member. He's a sort of real-life, more effective Captain Hook. He actually looks like Captain Hook: in his most common portrait, he wears a ruffled, gold-buttoned dress jacket, and his long, aquiline nose and sharp black eyes are framed by a long mass of wavy black hair. All he lacks is the ticking crocodile following him around.

La Salle, of course, saw Niagara Falls and immediately figured out that anyone who controlled that point controlled trade in the upper Great Lakes. Canoes on their way from the Great Lakes to Upper Canada could be stopped at the portage. Furthermore, the lakes above the Falls offered access to thousands of miles of fur-filled woods inhabited by Indians who would sell those furs at cheaper prices if they didn't have to paddle to Montreal. All the explorer needed was a fort where he could build a ship. But that was exactly the problem: as his previous experience testified, fort-building didn't sit well with the Indians. Constantly on the verge of war with the French, the Haudenosaunee were suspicious of military outposts in their territory. Besides, they wanted to control French access to the West and its beaver pelts. Already in the seventeenth century, beavers were scarce along the eastern seaboard. When they weren't at war with the Indians further west, the Haudenosaunee served as middlemen between them and the French. They disliked the idea of a big boat that would allow the French to trade directly with their enemies, or worse, make political alliances with them.

Still, La Salle wanted Haudenosaunee permission to build his boat, so while he was in Montreal with Tonti sorting out his business affairs, he sent his agent La Motte back to the Senecas to ask for permission to build a "great wooden canoe" on the river above the Falls. La Motte met with elders, handed out gifts, and promised that if they could build a fort at Niagara, the French would give the Senecas better prices for their furs than the English—who had recently wrested the Hudson River valley fur trade from the Dutch. The Senecas weren't having it. The goods the English traded for furs were generally cheaper and better than what was on offer at French posts—and unlike the priest-ridden French, the Brits were usually allowed to sell the Indians rum. More importantly, the Senecas were not about to simply hand over the Niagara portage. They were the keepers of the Western Door, not the French.

But La Salle was determined. He and Tonti sailed for Niagara. They sank their ship on Lake Ontario and lost most of their shipbuilding supplies, but somehow managed to get there in one piece. As soon as he arrived at Niagara, La Salle went to the Senecas himself, taking Tonti with him. This time, for some reason, the Senecas grudgingly agreed to let the French build a boat. La Salle and Tonti repaired immediately to the mouth of Cayuga Creek— the very spot where William T. Love would later dig a canal that would make his name a byword for environmental disaster. La Salle pounded in the ship's first bolt with great ceremony, then scrammed back to Montreal, where, even though creditors had seized his possessions, he undoubtedly spent a much more comfortable winter than the shipbuilders, left to labor under Tonti's watchful eye.

That winter on Cayuga Creek, hundreds of miles from the nearest fort, the small band of *voyageurs* built the first sailing ship to ply the upper Great Lakes. Winter on the Niagara frontier is moderated by its position between Lakes Erie and Ontario, but it still must have been difficult, lonely work. Living in bark huts, subsisting on parched corn, venison and whitefish, the men toiled away with paltry materials to build a small but sturdy ship. Hennepin led prayer meetings on Sundays and holidays, where the crew relaxed by singing Gregorian chants. Meanwhile, small bands of suspicious Senecas lurked ominously about, marveling at the mad Frenchmen and plotting to burn the "big canoe." The blacksmith was attacked, and protected himself with a red-hot poker. The Indians, who were always short of good metalwork, had been falsely promised a permanent blacksmith on the site, and Hennepin reports that one day he accompanied Tonti to the mouth of the Niagara, where Tonti "pretended to mark out a house for the blacksmith" for the benefit of the watching Indians. Even Hennepin seems to feel slightly ashamed of the subterfuge. "I cannot blame the Iroquois," he remarks, "for not believing all that had been promised at the embassy of the Sieur de La Salle."

When the ship was built, they named her the *Griffon*, broke a bottle of spirits over her prow and promptly moved aboard to protect themselves from the stewing Senecas.

In August 1679, La Salle returned and launched the *Griffon* from Niagara Falls, sailing across Lake Erie, up Lake Huron, through the Straits of Mackinac and down Lake Michigan. Perpetually in debt, the explorer loaded his new ship with furs and sent her home to his creditors while he forged onward into the Great Lakes region. The *Griffon*'s return journey was never completed; somewhere along the way, she sank below the waterline of history and into the depths of myth. Exactly what happened is not known: the ship was lost in a storm, or perhaps destroyed by the unhappy Haudenosaunee, or maybe, as La Salle came to believe, it was scuttled by a thieving pilot and crew. Its wreck has never been positively identified. La Salle went on to establish more forts and trek down the entire Mississippi River, claiming it and its watershed for France in the usual way, by burying commemorative plates in the ground. Pompous as ever, he was hounded by jealous Jesuits, badmouthed by rival explorers, and frequently deserted by his own men, who tried to kill him by putting hemlock in his salad. Only Tonti remained loyal. Finally, La Salle went back to France, outfitted four ships, and returned to try to find the mouth of the Mississippi via the Gulf of Mexico. He got lost, missed the river delta and landed instead in Texas, where he wandered fruitlessly, losing men to Indians, disease and alligators (the ticking crocodile at last!), before his crew finally mutinied and killed him. "*Te voilá*, you great Pasha, *Te voilá!*" his murderer cried as he shot him. The mutineers left his body unburied for the wild animals to eat.

Today, the working-class neighborhood in Niagara Falls near where the Griffon was built is called La Salle, but the man himself remains a mystery. Was he egomaniacal or bravely ambitious? Eloquent or cruelly violent? An idiot or a genius? But as inscrutable as La Salle is to us, the Senecas in his story are even more so. Why, after refusing to give La Motte permission for the "big canoe," did they change their minds? Did they truly take a liking to La Salle, or did they fear his iron-handed sidekick? Were they convinced by the eloquence the pro–La Salle historians attribute to him, or did they secretly plan on scuttling the braggart Frenchman's ship? Did they even really say yes? Their real story is more lost to us even than La Salle's. We don't even know their names.

Shortly after La Salle lost the *Griffon*, a man named Louis-Thomas Chabert de Joncaire arrived on the scene, assigned to improve French relations with the Iroquois. The Senecas decided relations would best be improved by burning Joncaire at the stake, and they kidnapped him to that end. They ended up adopting him instead. Legend has it they changed their minds when he bloodied the nose of the guy tying him to the stake: the Senecas were big fans of bravado. Of course, our authority for this story is Joncaire himself, so things may have unfolded in a slightly different way. In any case, Joncaire made himself popular with the Senecas, and by 1720, he convinced a breakaway group of them to let the French build a trading post—not a fort—below the Falls. Building a fort on the Niagara peninsula would have clearly been in violation of the 1701 treaty between the French and the Haudenosaunee, as well as the 1713 Treaty of Utrecht, which set the boundaries between French Canada and British New York. So Joncaire's trading post was a simple wood-bark outpost. Then, as the trade war with Britain was heating up, the sneaky French went right ahead and built a fort, which they called a "House of Peace," disguising it to look like a fancy trading post. Weapons were stored upstairs; cannons were neatly hidden in the attic. It was located on the spot where the Niagara River empties into Lake Ontario, the better to interdict canoes heading across the lake to English trading posts farther east. To lure the Indians to trade there, they even relaxed their rules against selling them rum.

What came to be called Fort Niagara was critical during the French and Indian War, which historians now like to call the Seven Years' War, to reflect the fact that it was actually a world war. The standoff in North America began in 1754, when a French expedition kicked some British fort-builders out of the Ohio River valley. The French then began to assert their claims on the entire Ohio River region; some of that commemorative tableware even turned up, intercepted at Niagara. The British resisted the claim, and battles for control of forts along the frontier ensued. Fort Niagara was besieged and eventually taken by the British in 1759 in a battle that gets reenacted annually on the very spot where it happened. With nearly 1,000 costumed reenactors turning up, it's the world's largest annual French and Indian War event.

Fort Niagara sits on a gorgeous piece of real estate, a high windy hill, overlooking the river mouth and the vast, glittering lake. When I arrive on day one of the reenactment, the whole place is swarming with French officers, Redcoats, rugged militiamen and Indians. A row of white tents hugs the garrison walls, and people scurry in and out among them. A posse of Redcoats is preparing for a council with the Indians. The head Indian, painted entirely black on one side, is wearing a loincloth, knee-high boots, and a tuft of feathers that looks like a cardinal and a blackbird fought to the death on his scalp. A sweaty soldier runs by, knees high, holding a musket over his head and chanting "I will not call the captain fat!" Clearly, these folks take their reenacting seriously.

Inside the fort, French soldiers are marching in formation and firing muskets, while fabulously got-up Indians—none of whom appear to be actual Native Americans—are charging visitors for posing in photos. On the center lawn, a lively market is spread out, and tourists in shorts and T-shirts mingle with reenactors in heavy wool jackets as they inspect leather goods, fondle linens and eye knives, hatchets and guns. Children scrabble about the ankles of bonneted women. A lone musician plays airs, a cup set out at his feet.

Fort Niagara is spectacular, its grounds perfectly groomed, every brick lovingly restored in an outburst of patriotism between the world wars. Standing there with the French and Indian War about to be acted out in real time, I realize that this conflict, which I always considered a dull chapter in high school history texts, was actually a thrillingly critical moment in the struggle for North America. Here are French, British and Iroquois soldiers ready to kill each other over a tiny spit of land, but what's at stake is really how the New World will look. Will it slouch around in cafés, drinking vermouth and smoking Gitanes, or will it purse its lips and drink tea with dry, unappetizing biscuits? The visitors, clambering onto the fort walls to see the assault, also seem to sense how much hangs in the balance. Families hoist cameras and slather sunscreen on impatient children. Down below, on the field of battle, white tents billow like sails. Indians dart here and there while the French crouch behind a berm, about to lose control of the continent. Anticipation rises from the ground with the smell of newly cut grass. Finally, some shots ring out, a crackly smattering, like fireworks. A haze of musket smoke wafts up as the British appear from behind the treeline, playing "Yankee Doodle" on a fife and drum. Round two in the reshaping of North America has begun.

Around the time of the French and Indian War, a story turns up that shares some elements with the Maid of the Mist tale. J. C. Bonnefons, a French soldier posted in the New World from 1751 to 1761, relates a "common report" of an Iroquois who, when his canoe is drawn into Niagara's ineluctable rapids, simply wraps himself in his blanket and rides down to his doom. The story is retold frequently in Falls narratives. By 1835, when it gets added to the second edition of Horatio Parsons's popular *Guide to Travelers Visiting the Falls of Niagara*, the author is quick to say that he believes the story to be fake, merely "a stereotype Indian story, told as having happened at all different falls in the country."

The stereotype of the "doomed Indian" was popular in the colonies, and later the young United States, because it downplayed the colonists' role in a people's extermination. "Removing" the Indians wasn't such a bad thing if they were already destined to vanish simply because their culture was inferior. The "doomed Iroquois" on the waterfall, and the Maid of the Mist who picks up his disappearing act, performs this particular white man's fancy as red man's fact: once he sees the inevitable fact of his demise looming ahead, he quietly and stoically goes to his end.

Later on, when Indian removal became national policy, the story took on unsavory aspects. Parsons's 1835 "doomed Indian" has a new accessory—a bottle of whiskey:

A story has frequently been told of an Indian, who fell asleep in his canoe some miles above, and awoke in the midst of the rapids; perceiving that all efforts at escape would be vain, he turned his bottle of whiskey down his throat, and composedly awaited the awful plunge.

The image of the "drunken Indian" was key to nineteenth-century justifications for removal and treaty-breaking. Indians were lazy drunks, the line went, who would simply let the land go to waste, instead of improving and farming it like white folks would. (Never mind that Europeans introduced them to liquor in the first place.) It was practically a moral duty to take their land away, and using treaties and money to do so quickly devolved into using guns.

In 1830, President Andrew Jackson pushed his Indian Removal bill through Congress, making the relocation of all southeastern Indians official government policy. In exchange for their productive farmland, they were to be given some nice property in Oklahoma. In 1838, three years after Parsons sent his doomed drunk over the brink, 17,000 Cherokees were ousted from their ancestral homes in Georgia and made to walk 800 miles west. After four thousand died on the way, the forced march was named the Trail of Tears. At Niagara that year, corrupt sachems were liquored up and tricked into selling off most of what remained of Seneca lands in the region, against the will of the majority, in the fraudulent Buffalo Creek Treaty.

Guidebooks continued telling the drunken Indian story. By 1842, in C. D. Ferris's *Pictorial Guide to the Falls of Niagara*, the drunken Indian has been given a mate, and the whole episode has become an unsavory joke:

> Tradition tells many a tale of persons going over the Falls; and among others, of an Indian and squaw, in a canoe, who were drawn into the rapids, and hurried down to destruction. It relates, that the Indian, when he found it impossible to escape, coolly laid down his paddle, and taking up a bottle of whisky, which had been the object of the voyage to procure, deliberately applied it to his lips, and kept sucking away, until he was himself sucked in, by the overwhelming flood; and, thus in a spiritual way, introduced himself to the world of spirits. Whether or not, he took a drop too much, it is impossible to say; but of this we are certain, that he was loath to lose a drop. The poor squaw paddled away till the last, and that was the last of both.

What's interesting is that even before the Maid of the Mist legend appears and sends a doomed maiden over the brink, the demise of the Iroquois is being associated with Niagara Falls. It's not just coincidence. After the French and Indian War, the balance of power shifted, in ways that were very nearly disastrous for the Haudenosaunee. Central to this loss of power and influence was what happened at Niagara. There the Haudenosaunee lost control of the Western Door, and with it, lost much of their world.

The heart of the Maid of the Mist legend is Indian displacement. When Lelawala comes back with the news about the poisonous snake, the whole town packs up and leaves. This aspect of it, at least, seems to reflect Indian reality. I'm convinced of this even more when, back at the American Antiquarian Society after my brief jailbreak, I find Henry Schoolcraft's 1846 *Notes on the Iroquois*. Schoolcraft, an ethnologist and superintendent of Indian affairs who married an Ojibwa woman, was the first European to attempt an anthropological study of the Haudenosaunee. In his surprisingly readable book, I find a Seneca tale about a poisonous snake that sounds like it could be the real kernel in the Maid of the Mist tale.

The Senecas, this story tells us, first lived in a village at the head of Lake Canandaigua. One day a young boy from the Canandaigua village found a small two-headed serpent. He caught it and kept it as a pet, feeding it the flesh of birds and small mammals. It grew, needing larger and larger meals, until eventually it became so big he was forced to hunt deer for it. Too big to live in the longhouse, the snake took up residence on a nearby hill, sometimes coming down to play in the lake.

The townspeople began to fear the two-headed snake. They resolved to move to get away from it, but when they woke the next day, the serpent had surrounded their village with its body, placing its open mouth at the gate. Anyone who tried to escape was eaten. Eventually, only one warrior and his sister remained. In a dream, the warrior was told to fledge an arrow with a hair from his sister and aim for the serpent's heart. He did it the next day, and the serpent was mortally wounded. In its death agonies, it rolled down the hill and into the lake, where it vomited up the heads of the people it had eaten. Those heads are now the stones that mark the bottom of Lake Canandaigua. The warrior and his sister moved the council fire to the western shore of Seneca Lake.

This tale sounds like a credible Seneca story to me; as soon as I read it, I'm convinced I've found the truth at the bottom of the Maid's fake legend. But it also sounds like a nice metaphor for what life must have felt like to the Senecas in the eighteenth century: like being hemmed in by a beast with two heads. Throughout the period, as the British and French struggled for control of North America, Indians were caught in the middle. It was in many ways a position of power—with diplomatic skills honed over centuries of Iroquois League politics, the Haudenosaunee were especially good at playing rival nations off each other to their own advantage. But theirs was a precarious position, and the Indians constantly worried that both nations' assurances of friendship were really just empty promises that would vanish once either side got the upper hand. Which is exactly what seemed to happen when the British won.

Though they had spent much of the previous century and a half at war with the French, many of the Haudenosaunee would have preferred to see a French victory. They had always respected French military power, and felt they had hammered out a fairly stable relationship with Onontio—their name for the French colonial governor. Furthermore, the French and British seem to have adhered to national stereotypes in colonizing North America. When not putting the torch to Indian towns, the French were colonizers in only the loosest sense; as long as the furs were coming in and the Jesuits were totting up enough souls, the rank and file hung out with the Indians, smoking and intermarrying with them, and engaging in the gift exchanges that were central to Native American cultures. They occasionally put on big shows of sovereignty—heavy on the feasting and fashion—but the Indians actually enjoyed the spectacle, because the French didn't seem to despise them.

The English, on the other hand, marched into North America to the tune of "Hail Brittania." They made no secret of their distaste for Indians, and the first North American governor after the French and Indian War, General Jeffrey Amherst, took what one historian calls a "shopkeeper's approach" to managing the colonies. One of his first moves was to slash the budget for gifts. He refused to engage in conciliatory gestures toward the Indians, instead treating them like subjugated savages. Relations between the English and Indians soured so quickly that the Indians couldn't help but feel the French had sold them out: rumors circulated among Indians that the French and British, like a two-headed snake, had actually staged the entire Seven Years' War just to extinguish the natives.

The way the British behaved after winning the war with France feels unnervingly familiar to Americans of the early twenty-first century: they entered a nation claiming they had no desire to dominate it, then acted like swaggering conquerors. They deposed a military bureaucracy built on cronyism and installed profiteering cronies of their own, refusing to hold their troops accountable for appalling behavior and making no bones about being more interested in profits than lasting peace. As a result, they provoked an insurgency.

In 1763, dozens of Indian nations attacked British forts and villages in a loosely coordinated effort to eject the British from the Great Lakes region. They managed to take every British fort in the area except the ones at Niagara, Detroit and present-day Pittsburgh. The war has gone down in history as Pontiac's Rebellion, named for the charismatic Ottawa chief who led the siege of Fort Detroit. But the first war belts—wampum beaded with symbols calling for an uprising—were actually sent around by some Senecas from the Geneseo region just south of Niagara. They were concerned about losing control of the Western Door.

Historians see Pontiac's Rebellion as a defining moment in the history of British–Native American relations. It's when things became really ugly: both sides succumbed to fantasies of genocide. The Indians, determined to kick the Europeans off the continent for good, laid waste to settlements. On the British side, Governor Amherst infamously condoned handouts of smallpox-infected blankets to besieging Indians at Fort Pitt. Writing to the colonel sent to relieve the fort, Amherst declared "You will Do well to try to Innoculate the Indians by means of Blankets, as well as to try Every other method that can serve to Extirpate this Execrable Race." He then went on to lament that they were too far from England to obtain some good hunting dogs to finish the job.

Ignoring the breakaway group of Senecas who had sent out war belts, the Haudenosaunee stayed technically neutral in Pontiac's Rebellion. It was an uprising of the midwestern Algonquian Indians. Nevertheless, some of the Senecas, especially on the border between Algonquian and Iroquois lands, took part in the skirmishes breaking out all over the Great Lakes region. One of these skirmishes happened at Niagara and has entered Niagara lore as a bizarre, ahistorical story of Indian barbarism. This is the famous Devil's Hole Massacre, in which a group of 300 Senecas, Ojibwas and Ottawas attacked a supply caravan at Devil's Hole, about four miles below the Falls.

Devil's Hole—the place—comes up a lot when you talk to Native Americans; it seems as important as the waterfall in Indian lore. In Darwin John's story, it's where the evil Falls serpent goes down a hole into the underworld. It's also where the Senecas lost title to Niagara Falls. The person who made that happen was an adopted Mohawk sachem named William Johnson.

William Johnson, like La Salle, is a complicated figure, equal parts hero, opportunist and cad. An Irish gentleman dispossessed by the Protestant ascendancy (his family was Catholic), he came to the British colonies to make his fortune. He turned an estate in the Mohawk Valley of upstate New York into a miniempire, in part by insinuating himself into the Haudenosaunee world. He learned the Mohawk language as well as the culture's rituals, eventually becoming an adopted Mohawk sachem. He had a couple of wives and a few more mistresses who bore him scads of children, but the woman he seemed most attached to was a Mohawk clan mother, Molly Brant, mother to eight of his kids. Britain's point man with the Indians, he insisted on fair treatment for his Haudenosaunee friends. Johnson led the British forces that took Fort Niagara in the Seven Years' War; his British and Iroquois troops completely devastated a French relief regiment that outnumbered them. His business success—his estate ultimately comprised about 400,000 acres—also hinged on his Haudenosaunee connections. But in 1764, he held a huge treaty convention at Fort Niagara, where he negotiated a treaty with the Senecas that gave control of the Western Door to the Brits. His pretext was the massacre at Devil's Hole.

Devil's Hole is about four miles north of the Falls, downstream on the Niagara River. It's an impressive spot, a semicircular natural amphitheater carved out of the gorge cliff in flaky striations. A path leads down along the cliff face to a trail at the river's edge.

You make your way down through the crisp scrub, the rocky face of Devil's Hole looming ever higher above you, until at bottom you break through the Arcadian woods to face the noise and fury of the Whirlpool Rapids. It's stunning.

September is especially beautiful in the Niagara region. The haze of summer sweeps out of town with the tourists and the landscape takes on a timeless, pastoral sheen: leaves settling into their brilliant autumn palette, clear fall light casting the cornfields in a golden glow, apples punctuating spiky trees with heavy, red dots. As they made their way down the Niagara Gorge rim from Fort Schlosser, just above the Falls, on the morning of September 14, 1763, the members of a British wagon train may have admired the Niagara frontier's beauty. They were escorted by 25 regulars, but no doubt they were still nervous. Portage master William Steadman had recently begun the use of Conestoga wagons—the famous "prairie schooners" used by pioneers—on the portage, and the local Senecas who had previously done all the portage's heavy lifting were unhappy at losing their jobs. So when they began peppering the caravan with bullets from the forest along the trail, it was partly an act of war allied to Pontiac's Rebellion and partly a really dramatic instance of labor unrest.

It was over quickly. The wagon train was caught between the forest and Devil's Hole: when around 300 armed Indians came charging out of the woods, many horses went over the ledge in panic, dragging their wagons with them. The people who weren't shot were tomahawked. Steadman escaped (the Senecas later deeded him some land, they were so impressed that he survived their onslaught), and the story tradition later inserts a drummer boy who falls over the cliff and survives when his drum straps catch in a tree. The Indians hung around long enough to dispatch 75 of the 85 troops who came rushing up the gorge from the outpost at Lewiston, a mile and a half away. Then they disappeared into the woods, where they continued a reign of terror for weeks afterward, sniping at people and cows in the region and plotting to take Fort Niagara.

The Devil's Hole Massacre quickly became a standard part of Niagara lore. The creek that seeps out of the rock face at Devil's

Hole and drains into the Niagara River became known as Bloody Run. The massacre itself, stripped of its historic context, entered regional history as a thrillingly awful example of Indian barbarity with no apparent cause. Nineteenth-century guidebooks all narrate it, but make no mention of Pontiac's Rebellion or Indians losing their livelihoods. Orr's 1842 *Pictorial Guide to the Falls of Niagara* is typical:

> Men, horses, wagons, cattle, stores, all in one promiscuous mass were forced over the bank, and dashed to pieces on the rocks below, while the fiendish yells of the savages drowned their shrieks and groans, and thundered from the rocks and cliffs above, wild, terrible, triumphant!

Traditionally, tourists love thrilling episodes where "savages" cruelly attack "men" just for the sake of violence. William Johnson was more pragmatic. He saw the Devil's Hole Massacre as a chance to wrest Niagara once and for all from the Senecas, thus ingratiating himself with the British government. At the 1764 treaty convention at Niagara Falls, he successfully divided the Indian nations, making treaties with each separately. From the Senecas, he demanded the biggest concession: what became known as the Mile Strip. It was actually a strip four miles wide, running the entire length of the Niagara River, two miles on each side. The Senecas threw in all the islands in the Niagara River, deeding them to Johnson personally. Ever the loyal subject, he turned them over to the Crown.

Seneca history—in which they lose the land around the Falls—seems related to the Seneca serpent myth—in which the poisonous serpent's attack means that the village must move. The serpent myth seems to have been geographically mobile; versions of it turn up that are set in other places besides Canandaigua. There's a serpent in Lake Ontario, and Henry Schoolcraft, in *Notes on the Iroquois*, even relates a similar story about the Chippewa River, near Niagara Falls. The Indians in that story move to Buffalo Creek (near present-day Buffalo) and the serpent follows them, at which point the Great Spirit zaps it with lightning. Similar serpent myths show up in many folklore books by Indians, always involving displacement. Seneca scholar Arthur Parker even includes "thunderer wars upon horned snake" as one of the major themes of Seneca folklore in his 1923 *Seneca Myths and Folk Tales*. A likely predecessor to the Maid of the Mist story, it has almost every key element: the deadly serpent, the Thunder God's help, the village that must move, the serpent's dead body causing a natural feature. It's only missing one thing: the maid.

As far as we know, the sacrificial maiden makes her print debut in 1850 in *Burke's Descriptive Guide*, under the heading "The White Canoes: An Indian Legend." It's easy to see how such a story tickled the fancies of its audience. It's mildly salacious in a prudish Victorian way: Burke says breathily of his tasty maid that "like a rose, she opened all her beauties to the maturing breath of Nature." In Burke's version, Lelawala's father rows himself over the Falls after her, a sentimental touch nineteenth-century audiences would have loved. The following year, the story appeared in an anthropological study: Lewis Henry Morgan's *League of the Ho-de-no-sau-nee or Iroquois*.

Morgan's hefty tome, published in 1851, is still considered the classic text of Iroquois ethnohistory. This is weird, given that Morgan was a lawyer whose interest in Iroquois culture began when he and some friends founded a literary and social men's club in Rochester called the Grand Order of the Iroquois. The gentlemen in the fraternity took Iroquois names, performed "Iroquois" ceremonies, and gave each other lectures on Iroquois culture. No doubt they had secret handshakes and used Iroquois words to tell dirty jokes in polite company. There's something Tom Sawyerish about the whole endeavor. Nonetheless, their constitution, penned by Morgan, declared their purpose was "to encourage a kinder feeling towards the Indian, founded upon a truer knowledge of his civil and domestic institutions, and of his capabilities for future elevation." This language later became the preface to his monumental study.

Morgan's prediction of the Indians' "future elevation" reveals his racist conviction that they must aspire to be like white folks,

but to give him credit, he did do his best to build a "truer knowledge" of Iroquois life. He was very fortunate to meet—in a
bookstore, the story goes—a highly educated and brilliant young
Seneca man from the Tonawanda Reservation, Ely Parker, who
would later join the staff of Ulysses Grant and become a brigadier
general in the Union army. The terms of the Confederate surrender
at Appomattox were handwritten in his elegant script, and probably composed by him too. Parker would also become a Seneca
sachem, and in 1869, Grant would appoint him the first Native
American commissioner of Indian affairs. With Parker as his collabo-
rator and interpreter, Morgan collected more data than anyone had
ever put together about the social organization, political practices,
domestic habits and stories of New York's Haudenosaunee. One
of the stories he included in *League of the Ho-de-no-sau-nee* is the
story of the Maid of the Mist. Interestingly, it has nothing to do
with human sacrifice. Rather, Morgan's luscious maiden paddles
to her own death because her family is forcing her to marry an
unpleasant old Indian.

The "suicidal bride" version of the Maid of the Mist tale is
historically just as popular as the sacrifice version: in fact, along
with another variant in which the maid paddles herself to her
death because she's a three-time widow, it is often presented as
the more politically correct, "authentic" version of the tale. It's
the one that appears in ABC-CLIO's 1992 *Dictionary of Native
American Mythology*, and that comes to dramatically re-created
life in the most-watched IMAX film ever made: *Niagara: Miracles,
Myths and Magic*, playing since 1986 at the Niagara Falls IMAX
Theatre. Suicide, with its noble overtones, is presumed to be less
insulting to the Native Americans than the notion that they took
part in human sacrifice.

The problem is, neither of these more "authentic" suicide versions rings true either, given the kinship structure and cultural
traditions of the Haudenosaunee. A mythology also reflects its
culture, and these stories just don't. The "forced marriage" idea
is particularly anachronistic: all of the Six Nations were highly
matrilineal. Not only were women always free to refuse a marriage,
but marriage wasn't even as central to female identity as it is tradi-

tionally in European culture. By all accounts, the Haudenosaunee treated marriage rather lightly: husbands and wives retained their matrilineal clan affiliations, and unhappy marriages were easily dissolved. They were, in fact, so sensible about marriage that Morgan claims love and passion must have been unknown to them.

But the thing that makes the suicidal maid look really unlikely to have an Indian source is the fact that she was already a stock character. Sexy squaws had been killing themselves for decades by 1850—on the American stage. Another take on the "dying race" myth, hugely popular "Indian plays" proliferated in theaters while the real Indians were being edged into the wings. We have records of at least fifty Indian plays that were performed between 1826 and 1860. They nearly always focused on a female protagonist, often Pocahontas. These beautiful, softhearted babes of the woods, precursors to Disney's animated sexpot, starred in what were basically sentimental novels spiced up with Indian characters. In Lewis Deffebach's 1821 play *Oolaita; or, The Indian Heroine*, for instance, a young maiden's father tries to make her give up the noble young warrior she loves and marry a conceited old chief. The old Indian hires assassins to kill his young rival and puts out the word they have succeeded. The news, though false, causes loyal Oolaita to leap to her death rather than marry her lover's killer.

The Indian plays could be seen as technicolor versions of the "doomed Indian" in his canoe. Awash in sentiment about children of nature and hopeless love, they are full-length versions of the vanishing Indian story. The most famous of them, *Metamora*, was a long-running star vehicle for the popular actor Edwin Forrest. Lewis Henry Morgan undoubtedly saw or heard of them.

At this point in my research, I'm convinced I have it all figured out. For his 1851 Maid of the Mist story, Lewis Henry Morgan took the traditional Seneca serpent tale—probably from Schoolcraft, whose book Morgan owned—and slathered on a tragic maid straight from the era's popular melodramas. Then he peppered the whole thing with the notion of the "vanishing race" by moving it to Niagara Falls, where there already was a "stereotype story" of an Indian and his squaw going over the brink. Since Morgan was

working on *League of the Ho-de-no-sau-nee* for years, and presenting bits of his research at public lectures and meetings in the secret
Iroquois clubhouse, no doubt word got out and some guidebook
writer stuck it in his Niagara Falls guide even before *League* was
published. I leave the American Antiquarian Society feeling tri-
umphant: I have traced the sources of Niagara's fake myth.

"Where did the Maid of the Mist legend come from? Ely Parker,"
Joseph Bruchac tells me over a bowl of French onion soup. "He
was really fond of telling that story."

Ely Parker? The brilliant Seneca sachem? I choke on my Gru-
yère.

An Abenaki Indian, Joseph Bruchac is what the nineteenth century, or the folks at the Antiquarian Society, would call "a man of
parts." Writer, editor, publisher, scholar, educator, storyteller, musician, flute-maker—he seems to throw himself with vigor into every
aspect of native lore and culture. He has advanced degrees in literature, and among his seventy-plus books are several collections of
Iroquois and Abenaki tales, which is why, one gray Tuesday, I travel
up to Saratoga Springs to talk to him about serpent myths, folklore
and the Falls. The fog is heavy on the Hudson as the train slithers
along its shore, following the only Amtrak route that offers not only
stunning Hudson River views, but the chance to roll right through
the middle of a maximum security prison—Ossining, previously
known as Sing-Sing, and home (incidentally) to Old Sparky, the
Auburn State Prison electric chair's identical twin.

"Sing-Sing is a Mohawk word originally," Bruchac tells me
within minutes of picking me up at the station. "The town changed
its name to Ossining because it was tired of being associated with
the prison. Then the prison changed its name too."

Joe is a tall, solid man with kind eyes and an air of extreme
composure. We settle in at a popular spot downtown, and as we
sit among Saratoga's ladies who lunch, he drops his Ely Parker
bombshell. Parker, Joe tells me, was considered one of the most
learned and articulate men of his generation. Conversant in both
European letters and Iroquois languages and lore, he contributed so much to Morgan's book that in dedicating *League of the*

Ho-de-no-sau-nee to Parker, Morgan called it "fruit of our joint researches."

But Ely Parker, a Seneca raised on the Tonawanda Reservation, an Indian who practiced law but was not allowed to pass the bar, circulating the obviously fake Maid of the Mist legend?

"How do you know?" I ask, having managed to swallow my soup.

"All the Indians know that," Joe says.

If Parker is the source of the suicidal bride story, that makes it an "authentic" Seneca story. But why would he relate a story that seems to be so at odds with Haudenosaunee traditions and reality?

"Stories are told for a certain reason," Joe tells me, smiling in the way teachers smile when they know more than they're saying. "Sometimes it's because you need to hear them."

Or because you *can* hear them. As much as I don't want to see even Morgan's slightly improved version of the Maid of the Mist story as an authentic tale, the idea of it coming from Parker makes sense. Good story collectors know that a story is always changed in the telling, and that change has a lot to do with who's listening. Ely Parker was as educated in the European tradition as his non-native hearers; no doubt he went to the theater too. Can we blame him if he shaped the story to appeal to his particular audience? Because if he was the source of the suicidal bride, he was certainly playing to popular tastes. I mention the Indian play tradition to Joe and he laughs.

"It's the 'lover's leap' story," he tells me. "It comes up again and again in American culture. Like that old Johnny Preston song 'Running Bear.' Do you know it?"

I do not. He starts singing. Running Bear, it seems, loves Little White Dove, but things don't go so well.

"And then these fake-sounding tom-tom things come in, oompa, oompa . . ." The tom-toms startle a few of the lunching ladies and they look at us, forks poised over chopped salads. Joe's wife Carol, who has come along, laughs and eats the orange slices off his plate.

I realize in an instant that I have simplified everything. It would be easy to see the "lover's leap" tale as pure white man's fancy, a substitution of European clichés for authentic Indian tales. But the reality is more complicated, and it reveals the entwined nature of two cultures we think of as separate. When Europeans arrived in North America, they adopted many native ways of being in the world, just as the Indians adopted European goods and practices. Together they created a unique frontier culture historian Richard White names "the middle ground." As the United States came of age, the "middle ground" was replaced by a more Europeanized culture, and Indians were relegated to history books, reservations and Westerns. Like the natural world, they were domesticated: contained, controlled and dominated, even as their former "wildness" was romanticized in myth. But what the Maid of the Mist story reveals is that many Indian influences remained—we just lost sight of their Indian-ness. The maid is a hybrid, the love child of European literary convention and Native American folklore, traditions introduced to one another, perhaps, by a Seneca sachem steeped in classical learning.

"When you come to Niagara Falls, you come to the end of the land," Joseph tells me. "To some, it's a metaphor for what happened to the native people." For some reason, it makes me think of the snake Darwin John mentioned, and its plunge down to the underworld at Devil's Hole. Like the serpent, the native tradition didn't disappear; it just went underground.

I bring up the Canandaigua horned-serpent story, and its migration to Niagara.

"Oh, that myth is not about Niagara," Joseph declares immediately. "That's a story about contact."

Blindsided again. Contact? The story seemed so folkloric, so primal somehow. Schoolcraft presented it as an originary tale. And yet it makes perfect sense. The two-headed snake—France and Great Britain—is small at first. The Indians feed it and it grows larger. Some Indians fear it; others want to continue placating it. The fearful are proved right at last when, with complete ingratitude for earlier care, the serpent begins to destroy the Indians.

"Contact works its way into native traditions in a lot of ways," Joseph tells me. "I've heard that story interpreted again and again by tribal elders, and it's always about contact. And it's not about Niagara, it's about Canandaigua, because that's where they made the treaty that drew a line down the center of town: on one side, Indians; on the other, whites." But of course, at Niagara too the Haudenosaunee were turned on by a snake they had fed.

"In native culture," Joseph says, "stories have two purposes: to entertain, and to educate or inform. They're used as a means of child-rearing and as a means of societal balance. When a story no longer has either of those qualities, something has been lost."

I'm taken by the idea of nineteenth-century ethnologists collecting "ancient myths" from a primitive people, only to have those "primitives" tell them morality tales worthy of Aesop. *You want a story? Here's a story about what you've done to our world.* And the eager ethnologists wrote it all down, without ever realizing that they were hearing not some primal fairy tale but a modern-day "*J'accuse.*" Red man's fancy, it seems, can also be taken as white man's fact.

On the train home, with night falling on the beautiful Hudson River valley and some newly released residents of Ossining engaging in fisticuffs in the aisle, I gaze out the window and think about America and its first peoples. They, like the waterfall at Niagara, have traditionally been seen as outside history. Their culture is unchanging and eternal, and any "civilizing" or "Europeanizing" acts on their part are inauthentic. To freeze a culture—or a natural wonder—like this is to kill it, to deny its status as a living, constantly changing entity. A culture, like a waterfall, is not a thing: it's an event. Today, Americans shake their heads and sigh at past horrors like the Trail of Tears, but to see Native American history as a laundry list of crimes perpetrated by the government on a passive people adds one more crime to the list. And it continues a narrative tradition in which Indians, like the landscape, are only there to be acted on by the colonists.

"The history of Indian-white relations," writes Richard White, "has not usually produced complex stories. Indians are the rock, European peoples are the sea, and history seems a constant storm."

The Onondaga longhouse contains a four-foot-long wampum belt made in 1692. Its design is simple: two parallel rows of purple wampum shells are separated by white shells. The belt is called the Kas-wen-tha or Guswenta belt. It was made to record and commemorate a treaty with early Dutch settlers, and its meaning is straightforward: the two cultures, Indian and European, shall travel side by side, like brothers, without ever meeting. The Indians, in their birchbark canoe, will maintain their customs and ways, and the Europeans, in their sailing ship, will maintain theirs. Neither will interfere with the other's path, or seek to board the other's boat. A person attempting to stand with one foot on each boat will fall between them and drown.

And yet, that's exactly what the most fascinating characters in American history have done: Irish baronet and adopted Mohawk William Johnson, his Mohawk wife Molly Brant, soldier-scholar-sachem Ely Parker, even the ridiculous Lewis Morgan, donning his feathered cap and playing powwow, like one of Peter Pan's lost boys joining the Red Men's dance. William Johnson, who perhaps had his feet most firmly on both boats, fell into the waters of fiction. History can't contain him; he becomes instead an imagined character, turning up in novels by James Fenimore Cooper, James Kirk Paulding and Robert Louis Stevenson. Myth may not be true, but it's often good at describing new worlds and new possibilities.

"Contact was not a battle of primal forces in which only one could survive," writes White. "Something new could appear." That something was American history. Nowhere is that clearer than at Niagara, where the threads of separate histories are woven together too tightly to be broken apart. Indian and European may be on separate lines, but both lines share the same belt. Today the fate of Niagara Falls, New York, may hang on the ability of the Senecas to revive the economy with a downtown casino: some of the very land William Johnson forced the Senecas to yield was recently given back to them by the State of New York. Now tourists at the Seneca Niagara Casino can buy Native American dreamcatchers, drink cappuccinos in a marble lobby, and enjoy clams casino, oysters Rockefeller, Maryland crab cakes

and a 24-ounce porterhouse at a steakhouse called the Western
Door.

The Maid of the Mist myth continues to be told, though it
now includes culturally sensitive caveats about the difficulty of
identifying authentic native tales. The American Niagara Tourism
and Convention Corporation tells the "desperate widow" version
on their Web site, calling it "a dim reflection of the richness of
Niagara's native culture." Here is how it begins:

> When people knew the wholeness of the world, they knew
> that all are one with the world. They spoke with the earth
> and the sky, and knew them as themselves. The sun, the
> moon, and the stars spoke with them, and people were one
> with them. They knew the animals and the plants as their
> brothers and sisters. The thunder taught them about what
> is and what will happen. People knew all these things,
> and knew the wholeness of the world. But people forgot.
> The earth and the stars and the animals and the Thunder
> continued to talk to them, but people didn't always lis-
> ten. . . . This story tells about the last time that the Thun-
> der ever spoke to a human.

The Haudenosaunee had—and have—a complex and politically sophisticated culture. Even in the dim reflection of their
history we can glean from early accounts, it's clear they recognized the political and commercial value of the Falls, and fought
hard to maintain control of that asset. Still, they are used to this
day to represent humans in a "natural" state, people listening to
the voice of the landscape in prelinguistic, Edenic wholeness.
Early pictures of Niagara almost always included an Indian or
two. Like the waterfall, they were symbols of the New World's
wildness, a wildness just waiting to be tamed. Envisioning the
landscape in this way was the first step toward mastering it, just
as imagining Native Americans as "nature's children," subjects of
a world not ordered by humans, was to take the first step toward
genocide. To envision some people in a state of nature, while
others partake of human time, is to justify extermination as

merely progress. Welcome to history; here's your prize: a small-pox blanket and a gun.

As the nineteenth century began, settlers, land speculators and entrepreneurs would arrive at the Falls and begin the process of taming the landscape. The myth of Niagara's wildness would become increasingly difficult—and necessary—to maintain.

Two

THE EIGHTH WONDER
OF THE WORLD

So you're going to Niagara Falls! Maybe you've never been before—you feel a little sheepish about that if you're American or Canadian. *Actually*, you say, raising your eyebrows in mock disbelief, *I've never been to Niagara!* Then again, maybe you went when you were a child. At least you think so. You have an image of loud falling water in your head—did you visit on that childhood car trip, the one where you threw up at a rest area, and your brother slipped on a toad? Or does your mental image come from the panoramic picture on the wall of your favorite Chinese restaurant? And doesn't that picture have blinking lights behind it, so the Falls look as though they're in motion? Never mind, better late than never. The world is packed with natural wonders, but there's only one Niagara Falls.

Follow the interstate signs, and you'll skirt Buffalo, zip across Grand Island in the Niagara River (toll 75 cents) and glide up the Robert Moses Parkway past several Superfund sites and a row of chemical factories wafting an acrid, sulfurous smell over the upper river. Keep your windows closed. Or maybe you'll come into town on Niagara Falls Boulevard, skirting a forest of transmission towers and a mountainous landfill. If you come from the north, you'll pass by the Tuscarora Nation, advertised by billboards accusing New York State of breaking treaties, and a flashing sign announcing Smokin Joes Trading Post: Gas! Cigarettes! Indian Souvenirs! Tax-Free! Or you could take the Seaway Trail, which enters town at the edge of a huge sheetcake-shaped landfill surrounded by chain link and razor wire. That's Hooker–102nd Street, the lesser-known end of Love Canal. To your right is a sign: Welcome to Niagara Falls.

However you enter town, head for the riverfront in the spirit of awed anticipation; you are about to experience the sublimity of nature. The blue signs with what looks like Malibu Barbie's hair will point you the way. A high school kid in sunglasses and an orange vest will try to divert you into a private parking lot by flailing an orange flag at you. Ignore him, even if he blows a whistle. That's the oldest trick in the book. What you are looking for is Niagara Falls State Park, the nation's first, opened in 1885 for the purpose of making this sublime spectacle "free to all mankind forever." You know you are there when you see a vast plain of pavement, two squat toll booths and a sign: Parking $10.

Once you find a parking spot, proceed through the Great Lakes Garden—flower beds laid out in a map—and cross the pedestrian bridge to Goat Island. Veer right at the portable snack and souvenir stand at the end of the bridge. You are now on Goat Island, a little slice of Eden sitting in the Niagara River on the very brink of the Falls. As you enter this pristine parkland, maintained in a state of unspoiled nature, watch out for cars. No doubt you are all eagerness for the vision of wonder that awaits you, and may fail to hear the People Mover roaring by on the recently widened road.

Take time to appreciate the flora and fauna of this magical place. When you see a giant parking lot and a huge bronze seated statue—that's Nikola Tesla, who harnessed Niagara's watts—you're at the visitor center. Veer right to avoid the snack-bar lines, and you will see a large interpretive marker and some quarter-powered telescopes. Here at last the object of your anxious expectation is before you: Niagara Falls!

Slowly you turn. You are overlooking the southern end of the American Falls. Between you and the vast thundering water, a small railing-bound rectangle of land sits in the rapids like a scuttled barge, tourists crowding to its prow. That's Luna Island, dividing the slender Bridal Veil Falls from the rest of the American Falls. Early guides tell us to note the three profiles that can be traced in Luna's rocky outcropping. Don't bother to look for those now: Luna's face is flat, and flush with the brink. The Army Corps of Engineers blasted off its overhangs to make it safer for tourists below. Early prints show Luna covered with trees. There are nine there now; admire their artful arrangement on the island's neatly mown lawn.

No doubt you will want to get closer to this natural wonder, so descend the cement staircase and cross the bridge onto the island. Luna once shook with the force of pounding water. You can't feel this today, because hydro diversion has removed more than half the water, and the Army Corps engineers stabilized the island with drains, bolts, cables and dowels. It's perfectly safe today, and doesn't move at all.

Our next stop is the Cave of the Winds. But first, you must be outfitted. Stand in line to be issued your thin plastic poncho, stamped Cave of the Winds, and a pair of souvenir water shoes with nonslip soles. The shoes come stuffed with paper and cardboard, several inches of which covers the floor of the group dressing room. Wade through this and outside to the elevator. Before you go down, you will have the opportunity to have your picture taken in front of a large blue painting of the Falls you are about to see. Remember, there's no obligation to buy.

At the bottom of the gorge, the elevator ejects you into a long tunnel, from which you emerge onto a sunlit deck. After some introductory words from your guide, proceed along wooden walkways that take you into the spray. Nothing can describe the dread roar with which this deluge pounds down from above. The cliffs hang over you like destiny, frowning with nature's imposing brow and a huge sign that reads No Smoking. Of course, the overhangs that made the Cave of the Winds cavelike have been dynamited away for safety. The place maintains its early reputation as an excellent fishing spot though: in 1984, on this very walkway, Mr. C. J. Ann of Seoul was hit by a falling salmon (Chinook, 15 pounds!), which he enterprisingly grabbed. We hope he examined the mercury advisories for Lake Erie before eating his prize.

Upon your return to the top of the island, hasten to Terrapin Point. Here, at the American edge of the thundering Horseshoe Falls, you will be impressed most forcefully with the wild majesty of nature. Terrapin Point used to be Terrapin Rocks, a series of stone outcroppings in the rapids just above the brink, connected to Goat Island by wooden walkways. Today we have something far safer: a neatly mown triangle of artificial land extending into what used to be waterfall. The Corps of Engineers built this spot of land to improve your view. A ramp leads down to the railinged sidewalk. At the flank of the waterfall, you can observe the straight-edged stone wall built to make the Horseshoe Falls look nice at their American edge.

Stand still on this spot that used to be waterfall and you will experience the sublime sensation of human smallness. "And what are you?" asks an 1842 guidebook: "an atom in the midst of immensity; a breath of time on the brow of Eternity. How awful is the scene!" The tourists agree with the awful part. When the wind blows mist in their direction, they run screaming up the gently sloped lawn.

You could linger here for hours, but onward you must go, to the Three Sisters, once called the Moss Islands, for their green-blanketed misty glades. Water diversions for power have eliminated this inconvenience. Then onward again, to the upper end of Goat Island, now eight acres larger through the addition of fill, again to disguise the effects of power plant water diversions. What the Indians called the "parting of the waters," a shallow sandbar that allowed for canoe navigation onto the island, is no more. No need to mourn its passing; a nicely landscaped parking lot now occupies the spot, servicing more modern modes of transport.

Back to the mainland! At Prospect Point, you will enjoy the most panoramic view from the American side: the sweep of the American Falls at your feet and in the distance, the curve of the Horseshoe. How much better the vista since the 1961 opening of a 280-foot tower, with observation deck and four high-speed elevators inside to whisk you to the *Maid of the Mist* landing. This structure projects into the river gorge like a stuck-out tongue, but the park directors are sensitive to its impact. They recently clad it in green mirrors, so it would blend in better, and lowered it by 55 feet to reduce its imposition on the view.

And now we leave the American side, and visit friendly Canada. Directly across the Rainbow Bridge is the famous view of the American Falls from what used to be Clifton House, now the Sheraton. This scene, which one venerable author calls "lovely beyond all conception," is now nicely framed by snack-serving pushcarts. The Canadians have also increased its loveliness through the addition of heavy landscaping; they plant 200,000 flowers a year in Queen Victoria Park.

A pleasant ten-minute stroll away, and you are at the famous Table Rock. Of course, Table Rock is no more—the last vestiges of this rocky outcropping were blasted away in 1934, but the Table Rock Restaurant offers a lovely view of the Horseshoe, and Yorkshire puddings too. Hail Britannia! Afterward, you must take part in the longstanding tradition of going down into the gorge from Table Rock House and passing behind the waterfall. "Where may the ambitious, the proud, and the arrogant," asks an 1851 guide, "so perfectly judge of their own excessive littleness, as in the giant presence of this sacred shrine?" You may experience this divine humility too, especially if, like me, you can't get the audio headset they give you to work in the echoing tunnel.

How did this happen? How did a landscape heralded as an example of the awesome power of nature come to be so altered and controlled by humans? If you visit the Falls, or read one of the popular histories of Niagara, here's the explanation you'll get: Before the Europeans came, Native Americans revered the waterfall as a sacred place. But the inevitable advance of the white man meant that the land around the Falls passed into the hands of the nature-loving, respectful Porter family. These founding settlers left the Falls pristine, and early tourists came to experience Nature in her undiminished beauty. But the family couldn't fight the forces of trade. After the Civil War, commerce began to impinge on the waterfall. Small-time con men built a honky-tonk carnival of exploitation at the brink of the waterfall, but luckily, a group of high-minded public men formed a movement called Free Niagara to save it. They established the Niagara Reservation, the nation's first state park, and returned the natural landscape to its former glory. The Falls were saved for posterity.

This story is no more authentic than the rolling lawns of Terrapin Point. The urge to change Niagara Falls—to reshape the landscape to make it safer, prettier, more fun and easier to access—began with the first inklings of tourism. In fact, even as Niagara was being touted around the world as the symbol of American nature, it was being transformed by preservationists and artists no less than industrialists and entrepreneurs into something dollarable. The real history of Niagara is a history of commerce.

The Europeans who colonized North America were on a sacred mission. They were here to subdue the land. The so-called New World was impressive in its catalog of ready resources—trees, furs, fish, salt, birds, and water just for starters—but its wildness was not admired. William Bradford, governor of the Plymouth Colony, famously described his new home as "a hideous and desolate wilderness, full of wild beasts and wild men." Taming this savage land was not simply necessary to survival; it was God's plan. Clearing woods, planting fields, eliminating predators, harnessing rivers, dredging harbors and fencing off land were moral imperatives, equivalent to conquering evil. "What is not useful, is vicious," declared Puritan minister Cotton Mather, encouraging seventeenth-century settlers to continue the process of subjugating the vast continent.

In this worldview, a giant waterfall, its motive power going to waste, was not inspiring but awful, as made clear in Father Hennepin's description of the Falls, like Bradford's wilderness, as "hideous." Other early visitors agreed. The Baron de Lahontan, Louis-Armand de Lom d'Arce, called it "the most dreadful Heap in the world." Pierre-François-Xavier de Charlevoix, writing home in 1744, declared that "on whatever side you turn your eyes, you discover nothing which does not inspire a secret horror."

Horrible, and deadly too. Hennepin points out that the raging river above the cataract "violently hurries down the Wild Beasts while endeavouring to pass it." He's not the only one to notice this. Early accounts all tell tales of waterfowl swept over the brink, swans dazzled to death by the spray, even deer and bears hurled down to violent ends, as if the waterfall itself were a vicious predator. The downriver Indians are often reported to reap the benefit of this brutal harvest, eating the dead animals that drift downstream—according to the Baron de Lahontan, "they take 'em out of the river with their canows." Even the stolidly factual Swedish botanist Peter Kalm, in his "correction" to the exaggerated reports preceding him, tells us that the entire French garrison below the Falls lived on the river's harvest of waterfowl in autumn, as well as "deer, bears, and other animals which have tried to cross the water above the fall."

What would cause this awful death machine to become something every American dreamed of seeing? The typical answer to that question is that it was Romantic notions of the sublime: the idea that the things most worthy of admiration were not merely beautiful, but a little bit frightening too. Joseph Addison, writing in *The Spectator*, famously associated sublimity with the unfathomable: our imagination, he explained, loved "to grasp at any thing that is too big for its capacity." Too large and powerful to be tamed, too stupendous even to be perceived, sublime objects made us aware of our own puny insignificance. They put us in the right frame of mind to contemplate the Creator. In this way, they weren't just nice to look at, but ennobling to contemplate. Sublimity was a religious experience. It was beauty plus moral, prettiness with a point.

The idea of the sublime had been kicking around since ancient Rome, but essayists like Joseph Addison and Edmund Burke revived it in the eighteenth century. Romantic poets like

Wordsworth and Byron gave poetic voice to sublime landscapes in the early 1800s, and for nearly a century afterward, the English-speaking world was crazy for sublime sights. Niagara—huge, awe-inspiring, unfathomable—fit the bill. By the mid-1800s, it was commonplace to say, as Charles Dickens did in 1843, that the waterfall was a "continual illustration of God's mighty power."

But even as a desire for sublime scenery would create the desire to see Niagara, actually seeing the place required the opposite of sublimity. In order for Niagara to be admired for its wildness, it would have to be partly tamed. Niagara's rise as a tourist site would hinge on "progress": transportation improvements such as roads, canals and railroads, as well as treaties with the Six Nations that would open western New York to land speculation and settlement. But it would also require an entrepreneurial spirit to transform the raw nature of Niagara into an experience that could be had, or rather, bought.

As you come off the pedestrian bridge onto Goat Island, the chunk of land between the American Falls and the Canadian Horseshoe Falls, three faces frown out at you from an interpretive marker. Augustus Porter, stiff-collared and white-haired, broods beneath a high forehead like the stout, gloomy judge he is; his younger brother Peter, the hothead, has the same pointed nose beneath a tousle of black hair. Below Peter, Frederick Law Olmsted, a glowering, bewhiskered Victorian, leans moodily into his walking stick amid a grove of leaves and flowers. In Niagara County, you can't escape any of these guys. They are, according to history books, monuments, visitor centers and souvenir guides, the saviors of Niagara Falls.

The Porters come first; they settled the town. After buying Goat Island, they kept it in the family for seventy years, until the state bought it back and turned it into parkland, which means they are universally held up as Niagara's first champions. Thomas Holder's *Guide to Niagara Falls*, 1882, compliments the Porter family for having "refrained from making their splendid property a mere mercenary scheme." As the interpretive marker on Goat

Island declares, the Porters "respected the island's natural beauty and preserved it as a scenic spot." Thanks to these prescient conservationists, Holder declared, Goat Island was "found to-day covered with virgin forest and almost in a state of nature."

This is the story told by every guidebook after 1880: the Porters preserved Goat Island as virgin forest. Nothing could be further from the truth. The Porters set out to subdue Niagara with a zeal Cotton Mather would have loved. They made extensive alterations to Goat Island, catering to both tourists and industry. Far from maintaining the Falls in a "state of nature," they constantly attempted to alter and monetize their properties, and when they failed, they tried to sell. History has remade them as idealistic lovers of Niagara's natural wonder, when in fact they were wily entrepreneurs who came to the region with one thing in mind: money. The Porter brothers launched the tradition of altering Niagara in order to sell an experience of nature.

Augustus Porter first laid eyes on Niagara Falls in 1795; he was traveling with a group of surveyors to Ohio's Case Western Reserve. Once he'd seen the Falls, though, he quickly lost interest in Ohio and focused his attention on western New York. He bought thousands of acres in the state, but his speculative interest was centered on Niagara. What struck him most was its water-power potential. In 1805, he bought the Mile Strip ceded by the Senecas and built a sawmill on the Niagara River. The following year, he moved his family from the town of Canandaigua to the Falls and got down to business, soon adding a gristmill, a ropewalk and a tannery. Having founded the town, he went on to be its leading citizen, its only judge and, for many years, postmaster too. His brother Peter soon joined him and launched his own little fiefdom at Black Rock, a few miles upstream.

In 1811, the Porter brothers tried to get their hands on Goat Island, the wooded hunk of land dividing the Canadian Horseshoe Falls from the American Falls. Augustus wrote to the state legislature declaring that there were too many wolves and bears around Niagara Falls for him to raise sheep. Goat Island, he said, would offer a safe haven for his grazing flock. The state surveyor general reported back that the island might serve well for sheep, providing "that the Indian title to it be first extinguished." (The Senecas had renounced the earlier land grant to William Johnson.)

Like most land speculators of the time, the Porters had little concern for Indian title. Neither did the State of New York: ultimately they decided not to sell Goat Island to the Porters on the grounds that the state might want it for a prison or an arsenal.

Temporarily foiled in their scheme to get the choicest land for developing Niagara's water power, Peter and Augustus focused on their portage business. Augustus obtained the lease on what was formerly the Indians' Niagara portage and built a warehouse at Fort Schlosser, less than two miles upstream of the Falls. Peter built a warehouse at Black Rock. The brothers had a large salt depot and a lively transportation business; as settlement moved westward, the Great Lakes were becoming more and more vital to commerce in the young nation. Controlling the Niagara Falls portage gave them an advantage in the burgeoning Great Lakes transport trade; eventually they would own more than half the ships on Lake Erie. The Porters wanted to make Black Rock the hub between points east and the growing towns on the upper Great Lakes—they planned to be the new keepers of the Western Door.

Recalling Peter B. Porter in his autobiography, Martin Van Buren declared that "the acquisition of wealth was his master passion, to which every other was made subsidiary." Looking at the man's political career, it's not hard to believe. Getting himself elected to Congress in 1809, Peter Porter went to work at once forwarding the family's entrepreneurial goals: in 1810 he was appointed to the committee to study the feasibility of an inland canal to the Great Lakes. He immediately began proposing strategies that would bolster his Falls portage monopoly. Determined to advance the fortunes of Black Rock at the expense of upstart Buffalo, he got the U.S. Customs House moved there in 1811. But then the looming war with Great Britain offered even better opportunities for profit.

· · ·

Fifty percent of the casualties in the War of 1812 happened on the Niagara frontier. The Americans expected no difficulty in occupying Canada; Thomas Jefferson claimed it would be "a mere matter of marching." Canada was expected to join the United States soon anyway; invading them would simply speed up the inevitable. In fact, the opposite happened: defending their nation gave Canadians a new sense of national pride. French Canadians and British settlers forgot their differences in joining to fend off the invading Yanks. If it weren't for the War of 1812, in other words, the United States today might dominate world hockey, and senior citizens in Ottawa would send away to Mexico for cheap prescription drugs.

An early hawk, Peter Porter was bullish on a Canadian invasion. He wrote a memo in early 1812 arguing that a swift conquest of Upper Canada should start with the taking of forts on the Detroit and Niagara rivers by local militias—never mind that constitutionally, they could not be made to fight abroad. He helped draft the official 1812 declaration of war, then left Washington to become quartermaster general of New York. While using his shipping business connections to source supplies for the American army, he enrolled as a militia officer and more or less told the British to "bring it on," bragging he would lay out a "war feast" and invite them once the table was set. The Brits responded by lobbing a cannonball into his Black Rock house while he and some guests were eating dinner; it blasted through the chimney and lodged in the ornamental work over the dining room. They went on to burn down the entire Niagara frontier, nearly capturing Peter in his pajamas. His housekeeper tipped him off that the enemy was at the door, and he skedaddled, half-dressed, leaving his breakfast on the table. The Brits finished eating his eggs—not quite the invitation he had issued.

Porter was raked over the coals by the early American press for the "war feast" comment, with some papers pointing out that as quartermaster, he was feasting on the war himself: the government had purchased all the Porters' ships for the war effort, and Peter was accused of selling supplies to the army at a profit. Worse yet, he had helped mastermind the disastrous first attempt to invade Canada a month earlier. The Americans, with Porter leading a local militia brigade, had mounted a sneak attack on Queenston Heights, the Canadian vantage point at the top of the Niagara Escarpment seven miles below the Falls. It had started out well, with the Americans rowing across in the dark and capturing a small battery below Queenston Heights. British General Isaac Brock, roused from his bed at Fort George, got on his horse Alfred and galloped the seven miles from Niagara-on-the-Lake. Without backup, he charged into battle and was almost immediately felled by a musket ball to the chest. His aide-de-camp, Lieutenant Colonel James Macdonell, took Brock's horse Alfred and waded into the fray, quickly getting both himself and poor Alfred killed.

But things quickly went sour for the Americans. Rallied, the Canadian troops began raining a hail of grapeshot and musket balls on the landing Americans, and their Mohawk allies started in with scary war whoops. At this point, American militia soldiers still waiting to cross the river had an attack of clarity about the Constitution and refused to cross the river, pointing out that Canada was foreign soil. With no more backup, the American troops in Canada beat a hasty retreat, and many were taken prisoner. After this rousing defeat, Peter Porter had to fight a duel defending the honor of his reluctant troops when an army captain named Alexander Smyth impugned their courage. The duelists missed each other—perhaps another reason for the Americans' ill luck at battle—and then Smyth's father stepped in and stopped any further fisticuffs.

Today, Queenston Heights is a war memorial, and General Brock stands firmly on a 185-foot column, caped, booted and sporting a schooner-shaped helmet. He has one arm outstretched toward the vineyards of the Canadian fruit belt, as if asking for a glass of their famed ice wine. At the base of the column, in a huge square plinth bristling with shields, weapons and lions rampant, Brock and Macdonell are buried. On a green below the escarpment, there are two additional monuments, one for the Canadians' Indian allies and another for Alfred, the horse.

From its 1826 construction, Brock's Monument was a hit with tourists. The War of 1812 changed the landscape of the Niagara frontier, giving it historic and patriotic significance, and bolstering Niagara's position as national icon for both countries. Two other Canadian battlefields, Lundy's Lane in Niagara Falls and Chippawa a few miles upstream, also became popular tourist sites. Peter Porter had the good fortune to be involved in both of those battles, which were—if not outright victories—face-saving fights for the Americans. They also salvaged Porter's reputation for valor; he and his Iroquois and New York volunteers fought bravely.

Throughout all of it, Porter never seems to have lost his penchant for eating well: the Niagara Historical Society Museum in Niagara-on-the-Lake today proudly displays an elaborate silver serving basket said to have been taken from General Porter's tent during the Battle of Queenston Heights.

One afternoon at the Niagara Falls Public Library, I decide to ask Maureen Fennie about the Porters. Anyone who does historical research on Niagara Falls knows Maureen. Skirted, bespectacled, and usually sporting a strikingly arty piece of jewelry, she looks like she arrived from central casting after someone ordered up a librarian. That is, until she opens her mouth. A sharp-eyed observer of local affairs, Maureen has a tart way with words belied by her somewhat matronly laugh. She's responsible for having recovered the Civil War sword of Colonel Peter Augustus Porter, son of Peter B. Porter. The sword was one of many artifacts owned by the Niagara Falls Historical Society. In a saga many see as depressingly typical of the town's attitude toward its history, the sword ended up in private hands after the bankrupt Historical Society divvied up its items for safekeeping. Someone's idea of safekeeping was to sell the sword, and it passed to an Ohio auctioneer. The auctioneer called the Niagara Falls Public Library to ask about the sword's background, at which point Maureen demanded it back. The auctioneer resisted handing over his prize, and eventually, the state attorney general had to be brought in.

He pronounced the sword public property, and with much grumbling it was returned to the people of Niagara Falls.

Today the sword sits proudly in a glass case on the second floor of the library. Maureen and the other librarians continue to keep an eye out for missing artifacts. They also actively collect documents of local history; not just books and newspaper articles, but papers and ephemera others consider worthless. When Carborundum, one of Niagara's most longstanding corporations, closed their regional factory, the librarians went directly to the plant and scooped up all the corporate documents that were sitting around in garbage bins waiting to be shredded. I love this vision: a van pulling up, blue light flashing, three or four librarians in sensible shoes jumping out and racing into the lobby and shouting "Hold it right there, sir! Hands off that company newsletter!" Okay, so maybe it didn't really happen that way (I could be going too far with the blue light), but it's a great thing to imagine, and it makes my heart swell with bottomless admiration for librarians and the noble work they do.

I express this admiration by spending a lot of time at the library bugging the librarians. A seventies-style cement cathedral on a run-down stretch of Main Street, the library is surprisingly nice inside, with a bright reading room and a sprawling feel. Local History, on the third floor, has long tables strewn with treats for the Niagaraphile: maps, old guidebooks, obscure histories. There's a newspaper index, a picture file, closets full of goodies like postcards and glass lantern slides, and shelf after shelf of scrapbooks in which the librarians still paste articles under headings like "Industries," "Daredevils," "Hydropower" and "Snakes." And there's Maureen, who knows about arcane documents or Ph.D. dissertations on Niagara industries, and who, even in the midst of the apparently endless task of sorting and cataloging the library's collection, is always willing to stop and chat about things Niagara.

So when I'm reading old journal articles about the Porters and she walks by my table, I call her over.

"Maureen, what do you think of the Porters?" I ask her. "Augustus and Peter B.?"

"Well, Peter B. was a big guy," she says right away. "An interesting guy, but I don't really know much about him. Or Augustus really." She pauses, and I wait silently. This is the critical moment. She has some folders in her hand, but after a minute she sits down at the table next to me and I know I've succeeded in distracting her.

"Somebody should write a book," she says. "They weren't exactly philanthropists—let's put it that way."

When she sees me taking notes, she snaps her mouth shut. I ask her to say more, for the record, but she won't. She doesn't want to badmouth the local eminence.

Down at least one piece of tableware, Peter Porter returned to the rubble of his home county after the War of 1812. The war had changed his profile from grasping land speculator to respected patriot, a reputation he has enjoyed ever since. But his actions after the war were even more blatantly self-interested than before. Back at the Niagara frontier, he and Augustus—no doubt eager to get back to entertaining—began to rebuild. Peter entered state politics, where he could forward their causes more effectively. In 1815, he acted as state commissioner for a New York State treaty extinguishing Seneca title to the islands in the Niagara River—a nice way of repaying the Iroquois volunteers who had helped him gain military glory. A few weeks later, he and Augustus tricked the state into handing the islands over to them. They found a man with a "float": an IOU from the state promising him 200 acres of his choice. The sneaky Porters bought the float and used it to demand Goat Island and the other small islands around it.

In 1816, Peter got himself appointed to the Joint Mixed Boundary Commission to resolve lingering disputes over the U.S.—Canadian border. One of the issues to be resolved was whether the islands in the Niagara River belonged to the United States or Canada. Some members of Congress pointed out that since Peter owned many of those very islands, his appointment to this commission created a teeny-tiny conflict of interest. They were rebuffed. In the subsequent unsurprising report of June, 1822, the commissioners declared that all the Niagara River islands except for Navy Island—which hugs the Canadian shore and was not owned by the Porters—should be considered U.S. territory.

After an unsuccessful run for governor in 1817, Peter married into a fancy Kentucky family—his father-in-law, John Breckenridge, was President Jefferson's attorney-general—and turned his attention to business. With Black Rock not quite the thriving metropolis they imagined, Peter and Augustus focused on Niagara Falls, which they named Manchester, in hopes of making it a great manufacturing center like its English namesake. Things got off to a promising start: factory-owners saw the water-power potential in the thundering falls, and Manchester quickly added to its industries a woolen factory, a forge-rolling mill and nail factory, and a paper mill.

At the same time, the Porters didn't ignore the area's potential for tourism. American hotelier Parkhurst Whitney built a staircase down to the river from his hotel in 1817. Loyalist and ex-con William Forsyth, who fled to Canada after the Revolution and opened the Niagara Hotel near Table Rock, built another. Forsyth and Whitney connected their stairs with a ferry service, launching the tradition that would become the *Maid of the Mist*. Whitney also built a log bridge to Goat Island and when, in early 1818, it was destroyed by ice, the Porters got into the tourism game by rebuilding it, and instituting a 25-cent toll for passage. In 1821, Augustus constructed a gristmill and private bathing facilities on the little island between the mainland and Goat Island. He also decided to put a hotel on Goat Island and wrote to Peter asking him to draw up the plans.

The hotel scheme languished. At this point, the Porters were still mainly interested in the area's industrial potential. There were visitors coming to see the Falls, but they were a trickle, not a steady stream. The Niagara frontier was still just that, the frontier. It was dangerous, distant and difficult to reach. In a few short years, all that would change.

If you go to Niagara Falls from New York today, you pretty much follow the same route early travelers took. You roar north on the New York State Thruway along the mighty Hudson River, up which early travelers sailed by steamship. At Albany, you hang a left and head straight west to Buffalo. The Thruway follows the old Iroquois trail up the center of the Mohawk Valley, a broad, statewide plain dotted, now as in the 1800s, with riverfront towns and intermittently hardscrabble farms. Place names are the most persistent sign of the region's former citizens: Oneida County, Cayuga Lake, Seneca Falls, and my favorite, the Iroquois Travel Plaza. The Mohawk River occasionally slithers up to the Thruway, and at one point a set of stone locks stands high and dry next to the road, reminding the modern-day traveler, zooming along at 83 miles an hour (as officially clocked by the New York State Police to her great chagrin) that this journey, round-trip, once took fifteen days on the Erie Canal.

The Erie Canal opened in 1825. The celebrations marking the end of the eight-year project were grandiose. A cannon was fired in Buffalo, and then every 10 or 15 miles along the canal's 363-mile route to Albany and down the Hudson, finally reaching the Battery in New York City an hour and twenty minutes later. The cannon signal then returned by the same route. After that, a flotilla of four boats—the *Seneca Chief*, the *Noah's Ark*, the *Niagara of Black Rock* and the *Young Lion of the West*—sailed from Buffalo to New York carrying a bevy of dignitaries and a representative sample of upstate natural resources: birds, fish, apples, flour, butter, foxes, raccoons, a bear cub, two eagles, two fawns and two Seneca boys, "all of them," crowed the newspaper account, "*products of the west.*" Upon arrival in New York, Governor DeWitt Clinton, with great pomp, poured a keg of Lake Erie water into the Atlantic Ocean to signify the canal's wedding of ocean and upper Great Lakes. Speeches were made and toasts drunk. Unfortunately, whatever ceremonial use was planned for the Seneca boys was scotched: the *Noah's Ark*, weighed down with all that flora and fauna, had bottomed out in the 5-foot-deep canal.

The Porters had opposed the Erie Canal. If barges could travel from the Atlantic to Lake Erie, their portage monopoly would be useless. Peter even drew up an alternate plan for a ship canal that would connect Lake Ontario to Lake Erie, allowing sailing ships to circumvent the Falls and reach the upper Great

Lakes. Incidentally, it would also have made Black Rock even more decisively the Western Door. When Congress didn't go for the ship canal, he lobbied hard to get the western terminus of the Erie Canal located at Black Rock, arguing that the Buffalo harbor was too shallow. Incensed, a group of Buffalo advocates paid to refit the Buffalo harbor at the last minute, and the canal was terminated there. The Porters were still steaming about all of this when the canal opened—so much so that when Peter B. was invited along on the celebratory flotilla, he refused to ride on the *Seneca Chief* with Governor Clinton, father of the canal. He and some Black Rock buddies commissioned the pointedly named *Niagara of Black Rock* instead, aboard which they undoubtedly made some toasts of their own.

However, even if it eliminated their portage business, the Erie Canal excited the Porters' entrepreneurial instincts. It immediately created new possibilities for commerce—western New Yorkers could sell their farm products to the much bigger markets down-state, and could buy goods that hadn't previously been available to them. And it inflated upstate land values. Royal Navy officer and travel writer Captain Basil Hall reports in his *Travels in North America, in the Years 1827 and 1828*, that "property of every kind has risen in value, as might have been expected, in all those parts of the country through which the canal passes."

All that sounded good to the Porters. So, right on the heels of the canal's opening, they attempted once more to sell off Niagara Falls. They issued an "invitation to Eastern Capitalists" to come and develop the region's water power. "Practically speaking," they declared in the newspaper ad, "the extent to which water-power may be here applied is without limit." They pointed out the town's proximity to the Erie Canal terminus and to Lake Erie, and noted that the area's extensive forests would provide "a cheap and abundant supply of fuel for manufacturing purposes." They also envisioned the complete development of Goat Island. The upper half they saw "covered with machinery, propelled by water-power," and the lower half "converted into delightful seats for the residence of private gentlemen, or appropriated to hotels and pleasure grounds." They then offered to sell all their land and water rights at Niagara.

It seemed logical to the Porters that the opening of the Erie Canal would inspire further efforts to remake nature to better serve human ends. The canal was heralded by the citizens of New York not only as a new means of transport, but as a triumph of human design over nature's. With its locks and aqueducts it made ships float up mountains and rivers flow above roads. As a traveler wrote upon seeing the impressive "deep cut" at Lockport, where the canal edged through an artificial gorge and ascended an imposing 60-foot rock formation on two flights of five locks, "Here the great Erie Canal has defied nature and used it like a toy." Citizens of New York City could now feast on upstate apples, and western New Yorkers could indulge in Atlantic oysters. If a simple ditch so radically remade the world, what might be possible at Niagara, where, as the Porters assured investors, "a thousand mills can be erected and supplied with a never failing water power at a small expense"?

When no buyers came forward, the Porters continued their own industrial development, erecting more factories, building a road on Goat Island and even tapping the sugar maples. But little by little, their interest was shifting to tourism, as the Erie Canal's effect became clear. Before the canal, passengers en route to Niagara had to suffer fifteen days of jolting and bouncing along bad roads from Albany to Buffalo, often climbing out to help lever their stagecoach out of the mud when it got stuck. Once the canal was finished, packet boats departed on frequent schedules, and the journey took five to seven days at the heady pace of 4 miles an hour. If they were lucky, they'd get a captain willing to risk the $10 fine and kick it up to 5 miles an hour; even then, speeding was rampant. Of course, the era's travelers loved complaining about the packet boats as much as today's tourists love maligning air travel. The hot sun broiled them, the fellow passengers annoyed them, the food was dubious and there were frequent low bridges where you literally had to "hit the deck" to avoid being smashed on the overpass like a bug on a Hummer's windshield. But the trip time had been halved, and the packet boats were a great novelty. Ironically, the ditch that conquered nature made visiting nature easier than ever.

Within a couple of decades, millions of passengers had traveled on what was affectionately called "Clinton's ditch." The final destination for most of these early tourists was Niagara Falls, the climactic stop on the "Northern Tour," America's answer to the European "Grand Tour." The precanal trickle of tourism at the Falls was becoming a full-fledged flood. The Erie Canal brought a market economy to the farmlands of western New York, and it brought a new market to Niagara, ready to consume.

When he visited in 1827, Captain Basil Hall took a stroll around Goat Island with a man he describes as "the proprietor"— presumably Augustus Porter. Hall reported that Goat Island's owner "seemed unaffectedly desirous of rendering it an agreeable place of resort to strangers." Porter told Hall about the many improvements he had been advised to make: trimming the landscape, clearing the woods, and putting a tavern at the brink of the Horseshoe Falls. Captain Hall says he "expressed my indignation at such a barbarous set of proposals, and tried hard to explain how repugnant they were to all our notions of taste in Europe. His ideas, I was glad to see, appeared to coincide with mine; so that this conversation may have contributed, in some degree, to the salvation of the most interesting spot in all America."

Porter then asked Hall what alterations might be acceptable to these canons of taste, and Hall suggested adding a gravel walk, "broad enough for three persons to walk abreast," cutting paths through the woods to the best viewpoints, and installing "half a dozen commodious seats" for visitors to rest on. As for the unspeakable suggestion of a tavern at the Horseshoe, Hall was relieved to find that Porter's "own good taste revolted at such a combination of the sublime and the ridiculous." However, he noted pessimistically, such a descent in aesthetics "which we know from high authority and example costs but one step, will be made in the course of time."

Hall was right. The Porters would begin with roads, walking paths and bridges, and would move on to refreshment stands and pleasure gardens. As their vision of Goat Island half-covered with private homes and pleasure grounds shows, the Porters' ideal of tourism development was far from being based on the sanctity of the landscape. They weren't trying to maintain Goat Island in some sort of Edenic state, but to make it accessible and attractive enough to lure toll-paying tourists to town.

In 1827, as they were trying to lure those "eastern capitalists" to the Falls, the Porters took part in a scheme that would get more tourists to Niagara than had ever come at once before. They helped mount the first spectacle to be staged at Niagara: the wreck of the schooner *Michigan*. The odd undertones of this event demonstrate that the last thing on the Porters' minds was preserving nature.

The demise of the *Michigan* appears in every nineteenth-century guidebook; today, it's almost always left out. When it's mentioned, it's usually cast as the opening salvo in spectacle's attack on the sublime at Niagara—the moment crass commercialism began replacing natural wonder. The show was masterminded by Canadian hotelier William Forsyth, who had replaced his Niagara Hotel with the new, deluxe Pavilion Hotel in 1822. He got his two main rivals in the hotel business, John Brown, owner of the nearby Ontario House, and Parkhurst Whitney, proprietor of the American side's Eagle Tavern, to collaborate on pulling it off. This binational troika of entrepreneurs came up with a plan to do what Niagara tourism promoters have never ceased trying to do: extend the tourist season beyond the summer months. They scheduled their big show for September 8, 1827.

Posters advertising the event were very specific. The schooner *Michigan*, once a Lake Erie freighter partially owned by Peter Porter, would be decked out as a "Pirate" and loaded up with a cargo of "animals of the most ferocious kind, such as Panthers, Wild Cats, Bears and Wolves." The caged animals would be displayed on board the ship at Black Rock, where visitors would have the opportunity to come aboard and check them out, for a "trifling expense." On the morning of the eighth, the *Michigan* would be towed by steamship to the foot of Navy Island, a little more than four miles above the Falls. For the hefty sum of 50 cents, visitors could ride with the doomed critters. At Navy Island, the visitors would leave, and Peter Porter's business associate Captain James Rough, "the oldest navigator of the Upper Lakes," would tow the ship into the strong currents above the Falls and cut her loose, leaving her creaturely crew to its fate.

The organizers sent a card to the press asserting their belief that many of the animals would survive the descent: "great interest will be added to the closing scene," they declared, "in seeing them successively rise among the billows in the basin below . . . and shape their course to the shore." The *New York Sun* enthused that the intended spectacle "can hardly be equaled by the combinations of nature and art, in any other part of the world." They predicted that "the greatest part, and probably the whole" of the animals would survive the plunge without injury and "be seen, after a proper time, emerging from the abyss, and wending their way to the shores from which they were respectively taken"—nature returning to its domain.

Other commentators disagreed. The *Eastern Argus* declared that "it may be sport to the spectators, but unjustifiable cruelty to the animals," and then speculated on nature's potential revenge: "Why should the elements hush their commotion for the safety of men, or the storms forego their sporting, if man is deaf to the cries of things under his subjection?" Still others approved the idea of "a contest between the products of human art and the powers of nature." Would the ship survive the mighty Falls, proving man's ability to defeat the waterfall? Or would nature assert her primacy and smash the puny human craft to bits?

Expecting a huge turnout, Peter and Augustus exchanged letters about which boats to pull from regular service and load up with tourists. Augustus urged Peter to send the largest to the American side on what he called "the great day of the 8th." When the great day came, it was as good as they had hoped. The boats were packed, the roads thronged. Every hotel bed in town was booked, and people slept on tables and floors. Taverns ran out of food and liquor. Estimates of attendance ranged from 10,000 to 20,000 spectators. While they waited for the *Michigan* to meet her fate, the jostling masses were entertained by a ventriloquist, an astronomy lecturer, a menagerie, a learned pig and a card-playing dog named Apollo. Temperance lecturers railed against the evils of drink, violinists and pipe-players solicited donations, kino and three-card monte experts separated the gullible from their coins, pickpockets worked the crowd.

The hoteliers had been unable to lay hands on the promised ferocious panthers, wildcats and wolves. In the end, the crew consisted of two bears, a buffalo, two foxes, a raccoon, an eagle, a dog and fifteen honking geese. Apparently anticipating misgivings on behalf of the dog, the organizers assured the press that he, at least, deserved to die. He had bitten a reporter.

The ship was also fitted out with a human crew in effigy. A couple of scarecrows were dressed up in suits and labeled AJ and JA to represent recent presidential contenders Andrew Jackson and John Quincy Adams. The 1824 election had been ugly. It was, in fact, the first (but not the last) American election in which the winner of the popular vote did not become president. Andrew Jackson received more votes in both the popular election and the electoral college, but since neither candidate had garnered a majority, the House of Representatives had the final call and they appointed Adams President. Jackson cried foul, alleging that House Speaker Henry Clay had given his vote to Adams after making a deal to be appointed secretary of state.

Peter Porter was a great friend of Henry Clay, and had backed Clay's own bid for the presidential nomination. Clay was a supporter of the kinds of federally funded internal improvements that would encourage westward expansion and put money in the Porters' pockets. The ship's political references indicate a general disgust with a politics where backroom dealings replaced the will of the people, but they also grow directly out of Porter and his allies' frustrated ambitions. The spectacle even suggests they were still nursing the Erie Canal grudge. Like the ill-fated canal boat *Noah's Ark*, the *Michigan* was loaded with indigenous natural resources— advertised as "Living Animals of the Forests which surround the Upper Lakes." The ship went to her doom with an American flag on her bowsprit, a Union Jack astern, and flapping atop her mast, a Jolly Roger. The whole episode reeks of sour grapes.

The event went pretty much as planned. Captain Rough cut the ship loose and his men rowed like mad to safety. One bear, seeing the writing on the wall, jumped overboard and swam for shore. The other scaled the mast—an unlucky choice. The ship tossed and rolled as it hit the upper rapids; both masts broke off, water flooded aboard, and the schooner was completely submerged by the time she slipped over the brink and splintered into innumerable small pieces. On the riverbanks below, spectators raced to collect the scraps. Besides the bear who swam ashore before the plunge, the only animal definitely recovered was a one-eyed goose fished out of the river downstream. Both were promptly put on display, though by some accounts, the goose's stage career soon ended with a farewell performance on the dinner table.

Most contemporary viewers saw the descent of the *Michigan* as a succinct symbol for nature's mastery over man's pathetic creations: waterfall one, ship zero. "The power of the Almighty," declared the *Rochester Telegraph*, "was imposingly displayed over the workmanship of mere human hands." But it was now humans who staged nature's triumph. Nature's supremacy was already looking like an act.

Tourism is one of the earliest forms of consumer activity that is about acquiring experiences, not things. After the *Michigan* incident, more people than ever realized that there were experiences to be had at Niagara. Energized, the Porters got down to the business of providing them. They built walkways out to the Terrapin Rocks and "deflecting piers of logs and stones" to control erosion on the upstream end of Goat Island. In 1833, they erected Terrapin Tower, a stone pinnacle built at the very brink of the Horseshoe. Costing 10 cents to visit, the tower quickly became a popular attraction, and one of the most popular Falls images. Even as some saw it as an imposition on the landscape—British travel writer Anna Jameson declared it "detestably impudent and *mal-à-propos* . . . a signal yet puny monument of bad taste"—most visitors seemed to love the little tower; looking half a ruin in its prime, it perched bravely at the brink of the great fall. Like the *Michigan*, it pitted human art against nature; unlike the *Michigan*, it held its own—at least until its 1873 demolition.

In the 1830s, the Porters developed another new attraction: the Cave of the Winds. Discovered by three local men in a row-boat in 1834, the cave originally allowed visitors to go behind the downpour of the Bridal Veil Falls—the narrow waterfall separated from the bulk of the American Falls by Luna Island. It wasn't easy. According to an 1843 guidebook, the Porters went to "consider-able expense" and "excavated the rocks, erected steps, and con-tracted the stream above in such a manner that this cave can now with ease and safety be visited." By this time, they had also nearly doubled the size of Bath Island with fill, and their three-story mill there was producing 10,000 reams of paper a year.

Peter Porter moved to Niagara Falls in 1838, building himself a mansion across from the International Hotel. In 1839, a guide-book reported that General Porter was improving Goat Island fur-ther with a garden, an 8-acre park stocked with deer and other ani-mals, a pond filled with local fish, and a 4-acre poultry yard, sure to please "the traveling gourmand." To irrigate his waterworks and his gardens, he had built a dam, an embankment and a reservoir, all diverting water from the Niagara River. To top it all off, he was planning to add "a small, but elegant, romantic-like cottage, for occasional summer use." By 1862, that cottage would be remod-eled and turned into a refreshment and ice-cream stand, one of two on Goat Island.

The Porters' tourist alterations made it possible to sell a care-fully arranged experience of Niagara Falls, one that adhered to the pictorial conventions of the picturesque by organizing the wild natural landscape to create the right visual effects. The guidebooks that began to flourish in this period all recommended a standard tour with almost no variation. You followed the Porters' paths through the quiet glades of Goat Island, and emerged from the lush, sun-dappled woods to cross walkways or climb a tower to stunning, open vistas on the roaring Falls. You got closer to the massive waterfall by going down the staircase and entering the Cave of the Winds. Then you walked back onto the mainland

and descended the incline railway to the ferry landing, where you caught the *Maid of the Mist* and visited Canada's panoramic views. It was an organized tour that brought disparate effects into artistic counterpoint: far-off vistas with close-up encounters, shady woods with open white water, sylvan charm with impressive, roaring wildness.

The entire experience was meant to induce in the visitor a "correct" set of emotional responses, centered on the experience of the sublime. As the guidebooks explained, the waterfall was "the everlasting altar, at whose cloud-wrapt base the elements pay homage to Omnipotence!" The trip to the bottom of the Falls, or into the spray on the *Maid of the Mist*, was calculated to inspire a sense of smallness in the face of Creation. But the sweeping vistas achieved from Terrapin Tower and Table Rock on the Canadian side counteracted this with a distant, philosophical perspective. The experience was not all terror and vastness, nor beauty and charm, but a perfect combination of both. Niagara Falls—experienced in the "correct" way—was full of moral meaning. But it was also, in the hands of the Porters, a product that delivered—perhaps better than it ever has since.

General Peter B. Porter died in 1844; Judge Augustus Porter died in 1849. By then, they had been joined by other entrepreneurs who would help shape the tourist experience. The Niagara Falls Museum opened on the Canadian side around 1830, and grand hotels were built in the decade following: on the Canadian side, Clifton House, and on the American, Cataract House. Both featured fine dining, ballrooms, entertainment, billiards and gardens. The 1840s saw pagodas built on both sides of the gorge, and, on the Canadian side, a series of battlefield observation towers. Souvenir emporia and Indian curiosity shops sprang up along the riverfront on both sides, offering "authentic" beadwork and carvings. "Parks" and pleasure grounds—all with entrance fees—offered further access to the views and additional enhancements like restaurants, dancing pavilions, fountains and art galleries.

These antebellum additions to the scenery don't show up in prints and paintings; artists edited out what they considered unsightly. It isn't until the advent of photography that the Falls can be seen as they really were. In stark contrast to paintings and prints, photographs from the mid nineteenth century show observation towers, mills and souvenir shops crowding the Falls. There are tollbooths and signs everywhere: one shot from the late 1800s shows a walkway on Goat Island posted with a big sign reading Spare the Trees and Shrubs.

It became common later to badmouth all these additions to the scenery, as Henry James would do in 1871, snobbishly grumbling in *The Nation* that "the horribly vulgar shops and booths and catchpenny artifices . . . have pushed and elbowed to within the very spray of the Falls." James complained that the "importunities one suffers here . . . from hackmen and photographers and vendors of gimcracks, are simply hideous and infamous." Father Hennepin's word for the waterfall was now applied to the human accretions around it.

Frederick Law Olmsted and the "Free Niagara" movement of the 1870s would declare this subordination of Niagara's scenery to profit a national disgrace. But Free Niagara would not blame the Porters. In fact, the Free Niagara advocates would bolster their cause by claiming that the Porters—Niagara's only protectors—were about to sell Goat Island, opening it up to horrendous commercial development. The fact that it had been commercially developed for years was conveniently ignored: it didn't suit the story.

In 1893, Mark Twain wrote a short, hilarious sketch called "The First Authentic Mention of Niagara Falls" for a handsome souvenir volume called *The Niagara Book*. The sketch purports to be extracts from the diary of Adam as he hangs around in a place he persists in calling "The Garden of Eden." A "new creature" has recently arrived, however, who has other ideas. Adam makes note in his diary:

> Tuesday.—Been examining the great waterfall. It is the finest thing on the estate, I think. The new creature calls it Niagara Falls—why I am sure I do not know. Says it *looks* like Niagara Falls. That is not a reason, it is mere waywardness and imbecility.

The new creature, Eve, soon renames the place "Niagara Falls Park" and puts up a sign: Keep Off the Grass, which leads mopey Adam to note, "My life is not as happy as it was." The following week, things have gotten even worse:

> Tuesday.—She has littered the whole estate with execrable names and offensive signs: "This way to the Whirlpool." "This way to Goat Island." "Cave of the Winds this way." She says the park would make a tidy summer resort if there was any custom for it.

Twain neatly eviscerates the nineteenth-century guidebooks' propensity to equate Goat Island with the Garden of Eden. Many authors even quoted Milton's *Paradise Lost* when describing it—"Must I thus leave thee, Paradise?/—These happy walks and shades,/Fit haunt of gods?" And yet, as Twain's Adam makes clear, the transformation of this Garden of Eden into something much more mundane began with the act of naming and labeling it—with seeing it as a summer resort. Nature became a commodity, marketed and sold as if it were a beaded purse, or a shotglass.

Along with Twain's comic sketch, *The Niagara Book* includes a section on what to see at the Falls, and it declares Goat Island to be "still covered with original forest." The author explains why:

> That this is so is due no doubt to the fortunate fact that for generations all the Niagara islands, as well as part of the mainland, were owned by the wealthy family of Gen. Peter B. Porter, well known in the War of 1812. A summer hotel on the bank of Goat Island, overlooking the Horseshoe, would have been a source of enormous profit, but the sanctity of the place was always respected.

The Porters never got around to putting their planned hotel on Goat Island, and so history paints them as nobly resisting the temptation. This view of them was no doubt helped along by the fact that the second Peter Augustus Porter, grandson to Peter B., was an enthusiastic amateur historian who frequently wrote about the region, casting a rosy light on his own ancestors. More recent historians have simply followed in the footsteps of this family hagiographer. Pierre Berton, in his bestselling history of the region, *Niagara*, describes Augustus Porter as "the first conservationist," and insists that "until Goat Island was taken over by the state as part of a park system, the Porter family resisted all attempts to commercialize it." Apparently, the toll bridge, the tower, the paper mills, public baths, fish ponds and bird pen for eager gourmands are not commercial. Berton tells us the Porters resisted attempts to build taverns or turn Goat Island into planted parkland, but he doesn't mention the snack stands, gardens, or other "improvements" they made themselves, or how they tried to sell off the island to folks who would cover it with factories or private homes. Those plans have conveniently slid into the cracks of history. People want to believe, as a recent study commissioned by the Landmark Society of the Niagara Frontier asserts, that when Augustus Porter purchased Goat Island, "his intention was to preserve the thick primeval forest and unique flora on the island from commercial and industrial development."

Alas for Judge Porter's sheep. History has consigned them to oblivion.

Every region loves its local heroes. One fine day in late summer, I go to Oakwood Cemetery in Niagara Falls to visit the Porter brothers. I don't know where they are, but heading down the cemetery's gravel road, I see one plot fenced off with a black wrought-iron fence. As I get closer, I can see an obelisk bearing the name Porter.

"Can I help you?" calls out a young man from a work shed behind me. I wait for him to catch up to me, and explain that I'm looking for Peter Porter.

"Which one?" he asks.

"Peter B. Porter," I say. He nods and points to the fenced-off plot.

"The General," he says knowingly. "I remember reading about him in school." People in Niagara Falls still call Peter B. Porter "the General," to distinguish him from his son Peter A. Porter, "the Colonel," who died a Civil War hero and left behind the squabbled-over sword. The large obelisk belongs to the Colonel, but the cemetery guy confirms that the General is in the same plot. I thank him, but he stands there, surveying the cemetery with the air of an English baronet admiring his lands.

"A lot of history in this place," he says with a hint of local pride. Then he tells me that Annie Taylor, the first person to go over the Falls in a barrel, is buried in this cemetery too.

As I would have expected, the General's tomb is the grandest. Its red stone is carved with shields bearing *P*'s, and decorative *fleurs-de-lis*; the Porter family traces its lineage to French aristocracy. "Peter B. Porter, General in the armies of America," reads the tomb's inscription, "defending in the field what he had maintained in the council." The other side is even more grandiloquent:

A pioneer in Western New York. A statesman eloquent in the annals of the nation and the state. Honoured and renowned throughout that extended region which he had been amongst the foremost to explore and defend.

The transformation of the Porters from men who were minding the main chance to noble protoenvironmentalists is more than just sentimental nostalgia or local pride. It captures what we want to believe about Niagara: it's a natural wonder, untouched and untouchable by humans. Its beauty is a sign that, while we sometimes come close to ruining nature, in the end we always see the light. Goat Island today, enlarged and reshaped by fill, is ringed by two recently widened roads, with parking lots at both ends. Asphalt walkways lead from one viewpoint to the next, passing restaurants, snack bars and souvenir shops. Even as we pave paradise and put up a parking lot, we landscape it neatly and call our efforts conservation.

I sit for a while in the Porter plot. Occasionally, there's the whine overhead from a Niagara sightseeing helicopter. But mostly it's just birds and the rustle of leaves. In other parts of the cemetery, squirrels scamper up and down trees, noisily shredding the husks of walnuts. But here, as if honoring the great man, the squirrels are oddly silent.

Three

SKIPPER THE TWO-LEGGED DOG

IN 1999, ON A whim, a building contractor and shrunken-head collector named Billy Jamieson bought the contents of Canada's oldest museum. In spite of its age, the museum was hardly distinguished. In fact, it was considered a joke. Jamieson's purchase included around 700,000 objects: not just the animals, birds, shells, fossils and freaks of nature that had constituted the museum's original natural history collection, but Egyptian mummies, Chinese weapons, Japanese art, South Pacific war shields, Native American beadwork, model dinosaurs and the base of a giant redwood. As a collection, it was, literally, all over the map.

So when Billy turned around and sold the Egyptian artifacts to an American museum for a price rumored to be at least double what he had paid for the entire collection, the collecting world simply snickered. But when the American museum's curators declared one of the mummies to be the long-lost pharaoh Ramesses I, the same world reeled. Egyptologists professed amazement, and a flurry of art dealers and reporters declared they were shocked, shocked to find there were valuable objects in this outdated curiosity cabinet, a ragtag jumble of shoddy specimens, mislabeled artifacts and oddities, ancestor to Ripley's Believe It or

Not!, rather than the British Museum. No one imagined the place might hold items of value, let alone ancient kings. Its provenance, after all, was Niagara Falls.

As it turned out, Ramesses wasn't the only treasure to be found in the Niagara Falls Museum. Billy found two items casually draped around the neck of a wax Hawaiian warrior—a feather cape and a necklace made of whalebone, ivory and human hair. Rather nice, he thought. The museum catalog—full of maddeningly vague entries such as "Central African Bow," "Chinese Paper Fan" and "African Penile Cover"—didn't say what the cape and necklace were: it subsumed both under the heading "Wax Figures." Billy had the two items cleaned and listed them with Sotheby's. The necklace sold for $313,750, and the feather cape for $335,750. It was a new record for Polynesian art.

Somehow, Billy Jamieson, the contractor-turned-connoisseur, saw what a century of visitors and scholars had failed to notice: the curiosity cabinet at the brink of the waterfall was a treasure trove.

I start digging into the history of the Niagara Falls Museum because its reputation seems to track Niagara's; like the Falls, it went from class act to carnival to kitsch. Historical records aren't even clear on exactly when the museum was born. Its founder, Thomas Barnett, was born in Birmingham, England, in 1799. He trained as a cabinetmaker, but arrived in Canada in 1824 and opened a museum sometime around 1827 in Kingston, Ontario. A local newspaper paid a visit to his Kingston museum in 1830:

> We yesterday visited Mr. Barnett's Museum, in Church St., and were at once delighted and surprised to meet with so fine a collection of Natural Curiosities. It is only two years since Mr. Barnett commenced the laudable undertaking, and to his individual industry and skill are the public indebted for as beautiful a collection of Quadrupeds, Birds, Fishes, Insects, &c. as British North America can afford—all prepared in the best manner, and arranged with great taste and judgment. By frequently visiting the Museum, the inhabitants of Kingston will at once promote

the cause of science, and reward the unwearied exertions of a meritorious individual.

Kingston readers seem to have ignored the reporter's praise, because shortly thereafter, Barnett relocated to Niagara. The year 1831 found him at the Falls advertising "a splendid collection of natural and artificial curiosities" with "upward of 700 stuffed animals—from the hummingbird to the elk . . . including the choice specimens of birds, reptiles, fish, insects, and minerals of every hue and variety." Visitors to the new Niagara Falls Museum would find it educational, he assured them, as "the classical manner in which the numerous objects composing this selection are arranged affords a favourable opportunity for prosecuting the science of Natural History."

Thomas Barnett was a serious man: in the most commonly printed photograph of him, he peers out with an almost simian frown, face flanked by the bushy sideburns of an eminent Victorian, thick brows drawn together with what looks like worry. Overcoated and wool-trousered, lacking the mercurial air of the period's other great museum man, P. T. Barnum, Barnett looks the man of science, not the showman. It's said he used to walk his dog Skipper, born with no front legs, around Niagara Falls, the dog's legless front end propped on wheels. For Barnum this stroll would have been pure showmanship, the dog dressed in a coat with the museum's name on it, the wheeled contraption fitted out with bells. Thomas Barnett is different; he simply wanted to walk his dog. When Skipper died, Barnett mounted the dog and his skeleton separately, as Barnum had done with Jumbo the elephant, but without the attendant hoopla. Barnum issued progress reports on "the world's largest taxidermy job" and unveiled the over-stuffed elephant at a media gala featuring the elephant's mourning "widow" and a gelatin dessert said to be made from Jumbo's tusks. Former cabinetmaker Thomas Barnett simply mounted his dead dog beautifully and added him to his freaks of nature display.

At Billy Jamieson's apartment, I pick up Skipper. He's lighter than I expect; he looks so real, it's surprising to heft him and be reminded he's just a dog skin wrapped around a rag form. He has little bony stumps in the place of front legs. Barnett mounted him sitting up on his hind legs, and his face has an almost inquiring look, ears pert, snout lifted. Balanced between his ears is a label from the museum. Billy is upstairs, working in his study, and I feel vaguely furtive about touching his collection. I put Skipper down and take his picture, head-on. He looks undignified wearing the typed piece of paper, so I remove it and take his picture again. He regards me, so eager and hopeful that I can't help giving him a pat. His fur is coarse and dry. I put the label back where it was and go look at two lambs with deformed faces. One of them appears to have its head on upside down.

Throughout the nineteenth century, Mr. Barnett's museum was the second-best-known attraction at Niagara Falls. It's mentioned in the first Falls guidebook, and the second edition, printed in 1835, declares that "the rooms are arranged very tastefully so as to represent a forest scene . . . . There are bipeds and quadrupeds; birds, fishes, insects, shells and minerals; all calculated to delight the eye, improve the understanding, and mend the heart." The museum was one of the few spots early mapmakers labeled on the Canadian side. Guides pointed out its local interest—regional flora and fauna, as well as Native American artifacts—and recommended its souvenirs. Barnett would even mount dead animals brought in by visitors. "Few persons visit Niagara Falls without calling at Barnett's Museum," wrote the *Boston Journal* in 1852, "and few are disappointed."

The museum grew along with the Niagara tourist trade. Barnett built a new building in 1837. In 1848, the first bridge over the Niagara Gorge was completed, connecting the Canadian side more easily with the busier American town; visitors no longer had to wait for the *Maid of the Mist* ferry to cross the river. Hoping to capitalize on the Canadian side's subsequent growth, Barnett sent away to England in 1859 for architectural plans and built a larger and even more impressive museum. Said to have cost $140,000, the completed building was one of the grandest on either side of the river. Large windows let in light, and colonnaded terraces offered spectacular views. On its grounds were greenhouses, a pond stocked with waterfowl, Native American wigwams, and cages with buffalo, wolves, deer and birds. Barnett had an exclusive lease on a staircase down to the base of the Falls, where he rented boots, coats and guides to take visitors "behind the sheet" of water. Like the museum, "Behind the Sheet" quickly became a must-see.

As the number of visitors increased at the Falls, the number of attractions also mushroomed, creating a carnival atmosphere along both sides of the river. The American side was known as "the Midway," the Canadian side "the Notorious Front." Indian curiosity shops, observation towers and fenced-off vistas shared the streetscape with an array of sideshow attractions—freak shows, battle reenactments, panoramas, acrobatic acts, snake dens and Moorish palaces. And of course, there were drivers of hack cabs who took kickbacks for delivering passengers to certain attractions, barkers who ballyhooed patrons into shoddy shows, photographers who snapped a visitor's picture and then threatened him if he wouldn't buy it. By the middle of the nineteenth century, disparaging the rip-offs and tacky attractions had become almost as much a tradition as watching the waterfall. British crank George Warburton was typical: "The neighbourhood of the great wonder," he declared in 1847, "is overrun with every species of abominable fungus—the growth of rank bad taste, with equal luxuriance on the English and the American sides—Chinese pagoda, menagerie, camera obscura, museum watch tower, wooden monument and old curiosity shops." He doesn't include Barnett's museum in his list of travesties, only its new tower. Throughout the nineteenth century, the museum was held above the fray. It was, after all, designed to serve the same purpose for which people came to the Falls: the contemplation of nature, whether human, animal, vegetable or mineral.

"I have endeavored to establish an institution," Barnett later wrote, "to which any Canadian might point with pride, an institution that should rank with other great museums of the world." He collected endorsements from prominent scientific men of the era, including eminent Yale professor Benjamin Silliman, British dinosaur expert B. Waterhouse Hawkins, and naturalist Louis Agassiz, founder of Harvard's Museum of Comparative Zoology. Agassiz, who traded natural history specimens with Barnett, declared that the Niagara Falls Museum "unquestionably deserves the patronage of the public and the support of the government." In 1859, a year in which 20,000 people visited his museum, Barnett applied for just such help from the Canadian provincial legislature, hoping to enlarge his museum further and gain the respectability to exchange objects with other museums. Every member of the parliamentary select committee appointed to investigate concluded that the museum was a valuable addition to the cultural life of the dominion, and should receive governmental support. Caught up in political struggles between Upper and Lower Canada, the Canadian legislature never considered his request.

The first time I visit Billy Jamieson to see what remains of the Niagara Falls Museum, he's late for our appointment, because he's walking his dachshund Ramses. I sit outside his warehouse building in the trendy Toronto fashion district, and after fifteen minutes he zooms into the driveway in a yellow Austin-Healey convertible, top down, dog on his lap, waving like a pop star.

A robust, fiftyish man, Billy has sparkly black eyes and straight black hair not unlike that on some of the shrunken heads he collects. His face is round, with the broadly defined features of a Mayan stone carving. He says he's not one of the Seneca Jamiesons, though he looks like a Seneca, and his name is spelled in the Seneca way. He crackles with a gee-whiz sense of glee at his own luck, as you would expect of a man making loads of cash traveling to Amazonian jungles and South Pacific islands to buy carved skulls and shark-tooth daggers. He's terminally busy: when you get him on the phone, he's always on another phone too.

We take the elevator upstairs to his sprawling loft, packed with items from both the museum's collection and his own. In two downstairs rooms, he has painted the walls red and installed cabinets and objects from the Niagara Falls Museum, attempting to re-create the feel of the museum circa 1860. Before he takes me to see them, he shows me around his apartment, crammed with objects ranging from the gorgeous to the grisly.

"You wanna know what things cost?" he asks brightly, charging around with an excited Ramses at his heels. "A shrunken head goes for fifteen or twenty thousand dollars. That shirt (a beaded Cheyenne war shirt) about a hundred thousand dollars." He has just sold a baby mummy to a museum in Houston for $100,000, and he points it out in the corner of his living room. "They didn't even see it!" he cries. "They bought it based on a picture!"

Willingness to talk openly about money is just one of the things that makes Billy unlike your average art dealer. Another is his cheerfully cavalier attitude toward his artifacts. "You wanna hold a shrunken head?" he asks, pulling one out of a case and weighing it in his hand like a grapefruit. "This one's a white guy." He smiles down at the surprised little face. Headshrinking, he tells me, is the only form of posthumous preservation that lets you recognize someone you knew in life. Eyes and mouth stitched shut, red hair and mustache bright, this guy still looks amazed at having been reduced to a citrus-sized trophy.

Billy Jamieson was born in Etobicoke, a suburban neighborhood in Toronto's west end whose postwar sprawl reflected its middle class aspirations. His father was a brakeman for the Canadian National Railroad. When Billy was twelve, his parents divorced, and he went to live with his grandparents in Jacksonville, Florida. He didn't go to college; when I ask him if he graduated high school, he waffles. As an adult, he worked construction, eventually becoming a building contractor. He did well. He bought a nice car. He got engaged.

Then, like Thomas Barnett, Billy Jamieson left the safety of the civilized building trades and waded into a howling wilderness, only to discover his connoisseur's eye. It began in 1994, when he went to Ecuador to visit a shaman and drink some hallucinogenic *ayuhuasca*. His drug-fueled vision quest—*ayuhuasca*, according to Billy, is "like twenty years of therapy in one night"—had dramatic results: he canceled his marriage, quit his job and immersed himself in the life and art of the Shuar, an Ecuadorian warrior tribe known for shrinking heads. He got to know Tukúpi, a Shuar warrior and shaman known for killing twenty-two people. He attended healing ceremonies with Tukúpi and interviewed him about his infamous killing career. And he learned about headshrinking, becoming an expert in dating and distinguishing heads. He began to build a collection, which quickly branched out to include South American tribal art, then South Pacific and Indonesian artifacts. He bought what he liked, learning about it as he went. Back at home, he discovered an eager market for his heads, including buyers of the macabre-loving rock-star type as well as highbrow connoisseurs of tribal art.

He was still reinventing himself as a tribal art dealer on the fateful day in 1998 when he and a girlfriend took a stroll around the Niagara Falls Museum. The night before, he had drunk some opium tea and had a dream featuring Egyptian symbols and shapes. But he wasn't drawn to the Egyptian artifacts at the Niagara Falls Museum; he liked their tribal art. Billy was looking to expand his collection of tribal art. He noticed the museum didn't have a shrunken head. Maybe they could work out a trade?

Billy asked the man hanging around at the front desk if he was the manager. In fact, he was the owner, Jacob Sherman. Billy asked Sherman if he might be interested in trading some tribal artifacts for a shrunken head. Sherman said no, he didn't like to tamper with the collection. Well then, Billy said on impulse, how about selling the lot?

The question came at the right time. Sherman was tired. The museum was financially strapped. Its collections needed more upkeep than he could provide, and the building, an old corset factory, was in need of repairs. The displays were outdated and the display copy full of factual errors. He had been reduced to bringing in traveling exhibits—moving model dinosaurs, reproductions of the British crown jewels—to boost attendance. It wasn't working: visitorship lagged. A Nisga'a tribal council in northwestern British Columbia seemed to be the only party with any serious interest in the collection: they were demanding the return of a pair of native mummies. Scholars ignored the museum. Reporters made fun of it. Kids came to climb on the dinosaur models and ogle the three-eyed pig. Sherman had recently had to sandblast the tourist signatures off his whale skeleton.

"Make me an offer," he told Billy.

• • •

The Barnett museum was antiquated long before Jacob Sherman inherited it. Based on the European model of the curiosity cabinet, or *Wunderkammer* (wonder chamber), early museums collected objects that were beautiful or strange. They made little distinction between the natural and the man-made, including paintings, scientific instruments and exotic artifacts along with animals, rocks and birds, displaying all of it with an eye toward aesthetics rather than explanation.

All that changed after *The Origin of Species* was published in 1859. In the wake of Darwin and a new taxonomic understanding of the natural world, scholars came to see early museums like Barnett's, with their jumble of objects foreign and domestic, as signs of mental, if not moral, weakness. An article in an 1898 issue of *Science* magazine is typical: the author decries the "collecting instinct of man," which, if not regulated, "can produce the most fantastic and inane combinations of objects." Unlike the modern, truly scientific museum, which reflects "a *conspectus* of things, such as embodies the *consensus* of modern science," older museums were "mixtures of oddities, monstrosities and perversions." In such curiosity museums, the author declares, "art is not separated from natural history, nor from ethnology, and the eye of the beholder takes in at a glance the picture of a local worthy, a big fossil, a few cups and saucers, a piece of cloth from the South Seas, a war club or two, and very possibly a mummy." He could have been describing Barnett's museum exactly.

The corrective was large public museums like the Smithsonian, designed for education and research. These stately institutions, reflecting the era's zeal for social reform, were managed by scientists and scholars whose mission was to explain the world. It followed that the world must be orderly and explicable. The products of culture—art, design, industry, arms—were moved into their own museums, increasingly sorted and separated into neat categories of human production: art, artifact, technology. Nature—plants, rocks, trees, animals and "primitive" human cultures—was relegated to the natural history museum. Freaks and oddities had no place in either world. Lacking logical explanation, they flew in the face of this newly ordered universe, where the spread of science across the globe meant, as the *Science* writer put it, "the world, the universe and even the life of man fall into orderly and necessary arrays of evolutionary stages." So ceaseless was this march of knowledge that the author compares the advance of science to that of Alexander. Labeling the world—reducing its marvels to answers—is, after all, the first step in controlling it. It's a straight line from curating to conquest.

A child of the early nineteenth century, Thomas Barnett based his museum on the *Wunderkammer* model. His true passion, and the center of his collection, was natural history. But unlike later museum curators, he didn't exclude the works of man from that category. A self-taught collector like Billy Jamieson, he lined up shells, dried herbs, pinned insects and mounted animals for his museum. He was a gifted taxidermist, which is apparent when you look at the older specimens in Billy's apartment: the birds and owls about to lift themselves into flight, the alligator ready to clamp down on your leg, the two-headed calf and three-eyed pig regarding you mournfully with long-suffering eyes. Barnett even created "habitats," setting up realistic dioramalike displays with elaborate painted backdrops. He was proud of his northern whale skeleton and the mastodon he acquired after it was dug out of a marsh about 130 miles west of the Falls in 1857. But he was also proud of a collage made of moths and beans laid out in striking patterns, and another of dried seaweeds organized to look like a basket of flowers. For Barnett, the museum was not simply its collection, but the art used in displaying it.

"This past week I have been engaged most of the time in learning to stuff birds under my father's guidance," wrote his nineteen-year-old son Sidney. "I never imagined that it was so beautiful an art before now."

Sidney Barnett's journal offers up a gripping window on the life of a nineteenth-century museum family. The young Sidney, raised to take over his father's business, worked as a guide for the trip "Behind the Sheet," and as a salesman in the museum's store. Behind the scenes, he learned to wire up skeletons, mount animals and create displays. He sometimes spent days working on a single mount, trying hard to please his meticulous father.

In his free time, he took long walks with friends, sketched the Falls and read, always with an eye to improving his mind. He frequently visited one or the other of several young ladies in town—always with a nice bouquet from the museum's gardens— and always insisting to his journal later that he would never marry. He dreamed of bigger things. Like any young man, Sidney longed to step out of his father's footsteps and make his mark on the world. Upon turning twenty, he asked his journal, "Were I to die at this moment, would the world lament my death? No! for it does not even know me by name. I must now certainly do something more than I have been doing, or my existence on this earth will have been a drag, instead of a buoy and a light."

Even as he spent his days peddling Indian artifacts to tourists— he was especially good at chatting up the young ladies—Sidney cast about for his ticket to renown. He got some sketches published in *Frank Leslie's Illustrated Newspaper.* He took classes in daguerrotyping, struggling to master the difficult new technology. He set himself reading programs and wrote essays to improve his style. He thought up new lines of business for the museum and carefully noted the ups and downs of the tourist trade. But he also dreamed of exotic locales and distant cultures. He studied Spanish and pored over the travel journals of his hero, Prussian explorer Alexander von Humboldt. Travel, he wrote, "may be the idol that I worship."

Slowly, over the three years his journal records, Sidney Barnett figured out how to put the two things together. In August of 1855, he set it down. "I have now a great desire to travel," he wrote, "and I think I could be of some use to my father in so doing for I think I have a taste for collecting curiosities, both material and artificial. Thus if I were successful, I could materially aid our institution in raising it up higher and higher until it called the attention of all the scientific men of the world to its importance and sterling worth."

Two years later, he realized his wish. His father came up with the funds to send him on a trip to Europe and then down the Nile. His companion would be a colorful family friend, Dr. James

Douglas of Quebec; a man who, 140 years later, would provide the final key to Billy Jamieson's transformation from shrunken-head collector to art dealer.

Originally from Scotland, Dr. Douglas trained as a physician, but like Sidney Barnett, he craved far-flung adventure. He shipped out as a surgeon on a whaling ship, patching up harpoon injuries and treating sick sailors. Then he signed on as medical advisor for the principality of Poyais in Central America. This utopian new colony, funded by government bonds issued in London and ruled by a swashbuckling Scottish soldier, was said to be crammed with rich land, untapped resources and hardworking English-speaking natives. Poyais sounded too good to be true, and it was: it was the invention of a con man named Gregor MacGregor, who sold land, government appointments and Poyais scrip to a few hundred eager colonists, organized their departure and then skedaddled to Paris. Two boatloads of hopeful immigrants landed not in a thriving new nation but in the inhospitable wilderness of the Mosquito Coast. Most died of malaria and yellow fever; others committed suicide. The ones who could get out, did. Douglas, deathly ill, was shipped out on a boat that happened to be going to New York. Around fifty Poyais survivors eventually straggled back to London, where the newspapers jumped on their tale. The fraud became a national scandal and MacGregor was jailed. In the States, Dr. Douglas got well enough to take the Northern Tour. In Utica, he met a girl and, in no hurry to go home and take his place as one of the duped, decided to settle in upstate New York.

Highly admired as a surgeon, Douglas began teaching at the medical college in Auburn, New York. Unfortunately, like many nineteenth-century medical professors, Dr. Douglas had to side-step grave-robbing laws and prospect for cadavers for his teaching demonstrations. Medical professionals were careful to dig up indigent people or slaves; local authorities turned a blind eye to the practice. Dr. Douglas got into trouble when he took the body of what he thought was a homeless man. The poor stiff turned out to be a local eminence; the corpse was recognized by a stagecoach driver who wandered into Douglas's unlocked study.

"I guess I never expected to see my friend P. again," the driver remarked dryly. Douglas, who had already had one wrist-slapping for grave-robbing, extracted a vow of silence from the driver, but, on second thought, decided it prudent to hop in his sleigh and make for Canada. He and his wife hitched up the horses and crossed the frozen St. Lawrence, arriving in Montreal that night.

In Canada, Douglas again became a well-respected local doctor, eventually founding Quebec's first humane asylum for the mentally ill. But Canadian weather was a bit more than he had bargained for, a problem he solved by indulging his passion for all things Egypt every winter. In 1857, he took Sidney Barnett along.

For Sidney, the trip to Egypt was his life's turning point. He was no longer a dreamy youth but a traveling museum man, an explorer like his hero Humboldt. Local newspapers reported on his travels and published his letters from abroad. Upon his return, he was asked to give a public lecture about Egypt. His father's museum added his acquisitions to its collection. The ambitious young man was now an expert.

Sidney began to travel whenever there was money for it, collecting specimens wherever he went. He collected birds and other animals in Cuba and South America, coins in the ancient world, and pottery and swords from the Far East. In 1859, when the museum moved to its fancy new home, it advertised new collections of ancient and modern coins and Chinese relics, as well as some new mummies.

What makes any object valuable is its story. Museums call that story "provenance." At some point, someone made up provenances for the Niagara Falls mummies. They were clearly fake, as debunkers loved to point out. A newspaper headline from 1996 is typical: "Museum's Collections Are Bogus." The reporter does not moderate his derision. General Ossipumphneferu, who still bears a scar from fending off an elephant attack on King Tutmosis? Balderdash. Princess Amenhotep, daughter of the king who built Thebes? Not likely. As far back as the thirties, a visiting Egyptologist had called the Egyptian collection "comic." Modern institutions value truth and verifiability more than the ability to weave a good yarn. Sidney Barnett's mummies were tainted by their false tales.

"To tell you the truth, I was more interested in the Native American artifacts than the mummies," Billy tells me. "I knew the mummies were worth something, but I thought the American Indian material was worth more than it was." Although he won't disclose the amount of the offer he made for Sherman's collection—friends of his guess it was around half a million dollars—Billy cheerily admits he didn't have the money on hand. Needing to sell something immediately to fund the purchase, he called a few experts and asked about the museum's Native American artifacts and Egyptian relics. A curator from the Royal Ontario Museum named Gayle Gibson had spent some time with the museum's Egyptian collection while working on her master's degree, and she assured Billy that the coffins, at least, were worth something. Sotheby's appraised the coffins—policy forbids them from appraising mummies—at $200,000. Billy asked for $2 million. "I just liked that number," he says cheerily in *The Mummy Who Would Be King*, a *NOVA* documentary about the Ramesses mummy that aired in January 2006.

Billy had to offer the artifacts to Canadian institutions first. As museum after museum in Canada passed on the collection, Peter Lacovara heard about it. Newly appointed curator of ancient art at the Michael C. Carlos Museum of Emory University, Lacovara was eager to expand the museum's Egyptian holdings. He flew to Canada to look at the coffins, and promptly recommended buying them. Back home in Atlanta, the museum organized a hasty fund drive to raise the purchase price. Schoolkids sent in their pennies, museum members wrote checks, and local businesses came up with the rest.

"I had the people from the Carlos Museum in one room and the people from the Niagara Falls Museum in another room, and I was going back and forth between them," Billy tells me, grinning. "I closed on the museum purchase and the sale of the mummies at the same time."

Part of why Billy asked so much for the Egyptian artifacts was that he had some reason to believe one of the mummies might be an interesting find. Gail had told him that the mummy with the crossed arms looked royal. Earlier Egyptologists had taken an interest in it; one German scholar had even notarized a statement in which he declared his belief that it was a pharaoh. Radiocarbon analysis had confirmed that the mummy was at least 3,000 years old, which indicated royalty: before 600 B.C., crossed arms were reserved for pharaohs. But even that was not enough for scholars to take seriously. Then Billy was contacted by an archivist and book-dealer named Hugh MacMillan. MacMillan told Billy that the grave-robber-cum-relic-finder Dr. Douglas had written a travel journal about his trip to Egypt called *Honeymoon on the Nile.* As soon as Billy saw it, he knew it would make a difference to the Michael Carlos Museum. It was the kind of story they could tell.

James Douglas published *Honeymoon on the Nile* in 1861. In it, he described how he acquired an excellent mummy for the Barnett museum from a well-known antiquities trader named Mustapha Aga Ayat. Ayat was the middleman for deals between European tourists eager to own a piece of ancient Egypt and Egyptian sellers who had "come into" artifacts. It was widely known that one of Ayat's mummy connections was a family of tomb robbers with the name Abd el-Rassul. The Abd el-Rassuls—allegedly while hunting up a lost goat—had stumbled upon a cache of royal mummies in the cliffs of Deir el-Bahri. They lived off the find for years, selling mummies and tomb artifacts to people like Sidney Barnett and James Douglas. Eventually, authorities grew suspicious at the number of royal artifacts coming onto the market, and family members were questioned. One of the clan ratted the others out and the jig was up. The cache was "officially" discovered in 1881. The coffin of Ramesses I was in it. It was empty.

Billy sent the Michael Carlos Museum a copy of Dr. Douglas's journal. For the first time, they had a plausible explanation of how a royal mummy made its way to the Niagara Falls Museum: through Mustapha Aga Ayat, the Abd el-Rassuls sold a royal mummy to Dr. Douglas for the Barnetts. The curators began to look at their mummy. At the Emory medical center, CAT scans showed the mummy's preparation was consistent with procedures reserved for kings. A computerized analysis of the mummy's skull placed him squarely in the New Kingdom's spectacular 19th Dynasty, a family that ruled from 1292 to 1185 B.C., and whose famous rulers included Seti I and Ramesses II. Most of the 19th Dynasty's mummies were accounted for, but its founder, Ramesses I, was still at large. All in all, it was enough to interest the Egyptian experts. The final determination fell to Zahi Hawass of Egypt's Supreme Council of Antiquities. Hawass flew to Atlanta and examined the mummy personally. Actually, he sniffed it; Hawass claims to be able to smell the difference between well-prepared royal mummies and their reeking plebeian counterparts. One look, a couple of whiffs, and Hawass declared the mummy likely to be Ramesses I.

Sidney Barnett had succeeded beyond his wildest dreams in acquiring for his father a curiosity that could make his name. He had managed at last to call "the attention of all the scientific men of the world" to the Niagara Falls Museum. But, alas, it did not confirm the museum's "importance and sterling worth," as he had hoped it would a century and a half earlier. Instead, the find was trumpeted as a bizarre anomaly, and Thomas Barnett, rather than being hailed as a man of taste and vision, was recalled as the father of a freak show. An article on the sale of the mummies in *Toronto Life* called Barnett "a man with all the acumen of a sideshow barker" who had "neither scruples nor the faintest idea what he owned." In the *NOVA* documentary, scholars and Egyptologists have fun taking pot shots at the pharaoh's former home. Peter Lacovara calls it "an ignominious kind of display," and University of Bristol Egyptologist Aidan Dodson declares it "looked like the cases in a cheap jewelry store." As footage shows Ramesses being packed into a box headed for Atlanta, the narrator intones that he is "no longer a creepy curiosity," but "now a valuable archaeological artifact," as if merely the fact of the mummy's purchase has magically transformed him into something worth buying.

The Carlos Museum exhibited Ramesses for a season and then returned him to Egypt with fanfare worthy of P. T. Barnum. They subsequently posted the whole history of the mummy's discovery on their Web site. But they wrote Billy Jamieson out of the story. In their version, they bought Ramesses directly from the Niagara Falls Museum. They too have a kind of story they like to tell.

The second time I visit Billy Jamieson, I ask to see any files he has on the Niagara Falls Museum. When I get there, he has unloaded a filing cabinet's worth of paper onto his dining room table.

"Go through it if you want," he says cheerily. A college film crew is hovering about; one of them is the son of an artist friend of Billy's, and they're making a documentary about him for school. He's letting them film the electric chair he recently bought. They have dragged the chair into his living room.

"Oh my God, it's Old Sparky," I say when I see it.

"It's one of the three original electric chairs made by Gustav Stickley for the State of New York," Billy tells me. "Old Sparky is at Sing-Sing. This one was at Auburn Prison." He tells me that one of Auburn's prisoners, while waiting to be executed in the chair, carved a cane for the prison warden with the names of all the chair's victims. He goes to his study and gets the cane. Then he launches into the story of how he believes the Auburn electric chair—said to have been destroyed in a 1929 prison riot—was snuck out and saved for decades. The confirmation has yet to occur; an ex–prison guard, currently on his death bed, is supposed to leave Billy a letter telling all. It can only be opened when he dies. As Billy talks, the college film crew follows him around, practically beside themselves with awe.

I take an armload of files to Billy's study so the students can get on with their interview without me rattling paper in the background. I sit at his huge desk. A giant warthog glares down at me as I read. Just outside the door, the shrunken heads grimace from their glass cabinet, eyes and mouths sewn shut with angry black stitches. According to Billy, it keeps their souls trapped inside. In the living room, camera lights go on and Billy begins to talk.

"It all started about fifteen years ago," I hear him say. "I was very interested in hallucinogenics. . . ."

Billy's files are full of letters from various experts on the objects in the Barnett collection. Some of the artifacts are incredibly valuable. Others might be: some of the South Sea items may have been acquired from an English museum that bought them from Captain Cook. A saddle may have been used by Wild Bill Hickock. Sitting Bull's moccasins are almost surely authentic; with other items it's impossible to say. Many things are barely worth anything, tourist trinkets acquired in China or South America by the wide-eyed Sidney or someone after him. Others are valuable but tricky to sell. The Nisga'a mummies, for instance, turned out to be real: Billy had them authenticated, then returned them to the tribal council. At one point, he paid a fine for putting a mounted curlew up for sale on eBay: it turned out to be an endangered species.

As I read, Billy periodically bounds through the room on his way to answer a phone or find a book he needs.

"You need a beer or something?" he never fails to ask.

When I'm done, I go downstairs again and sit among the Niagara Falls Museum objects. Near the animals, Billy has lined up a row of small terrariums holding beautiful dioramas of local birds, posed amid forest detritus. They have intricate watercolor backdrops, similar in style to young Sidney's sketches, which I one day requested from cold storage at the Archives of Ontario. Like the journey Behind the Sheet, the minidioramas offer the viewer a chance to look up close at something you see every day. For the Barnetts, the birds of Upper Canada were no less worthy of wonder than ceramic pagodas from Japan, a dead Egyptian king or a spectacular waterfall. The world, both near and far, is full of marvels.

Billy's loft also mingles the near and the far, the personal and the precious. A crouched Mayan mummy is lit by a crystal chandelier salvaged from a Toronto dance hall. Carved skulls from his trips south mingle with Erté prints (one of Billy's old girlfriends sold Art Deco). The collection invokes a feeling of wandering, not the armies of Alexander or the march of science, but a single soul charting its course through brave new worlds. Some objects are valuable, but their value is inherent in their stories: there's a Bornean war shield, for instance, painted with comic book hero the Phantom. Billy finds me looking at it and launches into a tale about how American soldiers gave comic books to Bornean locals when posted there during World War II. American superheroes thus turn up on authentic tribal shields—another instance of the middle ground.

"You want a Bloody Caesar?" Billy says at the end of the story. "It's the national drink of Canada."

Decked out with the accoutrements of a Victorian gentleman—leather sofas, Persian rugs, velvet drapes, gilt mirrors, mounted jaguar lounging on his bed—Billy's place probably looks a lot like Thomas Barnett's did. In fact, the Niagara Falls collection is right at home here. It's as if the drug-taking, convertible-driving art and oddity dealer reached out across one and a half centuries for a meeting of minds with the suited, bewhiskered museum man, scowling out of his photographs as if foreseeing his life's disappointing end.

Thomas and Sidney Barnett lost their museum for one simple reason: they ran out of money. The Barnett papers at the Ontario Archives are replete with bills and collection notices. Some historians claim that Barnett could not stop collecting, even when he ran low on funds. Others lay the blame on Sidney, who turned toward pricey, Barnum-style entertainments to draw in visitors. In 1872, he spent much of the museum's savings organizing a Great Buffalo Hunt and Wild West Show. He signed up Buffalo Bill Cody as headliner, but Buffalo Bill drank Sidney's advance payments without ever really intending to catch a single buffalo. After months of expensive delays, Sidney substituted Wild Bill Hickock as leading man and went to Nebraska to oversee the final arrangements himself. "Should I fail in this," he wrote home to his wife, "the consequences would be fearful."

The show was scheduled for August. Sidney ran ads touting Wild Bill as "the most famous scout on the plains," and promising a backup line of "over fifty Indians of different tribes . . . in full war dress," and a Mexican "band of Lasso Men mounted on their Mustang ponies." He built a makeshift arena with room for 50,000 spectators. The few thousand who turned up were treated to Hickock, four Mexicans and four Indians pelting three lazy buffalo with arrows to get them to run away. The *Welland Tribune* declared it "a perfect success—as a swindle." But even as a swindle it failed: the Barnetts lost money.

The failure of the Wild West show demoralized the Barnetts. But they had been losing money for years—in large part due to the exertions of their neighbor, Saul Davis. Davis arrived in Niagara Falls around 1850 and built the Prospect House Hotel. Then he moved right next door to the Barnetts and opened Table Rock House, where he offered a competing behind-the-Falls tour. Davis is often depicted as an exploitative interloper. Whereas the Barnetts maintained a carefully tended attraction with reasonable fees, Davis lured gullible travelers into his establishment by assuring them admission was free. He would outfit them with boots, hats, coats and a guide and give them a tour. At the end, he would present them with a bill charging them for the boots, the hats, the guide—everything *but* admission—while his thuggish sons stood by to make sure they paid. These accounts of his activities come primarily from the Barnetts.

The battle between the Davis and Barnett clans became epic, a sort of Hatfield-McCoy standoff at the brink of the Horseshoe. The Barnetts paid off hackmen to bring customers only to their museum; Davis paid them more to bring them to him. Davis and his sons posted signs declaring Barnett's staircase was dangerous; the Barnetts tore them up and threw them over the cliff. Davis told visitors a ticket from him also got them admission to the Barnetts' museum; the Barnetts sent the disappointed visitors to the police to complain. The two families dragged each other into court constantly over stray hogs, broken fences, customer harassment and personal assaults. Sidney tells how one Monday in 1855, after the Barnetts broke the law by staying open on a Sunday, Thomas Barnett sent one of his own employees down to the magistrate to report him, just to deprive Davis of the pleasure. Both men constantly petitioned the Crown for the exclusive lease on the Falls stairway. It seems to have passed back and forth between them with the whim of the provincial secretary. In 1870, the feud erupted in gunplay and one of Barnett's employees, a black man named William Price, was killed. After that, the fun was out of it.

Late in life, impoverished and bitter, Sidney Barnett claimed it was pure politics that caused his father's lease to be canceled in the 1870s. In 1875, the Liberals came into power in Ontario, and the Barnetts were well-known Conservatives. The lease was renewed in 1877 for $1,000 a year, an insupportable amount for the strapped family. Thomas Barnett accepted the terms only, he said, "because the alternative would be absolute ruin to me and the total destruction of an institution it has taken a lifetime to build up." Sidney wrote their creditors asking for permission to organize a joint stock company to keep the museum afloat; it was denied. The following year, Barnett went bankrupt, and his museum and its contents were auctioned off. Saul Davis bought it all for the fire-sale price of $48,000.

"Saul Davis went to the auction with his sons," Billy tells me over our Bloody Caesars—Bloody Marys with lots of tabasco. "They were these big bull-like guys, and they stood all around the room. Whenever anyone else bid on something, they would glare at them." This may or may not be true: according to the *Welland Tribune*—no friend to the Barnetts—Davis simply arrived at the auction and threw out a first bid of $45,000, which "had the effect of a wet blanket on the other bidders, some of whom turned on their heels and left." Three thousand dollars later it was sold, and the Barnett family had lost everything. Their Newfoundland dog declined to leave the premises. Even when a rope was put around his neck, he refused to be dragged from the Barnetts' former home.

A broken man, Sidney Barnett went to South America, where he spent the rest of his life selling Bibles and stereoview photographs, and shipping curios back for North American companies. A few years later, in 1888, Saul Davis more than doubled his money, selling the museum building and grounds to the provincial government for $102,000. While Ontario demolished the museum to build its park, Davis moved the collection into a new building on the American side of the Falls. His son Charles ran it thereafter. History casts them as villains, yet the Davis family ran the museum well. The sons traveled and added to the collection; they bought what remained from Wood's Museum in Chicago after Chicago's Great Fire, and a newspaper report from

1894 announces that they have just added "magnificent collections from Australia and Africa, and South California Indian relics and New Zealand curiosities." Like Barnett, they went out of their way to build the museum a beautiful home, this one on the Riverway, across from the Niagara Reservation. Five stories high, with an open atrium topped by a cupola, it held the collection for seventy years, until the New York State Parks Authority bought it and razed it to build a parking lot.

Curiosity cabinets celebrate wonder. Compelling mixtures of fact and fiction, they teach us not to name and to rule, but to marvel. Although museum history describes curiosity cabinets as ancestors of natural history museums, they are directly opposite in intent; they don't seek to explain and classify the world, but to celebrate it in all its strangeness. They propose an attitude toward nature that's as much about mystery as mastery. That's why they often feature the freakish and the bizarre.

It's also what made Barnett's museum such a perfect fit for Niagara Falls. What better place for a curiosity cabinet than at the flank of the Falls? Niagara itself is a great big noisy curiosity, like the *Wunderkammer* offering up death and beauty in equal measure. The museum completed the experience of sublime wonder by displaying objects from all over the world, collected for their ability to leave you speechless.

The post-Darwin world of empirical data and hard facts did not want to be awed. In this world, the Falls themselves were devalued as well as the museum. They were a famed sublime spectacle, but the sublime must be unknowable. So long as Niagara couldn't be fathomed or described, it maintained an aura of mystery. In the twentieth century, as the waterfall was explained, quantified, and placed under human control, the *Wunderkammer* beside them came to seem like the oddity itself, a dusty example of a worn-out worldview. There were occasional expressions of nostalgia for the old museum, but for the most part, people treated it with scorn.

Jacob Sherman, grandfather to the Jacob Sherman who sold the museum to Billy Jamieson, bought the Niagara Falls Museum in

1942. When State Parks claimed the building in 1957, he decided to move the collection back to Canada, buying the old Spirella Corset factory just north of the Rainbow Bridge. The Canadian newspapers trumpeted the museum's arrival "home again." But the world had changed. The *Niagara Falls Gazette* visited the museum in New York just before it moved and declared it "a weird collection of thousands of items," an "assortment of art and oddity." They pronounced the taxidermied animals "dusty and not too interesting," and cited the ancient Asian swords and samurai costumes as the most interesting and valuable part of the collection. They didn't mention the freaks of nature at all. For its new incarnation in Canada, the museum issued brochures advertising itself as "the oldest museum in North America," and playing up the mummies and the new daredevil relics—including a collection of stunters' barrels—while playing down the natural history collections.

Throughout the sixties and seventies, the Sherman family struggled to get visitors to come to the Niagara Falls Museum. The reason they had trouble was not that people were no longer interested in freaks and oddities. The problem was that there were plenty of newer freaks and oddities for them to visit at Niagara Falls. A 1964 Official Guidebook issued by the Niagara Falls Area Chamber of Commerce listed fifty must-see attractions on both the American and Canadian sides. The Niagara Falls Museum was not mentioned. Instead, there was Louis Tussaud's Wax Museum and Ripley's Believe It or Not!, with such must-see items as a guitar made of matchsticks, a shrunken head, the throne of a cannibal chief, and a model of Columbus's *Santa Maria* made of chicken bones. There was the Houdini Magical Hall of Fame, with its annual séances to contact the dead magician. And on Clifton Hill, there was the Burning Spring Museum, the Boris Karloff Wax Museum, the Biblical Wax Museum, the Sports Wax Museum, the Tower of London Wax Museum, and the Criminals Hall of Fame Wax Museum. All of them featured galleries dedicated to the freakish and awful: torture chambers, monsters, historical villains. A curmudgeon complained in the

Niagara Falls Review in 1977 that the craze for wax museums was "another creeping blight akin to the Honky Tonk days of the 1800s . . . God knows if it weren't for the Niagara Parks Commission, by now we'd have wax museums and freak shows right at the brink of the Horseshoe Falls."

But of course, that's just what they *did* have, 150 years earlier.

"If the museum was still in that location," Jacob Sherman tells me, "and had always stayed in that location, people could have looked at it differently, as part of Falls history."

A curly-haired blond man with a quick smile and a self-effacing air, Jacob Sherman has no regrets about the sale of his collection. He knows Billy Jamieson made a fortune flipping the mummies, but even that doesn't seem to irk him. "The one thing we never thought would come out of the Egyptian collection would be that Egypt would look at one of the mummies as being Ramesses," he tells me. "That was"—he casts about for the right word—"surprising."

I have found Jacob Sherman in his new position, less than three minutes' walk from the site of where his family's museum once stood. He is now retail manager for the *Maid of the Mist* souvenir store in the Niagara Falls State Park. In a shirt and tie, a silver pen perfectly tucked into his shirt pocket, he presides over a pin-neat store: shot glasses and souvenir mugs lined up in regiments, T-shirts stacked in order of size and *Maid of the Mist* key chains dangling in immaculate rows. It's all very orderly, down to the turnstiles and fences that corral tourists coming off the *Maid of the Mist* into the gift shop.

When I turn up, unannounced, Jacob very cordially invites me to his office, a windowless room behind the cash register. He tells me the retail business is as much a part of Sherman family legacy as the museum, perhaps more so.

"They were in the souvenir business," Jacob says of his grandparents. "They had four or five stores." In fact, his grandfather became interested in the Niagara Falls Museum because of the location: the beautiful building built by Davis sat right on the Riverway near the Falls.

"He thought it was a great spot for a souvenir store," Jacob says. The elder Mr. Sherman even told the newspaper he wasn't quite sure what was on the upper floors of the museum building.

In his even-keeled manner, Jacob speaks fondly of his grandparents. He got a degree from SUNY Buffalo in environmental design and planning, and says working with his grandmother, Louise, who managed the museum after her husband's death, was an invaluable experience. But he had no aspirations in the museum trade. He calls it "a curious business to be in" and seems downright modest about his family's role in the Niagara Falls Museum's history.

"We were just the keepers of it by the time it came down to us," he tells me. "It's in good hands, as far as I'm concerned. Billy's a collector and a trader. I was not a collector." The one thing he did keep for himself was the Niagara Falls heritage collection—material pertaining to power development, and an assortment of barrels and other daredevil relics. He says he does intend to put those items on display someday. But for now, the collection is in a warehouse a few minutes' drive away.

Later I call him and ask him if he'll show me the collection he still has. He pauses for a moment, and then gently, but firmly, declines.

On a sunny winter day, I visit another Niagara Falls museum man, Mark DeMarco, at the Evel Knievel Museum and Pawn Shop. Mark is a local motorcycle painter, and his private shrine to Evel and other gnarly stuff is now the closest thing to the old Barnett Museum at the Falls.

A shimmery disco-style curtain divides the museum from the pawnshop at the front. Through the curtain, five windowless rooms are crammed with curiosities of all kinds, including the remains of the defunct Ripley's "That's Incredible" museum, the world's largest collection of Evel cycles and memorabilia, objects with local history ties and a just-plain-weird assortment of collectibles, oddities and ephemera. Display cases are organized by theme: Elvis, gambling, Harley-Davidsons, samurai, skeletons, magician Raymond the Great, Indians, Dan Aykroyd, the *Titanic*, netsuke, Hitler.

I've called ahead, and Mark meets me cheerily to give me a tour around his place. He's a short, trim man with alert black eyes and a tendency to put his hand on your arm or shoulder as he talks. He takes me from case to case, pointing out objects.

"That game board was played on by Winston Churchill," he says, or "Elvis sent that necklace to my brother." At the *Titanic* case, he points out a photograph of a young woman in a navy uniform.

"That's my mother," he says, "who was in the navy during the war. Those plates are from the ship they called the Canadian *Titanic*, the *Empress of Ireland*."

Mark's museum makes no narrative sense at all. It's clearly completely personal, reflecting his own obsessions, interweaving biography and history. And yet it's fascinating. It's the sort of place where you could get lost for a couple of hours, staring out the window of somebody else's train of thought.

We look at a giant statue of the Alien standing near the world's smallest violin; Evel's X-2 Skycycle, used to jump Snake River Canyon; and a tiny netsuke figurine of two ladies getting it on with a tiger.

"This collection belonged to a doctor," Mark says at the netsuke case, grinning. "Some of them are pretty interesting."

We move on to a case full of bones. There's a skull carved with Freemasonic symbols, and Mark tells me a long and complicated story involving Freemasons, lawyers, virgins, corrupt cops and a local serial killer.

"An item is just an item unless there's a story about it," he tells me as we walk around, "the history behind it: Who made it? What was it used for? What lives did it change and how did they change? Everyone has a moral and ethical obligation to make sure injustice doesn't happen in the world. And objects can help."

We stop at his Hitler memorabilia case. A little sign inside it reads Least We Forget.

Mark looks sad for a moment.

"So much is lost," he says, "by not pausing for that one moment to look at what historical significance an object had."

Then he points at a small guitar.

"Some people don't know that Evel Knievel was a musician," he says, his face brightening.

What will be the future of Niagara's second-oldest attraction? That depends, as it always has, on the whims of its owner. Today's owner favors jeans and black silk shirts instead of the thick woolen coats that Thomas Barnett wore around town, or the regimental gear Sidney ordered from Toronto, but he's not so different from them. He too is an autodidact with a yen for institutional respectability. When the Michael C. Carlos Museum threw an opening party for their Ramesses exhibit, Billy flew to Atlanta to attend.

"The president of Emory University referred to the Niagara Falls Museum as a 'freak show,'" Billy says, indignation temporarily suspending his ebullience. The Carlos Museum still owed him $100,000, and he had been planning to make it a donation. On the spot, he changed his mind.

Billy always insists that the Niagara Falls Museum is not dead. He keeps a Web site and a phone number for it, and fields inquiries about it or its artifacts. He would like some part of the collection to stay together, as an example of what early museums were like. He's willing to donate some of it to a museum that will put it on permanent display. So far, he has found no takers.

The majority of the collection now idles in huge crates in a warehouse in St. Catharines, Ontario, a small city about eleven miles west of the Falls. After I leave Billy, I drive from Toronto to go to see it. The warehouse sits on a nondescript strip of back-office businesses abutting the Welland Canal, the ship canal that lets freighters bypass Niagara.

I'm met at the boxy brick building by a friendly, rotund guy named Tim Montreuil. He and his adult son lead me into a large, frigid warehouse bay stacked with car-sized crates. Along one side, open shelves hold what look like giant pieces of bark.

"That's the giant redwood tree," Tim tells me, and his son adds, "It took five of us guys fifteen hours to take it apart."

The tree hooks together with braces. When assembled, it's big enough that you can drive a car through the hole cut in its base. A picture of the tree fully assembled is duct taped to the shelves where it lies.

Tim and his son both say they visited the museum when it was open, and they seem proud of their role in its fate. Tim's son tells me he saw Billy Jamieson on TV.

"I told my wife, 'I know that guy!'" he says. "'That's Billy Jamieson.' I said it before they even said his name."

Together we stroll around the warehouse. They point out a shelf that holds a buffalo, and one where two taxidermied rhinos lie side by side, the foot of one rhino resting on the other one's head. I put my hand on the nearest rhino's rump—it feels hard like plastic. I have a thing for rhinos. The pert little ears on this one make me want to cry.

On a high shelf lies the five-legged cow. According to Billy, a taxidermist friend looked at the museum's freaks and declared them all real. This is probably the same five-legged cow that author William Dean Howells saw exhibited as a living calf in a tent at the Falls in 1860.

"I do not say that the picture of the calf on the outside of the tent was not as good as some pictures of Niagara I have seen," Howells wrote later. "It was, at least, as much like."

"The cow's fifth leg comes out of his neck," Tim tells me. "You want me to put you on the forklift so you can get a good look?"

What makes a look good? No museum today would show the five-legged cow, except perhaps a museum of anatomy, where looking at it might be considered educational, but only if you were a veterinary student, or some sort of biologist. Nature today is a world of rules, not exceptions.

"I'll take a look," I tell Tim.

His son loads a pallet onto the forklift and I climb on top of it. "What do I hold onto?" I ask.

"You just stand there nice and solid," Tim says, pulling a lever.

Seeing is never just looking. In late 2006, Ripley's Believe It or Not! outbid the Chicago History Museum for the Cook County gallows, built to hang the anarchist bombers of the Haymarket Square Riot. *The New York Times* began their story: "Morbid curiosity beat out history to lay claim to the infamous Cook County gallows." It's the same gallows in either place. But the act of seeing is different, just as the act of seeing Billy's collection—whether Skipper or the Auburn electric chair—is one thing in his apartment and something else entirely in a museum. In the museum, its meaning is fixed, just as Niagara's meaning is now fixed in statistics and dates pasted on placards. Perhaps looking at oddities in private hands, or even in a salacious sideshow like Ripley's, is the closest we can come to experiencing what early viewers felt when they looked at the Falls.

The forklift goes up, and the cow hoves into view. The fifth leg is not a full-sized leg, just a vestigial limb, hoofless, dangling over the side of the cow's thick neck like a misplaced tail. The cow's eyes are rolling and its mouth is slightly open, giving it a frantic look. Lying stiff-legged on its side, it looks as if it's saying Stop. I stand there, up in the air, marveling at the cow. Then Tim pulls the lever and slowly I ride back down.

Four

THE OTHER SIDE OF JORDAN

IMAGINE HARRY COLCORD, LOOKING at the rope. He helped string it across the Niagara Gorge. Now it stretches out before him, interlaced with so many guy lines it resembles a giant spiderweb. It's 2 inches thick and slopes downward in such a steep curve it looks as if it dips into the river below. Between Harry and the rope stands a small, muscular man, 5 feet 5 inches tall and around 130 pounds. Harry weighs 136. It's a hot summer day in 1859.

"All right," someone says. Harry puts one foot in the leather stirrup hanging from a harness over the man's shoulder and steps up. His other foot goes in the other stirrup. He puts his arms around the man's chest. He remembers how he once thought that after whaling, theatrical management would seem tame. He remembers how lucky he thought he was to become manager for the world's greatest tightrope artist.

"You are dead weight," the man tells Harry in his thick French accent. "If I sway or stumble, do not try to balance. You are not Colcord. You are Blondin." Then Blondin pulls his shoulders back to loosen Harry's grip and steps onto the rope. It's like jumping off a cliff. There's a sound, almost like the rustle of wind, as the crowd lining the bank behind them collectively draws its breath.

Blondin moves forward, one foot, then the other. The rope sways. Harry thinks of the sea.

Blondin told him not to look down, but he does. Beneath them, 190 feet of windy air, then a rushing river from which no one emerges alive. A tiny boat bobs like a toy on the water below, crammed with faces turned upward, waiting to see them drop. The sound of the wind, the sound of Niagara Falls.

One foot. Then the other foot. Every lift of the foot is like dying; every time it reconnects with the rope is like being saved. Don't move, Harry tells himself. He concentrates on Blondin's pole. It weighs 40 pounds; he's lifted it. When the two of them go right, the pole goes left. Harry stares at the pole and imagines he is that pole, leaning left. It helps him not lean left. The wind picks up, and the tails of his morning jacket flap against the back of his legs. He imagines melting. He can feel a heart pounding against Blondin's back and he doesn't know if it's Blondin's or his.

After a while, a kind of calm takes over. Harry is entirely focused on one thing: staying limp. One foot, then the other foot. He doesn't hear the Falls anymore.

And then Blondin stops. "Get off," he says.

Get off? The stocky man beneath him is the only thing between him and a fatal fall, and he wants Harry off. He needs Harry off. It's tough work reascending the steep hill to the other bank, even without a man on your back. Harry knows Blondin must rest. He can't get down. He has to.

Harry slides one foot out of the stirrup and reaches it—toward what? He's going to step off into nothingness. He can't breathe. Then his toe taps the rope. It's vibrating in the wind. He sets one foot on that vibration. His hands clench Blondin's shoulders. He can feel the aerialist shaking with exhaustion. He slides the other foot out of its stirrup and brings it down next to the first, shifting his weight to his feet. He stares at Blondin's back, rising and falling. If he loses his nerve, he will die.

After what seems like an endless time, Blondin says, "Get back on." Harry does and they move forward, one foot, then the other.

This happens five times.

The crossing takes forty-two minutes. It feels like a lifetime. The world has disappeared: the crisp blue sky above, the Falls roaring off to their right, the green river rushing below. After a while, Harry doesn't see any of it, just Blondin's back and the beads of sweat on the back of Blondin's neck. He doesn't see the dark mass of people lining the banks and nearby bridge until they are almost across the rope. Then he looks up and sees thousands of eyes, wide with something almost like horror, waiting to rush upon him. Some of them hold out their hands.

Blondin stops, and for the first time Harry feels him hesitate. Both men see the danger of the crowd; its eagerness could knock them off the rope at the very end. They freeze, staring at the sea of faces. No one moves.

"What should I do?" Blondin asks.

"Make a rush and drive right through them," Harry says. He's surprised to hear his voice sounding so low and calm.

Blondin tightens his grip on his pole. Every muscle in his body locks into place, and then they're moving fast, shoving through a sea of hands and faces; Harry sees ladies weeping, gentlemen pressing coins into his hand, children lofted above the fray to see him, and he realizes he's made it, he's going to be rich.

Now imagine another young man, the same age as Colcord—late twenties—and with a similar physique, small but muscular, well used to hard work. The setting is the same: the Niagara River. This man is crossing in the other direction, from the United States to Canada. This time it is dark. There are no eyes upon him. The person holding his hand is a woman, but she's such a powerful woman people call her Moses, and some even refer to her as "he." She and the man are both absolutely silent. They are not on a rope, but on the Suspension Bridge, less than 50 yards downstream from the wire Blondin crosses by day. This man can also feel his heart pounding. If he loses his nerve, he too will die. Not because he will fall, but because Harriet Tubman will shoot him.

Silent and swift, they make their way along the railroad tracks on the upper level of the bridge. The pedestrian roadway is below, on the lower level, but there's a toll collector there, and Harriet doesn't know him. She leads the way as she's done dozens of times.

When they arrive on the other side, the man drops to his knees and puts his hands on the ground, as if he expects it to reach out and embrace him. He's made it. He's going to be free.

People are fascinated by Niagara stunters. Whenever I mention my Niagara obsession, people almost inevitably bring up honeymoons or daredevils. "Oh, Niagara, you mean like people going over it in barrels?"

"No," I usually say, trying not to sound like a snob, "the *history*."

Even when I'm at the Falls, I tend to glance only briefly at the daredevils' commemorative markers, or the models of stunters in wax museums. I have never lingered at the IMAX Theatre's barrel exhibit the way I lingered over the freakish animals in Billy Jamieson's collection. I like the cheesy diorama of Father Louis Hennepin in the dusty wax museum on the American side, but the Daredevil Museum that's really a gas-station-sized souvenir store has always struck me as unbearably tacky. I am the proud purchaser of postcards, View-Master reels and a leather tie rack all bearing pictures of the waterfall, but while I bet you can buy a pen with a miniature Blondin inside sliding back and forth across his tightrope, I have never tried to acquire one.

I know the stories; you can't miss them. The town is rife with historic markers recounting daredevils and their dubious accomplishments, and the guidebooks are full of them too. Blondin is the most popular. But there's also Massachusetts millworker Sam Patch, who started it all in 1829, jumping into the lower Niagara from a platform between the Falls. Philadelphia cooper Carlisle Graham survived the Whirlpool Rapids in a barrel he built himself. Unemployed dancing teacher Annie Edson Taylor became the first person to go over the Horseshoe in a barrel, at the age of sixty-three. Maud Willard suffocated in her barrel because her dog stuffed his nose into its airhole; George Stathakis suffocated in his after getting caught in the Whirlpool for sixteen hours. The turtle he took with him survived. Roger Woodward, a seven-year-old boy, was an unwitting daredevil: after a boating accident in 1960, he went over the Horseshoe in a lifejacket and lived. He was the only person to survive an unprotected trip over the brink until 2003, when Kirk Jones, an unemployed salesman of auto industry tools, threw himself drunkenly into the rapids and somehow survived the plunge. Jones hadn't been intending to put on a show, he said; he'd been trying to kill himself. But his vodka-fueled survival earned him a spot in the long tradition of spectacular performances set against the backdrop of Niagara that began in 1827, with the schooner *Michigan*'s zooicidal plunge over the Horseshoe.

Niagara histories always treat such performances and stunts with an odd lack of wonder. *Of course* people want to go over the Falls in a barrel. *Of course* tightrope-walkers want to dare the Niagara Gorge. *Of course* thousands of people would turn up to watch a shipload of animals get dashed to bits. And of course, readers want to hear about who succeeded, who failed, and whether the turtle described the barrel ride afterward, as George Stathakis promised it would. (It didn't.) Daredevil history is everywhere on both sides of Niagara. Annie Taylor exits her barrel in an aging mural on New York's Niagara Street; little Roger Woodward plunges end-lessly over the brink in the taped narration on the *Maid of the Mist*, and an effigy Blondin stands eternally balanced on a high-wire strung over Ontario's Victoria Avenue. In the heavy summer traffic, it looks like a perfectly reasonable way to get across.

If you think you detect a superior tone, you're not far off. I take pride in resisting the allure of the daredevils, and I have to admit it comes partly out of snobbery, that long tradition of insisting that Niagara is gussied up with tawdry spectacle, but *one* is really inter-ested in the Falls. The claim is akin to the protestations of men who swear they read *Playboy* for the articles. I don't avert my eyes when I come upon Mr. Graham's barrel, but honestly, it doesn't do much for me. I am interested in meaning, and daredevil stunts don't have meanings, at least not complex ones. They're simply about the desire of certain individuals to make spectacles of them-selves by challenging nature in what, it has to be said, are some pretty dumb ways. Go over the Falls in a barrel? Who thought that up, anyway?

And yet, these meaningless spectacles carry odd symbolic undertones. The destruction of the *Michigan* acted out a relationship to nature. Barrel stunts are clustered around moments when humans succeed in further controlling the waterfall, as if the stunters are aping the domination of nature. Even Kirk Jones, the unemployed salesman, had a friend videotaping him as he slid toward his doom. Why would he leave a grisly record of his demise for the nightly news? Maybe he believed that an unemployed auto industry worker being dashed to bits on America's best-known icon might say something. Maybe he thought it would make a nice metaphor for Detroit's postglobalism attitude toward the working man. Or maybe, like the wreck of the *Michigan*, it was 90 percent pure spectacle with 10 percent's worth of subtext hiding in the wings. But it's enough to get me rethinking my attitude toward the daredevils. Given Niagara's propensity for hiding its real history, maybe there's something in all this stunting I've simply missed.

One night at dinner, I quiz my boyfriend, Bob.

"Who was Blondin?" I demand.

"The tightrope guy," he says right away. "He went across the river at Niagara Falls." Granted, Bob has an advantage: he's been dragged to Niagara multiple times, has seen the IMAX film *Niagara: Myths, Miracles and Magic* at least three times, has been conscripted onto the *Maid of the Mist* and hauled under the waterfall at the Cave of the Winds, and has suffered through so many long stories at commemorative rocks, scenic vistas and tombstones, he now declines all offers of free trips to Niagara. At home, he managed to muster a fake smile when he unwrapped the waterfall tie rack at Christmas, but after being subjected to dozens of horrible DVDs featuring the Falls, he did a search for *Niagara Falls* on the Internet Movie Database and banned any resulting films from our Netflix queue.

"When did Blondin cross?" I ask, and Bob looks baffled.

"The turn of the century?" he hazards.

I let the topic drop. Bob looks relieved, though later I find him shuffling through the latest Netflix arrivals with a nervous look, as if one of them might contain a bomb.

Blondin, born Jean-François Gravelet, may very well be the best aerialist who ever lived. His two summers at Niagara held America captive with suspense as he made more than a dozen crossings from the American to the Canadian side of the Niagara Gorge, and then back again. He did somersaults and headstands, drank champagne and cooked omelets, all on the tiny, swaying rope. Thousands of people traveled to Niagara Falls to see him, and newspapers nationwide reported on his every move. He had a truly unmatchable act. But was that really enough to hold the nation spellbound for two summers running? Those summers were 1859 and 1860. The more I read about Blondin, the more I'm convinced his feats over the Niagara River weren't just spectacular: they plugged right into the national mood. An anxious and divided America, hovering on the brink of war, worried together for a small man walking on a rope. But even more, what spectators were seeing was a succinct reenactment of a national spectacle all the more powerful for being unseen. America was transfixed by a man's impossible journeys across the very river slaves regularly crossed to freedom.

Performances were on Wednesdays or Thursdays. Around 4 P.M., a magnificent carriage would bear Blondin to an American park called White's Pleasure Grounds. From there, he would cross the tightrope to Canada, performing tricks and stunts along the way. Upon arriving in Canada, he would be taken by carriage to Clifton House, where he would rest up before his highwire journey back to the States. He would perform a new set of tricks on the return.

The overtones of a man taking a dangerous journey from the United States (*White's Pleasure Grounds*, no less!) to Canada had to be clear. For African Americans, Canada was synonymous with freedom. The British Emancipation Act of 1833 had banned slavery in the entire British Empire. But it was pretty much a moot point in Canada by then—abolitionist sentiment was strong, and in 1793 the legislature of Upper Canada—present-day Ontario—had passed a law mandating a gradual phasing out of slavery. By the time of the Emancipation Act, an estimated 12,000 fugitives already lived in Canada. The Canadians even regularly refused to extradite fugitives to the United States.

More than 20,000 blacks lived in Ontario at the time of Blondin's first performance, many of them emancipated slaves. Travelers to the area often visited their communities, remarking on the settlers' accomplishments in farming and education, and abolitionists published accounts such as Benjamin Drew's oral history *The Refugee; or, the Narratives of Fugitive Slaves in Canada*, printed in Boston in 1856. In 1858, the year Blondin came to check out the Falls, the radical abolitionist John Brown was in Ontario organizing an abolitionist convention, visiting Harriet Tubman and collecting volunteers for his planned raid on the federal arsenal at Harpers Ferry, Virginia.

The Niagara region was one of only a handful of places where fugitives could cross the border. There were four main routes into Canada: get on a Great Lakes steamship, cross the Detroit River to Windsor, cross the Niagara River, or hoof it from Quaker farm to Quaker farm all the way to northern Vermont. The route through the Ohio River valley led naturally to Detroit; the route up the eastern seaboard led to Niagara. There at Black Rock and Lewiston, the river narrowed to a manageable width. And in 1848, an even better crossing was completed—Charles Ellet's Suspension Bridge, the first bridge spanning the Niagara Gorge. It was quickly followed in 1855 by John Augustus Roebling's Railway Suspension Bridge. The bridge was so well known as a crossing point that Harriet Tubman's first biographer, Sarah Bradford, simply refers to it as "the Suspension Bridge," without bothering to name its town.

How many people crossed the Niagara River to freedom is not known; the Underground Railroad worked because it left so few traces. That may be one reason why the history of the Underground Railroad in the Niagara region is far less familiar than the history of stunting. Pierre Berton, in his fat bestseller *Niagara*, doesn't mention it at all. Geographer Patrick McGreevy, who analyzes the history of pilgrimage and utopia at the Falls in his book *Imagining Niagara*, says nothing about it. The official souvenir book from the Niagara Falls State Park mentions La Salle, the fur trade, the Iroquois Confederacy, the Porters, the Erie Canal, the Welland Canal, Frederick Law Olmsted, bridge-building, industrial development and tourism. It has whole chapters dedicated to daredevils and honeymoons but says nothing about the Underground Railroad. In the Niagara Falls State Park, you can find statues and portraits of the Porters, Olmsted, Nikola Tesla and Chief Clinton Rickard, founder of the Indian Defense League, but you can't find an image of Harriet Tubman.

"There has been slavery in other countries. But there has never been another country in the world that legalized slavery and institutionalized it, and that is a very difficult fact for a lot of Americans to swallow," Kate Koperski explains.

Kate is part of a recent movement to recover some of the region's lost history. Curator of folk arts at the Castellani Art Museum at Niagara University, she's one of the organizers of a new, permanent exhibit on the Underground Railroad there. "We got involved in this grant with Heritage New York because of our initial project with Houston Conwell," Kate tells me. This was a series of contemporary sculptures called *Stations* by Conwell and collaborators commemorating local sites on the Underground Railroad. They were unveiled in an early-nineties burst of interest after a local group, the Underground Railroad Committee of the Niagara Frontier, helped spearhead a 2,400-mile walk re-creating the fugitives' journey from Atlanta to St. Catharines.

Kate has long, straight blond hair, and she wears pearl earrings and a slightly cautious air. The exhibit, called "Freedom Crossing," was somewhat controversial: some donors weren't sure their contemporary art museum should be mounting shows about slavery. Aware of this, the museum has worked hard to make a strong connection between the Underground Railroad story and the Niagara region. The walls are painted a half mint, half battleship green that's meant to reproduce the color of the Niagara River. A glimmering light projection on the floor evokes sunlight on water. And the back wall is filled with a huge, beautiful photograph of woods on the river from John Pfahl's series *Arcadia Revisited*, a photographic study of the Niagara frontier.

"We're trying to create a sense of place," Kate tells me.

A sense of place is difficult to create for the Underground Railroad, because so many of its actual locations remain mysterious—it was, after all, a highly secretive operation. Records are scarce; photographs are essentially nonexistent. Most sites are identified as such through family lore, and many families, it seems, have a root cellar or a barn they fervently believe was used on the Underground Railroad. I find this easy to believe: I've had real estate brokers in New York City tell me a particular apartment building was "a station on the Underground Railroad." Rents were increased accordingly.

The *Stations* project did not include any private homes in its list of sites, and Heritage New York lists just one as part of its local Underground Railroad Heritage Trail: Murphy Orchards, a farm near the south shore of Lake Ontario. I ask Kate about verification of Underground Railroad sites and she laughs, shaking her head.

"It's very difficult to say 'verified,'" she tells me. "Unless there's a written record, you cannot say 'verified.'"

An example of an unverified station is the Tryon house on the river in Lewiston, seven miles below the Falls. The house was known as "the house of the seven basements" for its odd series of descending rooms built into the side of the gorge. Josiah Tryon, a deacon at the local church, is said to have been Lewiston's Underground Railroad stationmaster, and to have rowed many fugitives across the river there. There's no written record, so Tryon's participation can't be declared official. But Kate tells me when Josiah died, scores of African Americans turned up at his funeral and sang hymns.

One of the few places that can actually be verified as a critical Underground Railroad site is the Suspension Bridge. An enlarged picture looking across it hangs in the Castellani Art Museum's exhibit. It shows the tollbooth and the road for pedestrians and carriages; trains went across above, on the upper level. The picture is an enlargement of a stereoview—a double photograph that appears 3-D when you look at it in a special viewer. (Today's View-Master is the stereoview's direct descendant.) Mass produced by the millions, stereoviews hit stores in the 1850s and quickly became a national craze. In Niagara Falls, they immediately became a top souvenir. Views across the Suspension Bridge were among the most popular images. Looking at that stretch of bridge, were Americans thinking about fugitives, for whom that last quarter mile meant the difference between life and death?

In Sarah Bradford's Harriet Tubman biography, the bridge is the scene for the longest description of a fugitive's border crossing. It concerns a man named Joe, whom Harriet is taking across the border by train. Everything is going well, but Joe is filled with anxiety and seems despondent. As they cross the bridge, Harriet tries to get him to look out the window at the Falls, but he has his head in his hands. Only when they are safely in Canada, and he's told he's free, does he look up. He races off the train and weeps for joy, declaring he has only one journey left to make, the one to heaven. "You might have looked at the Falls first," Harriet is supposed to have wryly remarked, "and then gone to heaven afterwards."

Looking at the landscape is a privilege not easily shared by those in deadly peril. Yet comparatively, Joe had it easy. Not every fugitive had a cushy train ride across the border. Harriet herself often walked her charges across the Suspension Bridge at night, either bribing toll collectors or using the railroad tracks to avoid them.

"They used disguises, they traveled as train passengers, they were hidden on trains in luggage compartments," Kate tells me. "There's an exciting account of a wealthy citizen in Niagara Falls who had the fastest horses in town outrunning the police with someone in his carriage. To me that last getting over is where all the tension and suspense are."

The tension and suspense were also increased by the unique position of Niagara. Long a popular resort for southern gentry, many of whom traveled with enslaved attendants, the area saw many more slaves passing through than a typical northern town. At the same time, it was heavily populated with free blacks and progressive groups; Kate tells me there were 274 antislavery societies in New York State. On the Niagara frontier especially, public sentiment leaned toward liberty: the Niagara County Anti-Slavery Society had 21,000 members in 1837. Emboldened by this progressive environment, African-American hotel and restaurant workers in the area frequently helped fugitives make a dash for it.

As the Niagara frontier became well known as a crossing point for fugitives, it also saw an influx of opportunistic slavecatchers. The result was often fisticuffs. A group of the Cataract House's African-American employees trying to help a twenty-two-year-old woman escape in 1847 ended up clashing with a white mob. The girl was dragged onto the train, and one hotel employee jumped aboard and rode as far as Lockport, trying unsuccessfully to free her. That night, in Niagara Falls, a rowdy, drunken crowd of white workers destroyed many of the black workers' homes.

"For many decades the story of the Underground Railroad was the story of enslaved people being helped by virtuous white folks. But the Underground Railroad was started by black people," Kate tells me. "One of the things we wanted to do in this exhibit was put the black voices forward."

As an example of how powerful the black community could be, she mentions Solomon Moseby. In May of 1837, Moseby escaped bondage in Kentucky and made it to Niagara-on-the-Lake in Canada, using his master's horse. His outraged owner, David Castleman, reported the crime, and the Kentucky governor, eager to end the steady stream of fugitives out of his state, issued an extradition warrant for Moseby. A band of slavecatchers headed north. Kentucky and David Castleman had decided to make an example of Solomon Moseby. Instead, they ended up provoking Upper Canada's first race riot.

"The whole issue of the tension between the slavecatchers and the fugitives is also interesting," Kate says. "The role of the slave-catcher is still downplayed; it's very ugly. That's a piece of the story that can't be prettified."

You really can't prettify the story if, as in Niagara, the slavecatcher happens to be one of your local founding fathers. Not one single historian mentions it—or even seems aware of it—but the go-to guy for slavecatchers in the Niagara region was none other than Peter B. Porter, War of 1812 hero, alleged protector of Goat Island, connoisseur of war feasts and fine tableware.

Porter was intimately involved in the attempt to extradite Moseby. He was friends with David Castleman, Moseby's former owner, through his Kentucky in-laws, the Breckenridges. So when Moseby disappeared, naturally Castleman wrote Peter to ask his help in arresting him. His letter of early July was written in a breathless, angry tone: he asked Peter to "employ some man in whom you have confidence to decoy him over the line, have him apprehended and confined in jail as a fellon or a fugitive from justice—I will meet *whatever expense may be necessary.*" Anticipating Canadian resistance, he asked Peter "whether there is any arrangement between the governments" of the United States and Canada for extradition of fugitives, and noted, with further creative spelling, "It would be probably polacy not to speak of him as a *slave*, but as a *fellon.*" What was at stake for Castleman was clearly more than the value of one slave, or one horse. "It is important," he wrote, "that energetic measures should be used to put a stop to these escapes for they are becoming very common." In fact, Porter's parents-in-law had also recently lost a man named George Caball; Castleman was looking for him too.

Porter's friendly response invited Castleman to use his house as a base and advised him to get criminal indictments and extradition requests from the governor, preferably for horse-stealing, not self-stealing. Castleman acted on this advice immediately and wrote on August 13 to announce his imminent arrival with warrants for both men. He even added a third fugitive to his wish-list: a man named Jesse Happy who had fled a friend of Castleman's a few years back and was also in the Niagara region. "I have no desire to impose on you any further trouble," Castleman declared, "but if it should come in the way of some person who may be going over to enquire I should be glad to get holt of him." He promised to observe Porter's "suggestions about secrecy," and suggested back that Porter might warn his children against mentioning Castleman's name. He signed off "Truly your friend."

Castleman arrived in Canada in late August with three hired thugs and showed his warrants to the local authorities. Moseby was arrested in Niagara-on-the-Lake at once. The African-Canadian community was just as quick in coming to his defense. Led by a local pastor and teacher named Herbert Holmes, a group of black Canadians offered Castleman $1,000 to cover his horse (worth about $150) and his expenses. Castleman refused. They then petitioned the lieutenant governor: 17 African Canadians and 114 whites signed letters testifying to Moseby's good character and pleading that he not be sent back into bondage.

Meanwhile, the black community began to gather outside the Niagara-on-the-Lake jail. Runners went to nearby towns with the news, and the crowd swelled to hundreds. Living in tents, they kept 24-hour watch on Moseby and his captors. The women, led by a charismatic orator named Sally Carter, sang hymns. The group carefully devised a plan of resistance, agreeing, at the urging of the women, to remain unarmed.

The attorney-general of Upper Canada issued an order for Moseby's extradition on September 6. Buoyed by this success, Castleman went to Hamilton and filed the necessary papers against Jesse Happy. He too was accused of stealing a horse—four years earlier. Castleman didn't mention that Happy had left the horse in the United States and had even written his former master, telling him where to find it. Happy was quickly arrested in Hamilton.

After receiving the extradition order, Niagara-on-the-Lake deputy sheriff Alexander McLeod called in extra soldiers from nearby Fort George and notified Castleman to meet him at the Lewiston dock of the Niagara River ferry. On September 12, he attempted to take Moseby to the Canadian ferry dock in order to deliver him up. First, he ordered the crowd to withdraw. They did not. He ordered his soldiers to charge. People shouted "Don't hurt the poor soldiers!" and the crowd held its position without fighting back. Just then, a reprieve arrived: a letter from Toronto announced that the Executive Council was reconsidering the extradition decision. That letter was shortly followed by another saying that the decision to extradite had been confirmed. McLeod had the Riot Act read to the crowd. Then he and his constables led the handcuffed Moseby out of the Niagara jail and loaded him onto a waiting wagon.

The crowd followed its plan. Believing that soldiers would be reluctant to shoot females, the women charged first. One woman pinioned Sheriff McLeod. Pastor Holmes blocked the transport wagon's horses and a man named Jacob Green rammed a fence post in its wheels. Moseby took the opportunity to throw himself out of the wagon, leap a fence and flee. (His guards may have assisted by loosening or never fastening his handcuffs.) Enraged, Sheriff McLeod ordered his troops to fire on the crowd. Pastor Holmes and Jacob Green were killed. But Moseby was free. Later, he would make his way to Great Britain.

History has not recorded how the news reached David Castleman, waiting on the Lewiston dock for a delivery that never came. It's a nice scene to imagine. Perhaps he grumbled his way back to his friend Peter's that night, and Porter consoled him with a nice dinner. Castleman was doomed to further disappointment: following the riot at Niagara, the Canadian Governor's Executive Council took a closer look at the case of Jesse Happy. Given the underwhelming evidence of his guilt, they let him go free.

Solomon Moseby's arrest and escape became a rallying cry for Canadian antiextradition forces: the following year, the British government upheld Canada's refusal to extradite criminals whose "crimes" were not crimes in Canada. British traveler and memoirist Anna Jameson, who visited the Niagara region in 1839, was miserably disappointed by the Falls, but extremely impressed by Moseby's story. She especially admired the women, who had insisted on unarmed resistance but hadn't hesitated to put their bodies on the line.

Peter Porter was less pleased with the outcome. After the escape, he wrote a confidential letter to the governor of Upper Canada, lambasting the Canadians for their handling of the affair, including their refusal to render up Jesse Happy.

"I respect the members of the council for their humanity," Porter wrote. "I am as much opposed to slavery in the abstract as they are." But he went on to defend southern slavery on the grounds that a general emancipation would make it "impossible to sustain a moral and wholesome government." The answer, according to Porter, was not to free the slaves, but to send them back to Africa:

> You know something of the frivolous, improvident, reckless and, in extremities, desperate character of the African race. If you do not, the good people of your province seem in a way to become thoroughly and experimentally acquainted with it. The free negroes of the United States are decidedly, as a body, the most licentious, turbulent and worthless part of our population, and we are making, as you must have perceived, great efforts, at great expense, to remove them back to Africa and provide for them all the advantages of freedom that they are capable of enjoying.

Porter himself had already tried to contribute to the repatriation effort: after inheriting around twenty-five slaves as part of Laetitia Breckenridge's patrimony, he offered these folks their freedom, on the condition that they would scram to Liberia. No one seemed eager to go. Porter brought a few of the younger people to New York, under a state law by which slaves could be brought into the state as indentured apprentices and freed at age twenty-eight. They turned out to be "excellent servants," Porter told the Canadian governor, at least until "they were fastened upon by the emancipators and free blacks of Buffalo and Canada who persuaded them (with the exception of two only who served out their time) to flee across the river. Several of them are now in Canada and have become as worthless, I fear, as are most of that species of population."

Climb down into the memory hole, and you never know what you'll find. Porter's views—nominally abolitionist yet thoroughly racist—were hardly unusual for his time. That a war hero and town father of the 1840s should spout this rhetoric is not surprising. But that no one should ever mention it—even as Solomon Moseby's story is frequently retold—is a bit odd. The damning documents are not exactly hidden: they're in the Peter B. Porter papers at the Buffalo and Erie County Historical Society Library. There, among folder after folder of letters, contracts, deeds and steamship manifests, are the Kentucky governor's extradition warrants for Jesse Happy and Solomon Moseby.

General Porter is a hard guy to knock off his pedestal. He stays up there in part because slavecatching, like the destruction of nature, is one of those things we're inclined to sweep under the rug.

For the United States, things were nearing a head in the 1850s. The Compromise of 1850 included the infamous Fugitive Slave Act, which made it a crime, even in northern states, for citizens to help a runaway slave. This made getting to Canada imperative for fugitives. The act also had the unintended consequence of radicalizing abolitionists. Even northerners lukewarm on abolition were outraged at the idea that they were *required* to help slave-owners hunt down and capture fugitives. For those opposed to the institution, the whole notion of accommodating southern slavery began to seem ridiculous. The Kansas-Nebraska Act of 1854, engineered by Senator Stephen A. Douglas of Illinois, was meant to defuse conflict by letting new states choose for themselves whether to enter the union as slave states or free states. It only made things worse, polarizing the two sides and bringing violence into the mix as Free-Soilers and slavery advocates raced to settle Kansas. As pro-slavery sentiment increased, the Underground Railroad increasingly came out of the closet. By the time of the infamous Dred Scott decision of 1857, in which the U.S. Supreme Court declared that no person of African ancestry could ever be a citizen or sue in a federal court, northern stationmasters were advertising openly in newspapers.

With the radicalization of the 1850s, the plight of the fugitive slave went from hidden ordeal to national drama. Popular newspapers gave extensive coverage to chilling tales such as the 1856 tragedy of Margaret Garner, a fugitive who, on the verge of being recaptured, slit her two-year-old daughter's throat rather than see her sent back into bondage. (Toni Morrison later based her acclaimed novel *Beloved* on this event.) Blackface minstrel shows began openly referring to fugitives, performing songs about families torn apart and bondsmen determined to be free. And in a literal staging of the national spectacle, Harriet Beecher Stowe's abolitionist novel *Uncle Tom's Cabin* burst onto the scene in 1852 and was immediately adapted many times for the theater. Its popularity surpassed even the earlier vogue for Indian dramas.

Such was the state of the nation in 1859, the year Blondin chose to stage his performances. For his setting, he picked an American icon that happened to be a symbol of freedom for slaves, in a town where frequent fugitive escapes were reported with approval in the local paper.

Some historians suggest that Blondin's high-wire antics gripped Americans because the show gave them respite from ugly public debates and looming violence. Maybe, but descriptions of Blondin's act hardly make it sound relaxing. Thousands of people crammed the gorge rim and stood paralyzed with anxiety every time he crossed. Women screamed, wept and fainted; men swore and clenched their fists. The performance may have been an instance of mass projection—Americans transferring their anxiety from the nation's peril to the aerialist's—but this could only happen because there was something similar about the two.

Niagara chroniclers love describing Blondin's clever acts. He crossed the rope one day wearing a sack over his head. He pushed a wheelbarrow across, imitating a manual laborer. He crossed with an iron stove, wearing a chef's hat, and set it up and cooked omelets midway, which he passed down to the *Maid of the Mist* below. He crossed on stilts as the Prince of Wales watched. Most famously, he carried Harry Colcord over twice. Newspapers all over the nation reported on each new performance, always declaring that Blondin couldn't possibly surpass the latest feat.

Absent from later accounts is the act's historical context. But considered within the frame of the increasingly bitter slavery standoff, and in the light of Niagara's central role in that drama, the performances take on a different tone. When Blondin cooked omelets in a chef's outfit he had borrowed from "the head cook at the International," he made people think of the kitchens of Niagara's hotels—which were filled with black employees. When he crossed with a sack on his head, he looked like a fugitive being dragged back to slavery. When he crossed with Colcord on his back, he was within what we Michiganians call "spittin' distance" of the very Suspension Bridge across which Harriet Tubman "carried" scores of fugitives. The crowd's anxiety was all for his passenger: would Blondin get the man across?

The most powerfully suggestive performance was his crossing of the tightrope wearing an iron collar, chains, handcuffs and shackles. This getup was said to be the character of a "Siberian slave," but it must have suggested cruelties closer to home. If there was a universal symbol for slavery, it was a set of shackles. Abolitionists were often photographed holding broken ones, and abolitionist literature frequently included their image. Some states, like Ohio, even went to the trouble of outlawing shackles. Art historian Albert Gardner called the era's obsession with chains and shackles a "national mania." Abolitionists sometimes demonstrated the physical ravages of slavery by having former slaves display backs scarred from whippings. Shackles were a somewhat more genteel way of evoking this same brutality. Today, the one material object in the Castellani Art Museum's Underground Railroad exhibit is a set of shackles, with a tag neatly engraved, "T. H. Porter, dealer in horses and slaves."

Blondin never made any public statements about slavery, or any other aspect of American politics. He was a performer, here to entertain folks and make a lot of money. But imagine magician David Copperfield putting on a show somewhere in the desert along the Mexican border. Imagine he gets Regis and Kelly to come and tape segments of the show in which he builds a wall and makes someone disappear on one side of the wall and reappear on the other. Then he has himself straitjacketed, locked in a box, and dropped into the Rio Grande. He has to escape his bonds and swim to the other side. Say he does it when the Senate is hashing out a new immigration bill and immigrants are marching in the streets demanding a path to citizenship. Would people somehow get the idea that his performance *meant* something?

Blondin performed throughout the summer of 1859. That September, shortly after the aerialist packed up for the season, abolitionist John Brown led eighteen men in a doomed attempt to start a slave revolt by capturing the federal arsenal at Harpers Ferry. He and two of his accomplices were hanged in December. In April 1860, thousands of protestors, including Harriet Tubman, managed to free a fugitive from federal marshals in Troy, New York. Abraham Lincoln was the Republican party's nominee for president and war was looking inevitable in June 1860, when Blondin returned for another summer of shows. This year, he moved his tightrope farther from the Falls. He was now directly over the Whirlpool Rapids, water so turbulent the *Maid of the Mist* could no longer come underneath his rope. To kick off the year he arrived dressed as an Indian chief and danced across his new rope in eight minutes, "with scarcely more effort than another would put forth in going across the Suspension Bridge."

"On Saturday," reported the *Niagara Falls Gazette* on June 13, "twenty-five hundred dollars worth of bone and sinew, in the persons of Hill Burton and John Burt Purnell, two fugitives from Wooster County, Maryland, passed through Rochester *en route* for Vic's dominions via Suspension Bridge." Six days later, Blondin announced in the same paper that he would cross his tightrope that day "blindfolded, and tied up in a sack from head to foot." On the Fourth of July, he went across in the dark of night.

He had competition this year. On a tightrope closer to the Falls, a new aerialist who called himself the Great Farini was matching Blondin's antics trick for trick.

Farini and Blondin couldn't have been more different. Blondin was small and fair; Farini large, with olive skin, black hair and startling blue eyes. Blondin was married with children; Farini was a swaggering womanizer. Blondin was a distinguished Frenchman; Farini, who billed himself as a famed Italian ropewalker, was in fact a Canadian farm boy whose parents, embarrassed by his antics, refused to attend his shows. Blondin made everything he did look easy, but Farini's performances were a torment to watch. His slack rope pitched and swayed and his tricks pushed his abilities to the limit. He often had to stop and lie down to rest, and frequently caught himself from falling. The *Niagara Falls Gazette* declared his to be "the greatest slack rope performance on record," but asserted there was "no pleasure to the beholder" in it.

Throughout the summer, Blondin performed, and Farini tried to out-Blondin Blondin. Blondin cooked an omelet; Farini dressed up as an Irish washerwoman—with washing machine—and washed handkerchiefs on the rope. Blondin went over in a sack that covered his arms and legs; Farini went over in a sack that even enclosed his feet. Then he stood on his head in it. Blondin carried the small-framed Colcord across; Farini carried his friend, the long-legged, 150-pound tailor Rowland McMullen. In the middle of the crossing, Farini went under the rope, passed beneath McMullen, and then reloaded him for a return to the shore where they began.

Farini is famous today because he challenged Blondin, and because, for one magical season, two great circus artists attempted to outdo each other in amazing spectators at the Falls. But his act also served to underscore the perilousness of what both men were doing. Crossing Niagara was dangerous and difficult. Watching Farini, the audience really felt it.

Blondin shared the public stage with attractions other than Farini. In July of 1859 alone, Niagara region audiences could also go and see Sanford's Opera Troupe, a magician named Love, an equestrian drama, and a moving panorama called the "Panorama of Slavery" by a formerly enslaved minister named Tablos Gross. It was playing at the American Hall in Buffalo. In the wake of *Uncle Tom's Cabin*, abolitionist statements were increasingly common in theatrical venues. Was Blondin's act such a statement, and was it understood that way? The question is beginning to haunt me. It's time to go back to the Edith Wharton-meets-Homeland-Security atmosphere of the American Antiquarian Society.

It has been months since my last trip to the library, but the frock-coated attendant greets me charmingly by name, and patiently reexplains the tortuous sign-in policy, which I can never seem to keep straight. After you've consigned all your contraband to a locker, you sign in twice; once in a big logbook that is kept for all posterity to admire, and then on a sheet of paper. When you leave the library, you have to go and get a pink exit card from the reference desk, like an elementary schooler getting the bathroom pass. You hand the pink card to Frock Coat and sign out, noting the time of your departure. I get out my cell phone to check the time as I sign in, and Frock Coat points to it and says, "You can just turn that off now."

Back on my hard chair, I page through old newspapers from the Niagara region, looking for descriptions of Blondin's act. They all seem pretty much the same, even a long one in the *National Era*, Washington D.C.'s African-American newspaper. The *Era* praises the performance for its illustration of "the wonderful extent to which the human faculties may be trained," but like the other newspapers, it makes no claims about the performance's meaning. All the stories simply report on the spectacle: the size of the crowd, the details of the stunt. There are no allusions to subtexts or references to slavery.

Or are there? After a while, I notice that several newspapers mention the bands set up on both sides of the gorge, and identify the songs they played to accompany Blondin's journey. Most are what I'd expect: "Hail, Columbia" when he leaves the United States, "God Save the Queen" when he leaves Canada. But there's one I don't recognize, and it turns up several times. It's a song called "The Other Side of Jordan," said to have been played upon his first return from Canada. *The New York Times* reports that on the day of the very first crossing, a half-German, half-black band aboard the steamship to the Falls played so badly that "while dozens were under the impression they were 'doing' Hail Columbia, all the rest on board would have sworn it was the 'Other Side of Jordan.'"

Luckily, I'm at the American Antiquarian Society. I look up "The Other Side of Jordan" in the card catalog—there's a separate set of drawers for music—and pretty soon have several versions of the sheet music in front of me.

The song was popular. There are many versions of it; some are called "The Other Side of Jordan" and some are called "Jordan Is a Hard Road to Travel." The song itself is a fake spiritual, written by the blackface minstrel Dan Emmett, whose song "Dixie" became a Confederate anthem (allegedly to his dismay; he was a Union man). Written in the era's "negro dialect," the first verse goes:

> *I just arrived in town for to pass de time away*
> *and I settled all my bisness accordin*
> *But I found it so cold when I went up de street*
> *Dat I wish'd I was on de oder side ob Jordan.*

And then the chorus:

> *So take off your coat boys, and roll up your sleeves,*
> *For Jordan is a hard road to trabel*
> *So take off your coat boys, and roll up your sleeves*
> *For Jordan is a hard road to trabel, I believe.*

This is a song about fugitive slaves. Participants in the Underground Railroad used spirituals as a code to talk about the flight to freedom. Canaan means Canada; Moses means Harriet Tubman. Jordan meant the Ohio River. Crossing the Ohio River from the slave state of Kentucky to the free state of Ohio was crossing to freedom, a trip made famous by a dramatic escape across breaking-up ice in *Uncle Tom's Cabin*. Harriet Tubman sang about going to the other side of Jordan as a way of secretly informing her friends and family of her plans to escape to the free states. But after 1850 and the Fugitive Slave Act, of course, Jordan had to move north, to the Canadian border. The 1853 version of the song even gets in a joke about Canada's weather; it's so cold the fugitive wishes himself back in the United States. In fact, exaggerations about the harshness of Canadian winters were often used by slave-owners to discourage flights north.

The song is an ugly lampoon, and yet it also managed to capture some of the drama of the fugitive. Even an "Ethiopian Banjo Melody" version from 1852, titled "Jordan Am a Hard Road to Trabel," clearly references the flight north:

> *I look to de Norf, I look to de East*
> *Holler for de ox cart to come on*

Wid four grey horses driven on de lead
To take us to de order side of Jordan.

Ox carts, according to Kate Koperski, were one way to get fugitives across the Suspension Bridge. Certain toll collectors were known to be willing, for a small fee, to forgo inspection of your wagon when you had a load of "southern calico" aboard.

Like the minstrel tradition generally, "The Other Side of Jordan" is an odd amalgamation of racism and revolution. White performers "blacked up" with cork and using fake negro dialect were putting on a degrading spectacle founded on racist humor. But the shows also suggested the slipperiness of racial categories: If white people could be mistaken for blacks, why not the reverse? What does "race" mean, anyway? Minstrel shows bought into unsavory stereotypes, but they also subverted a "natural order" based on racial difference. In its own way, Blondin's high-wire act suggested the same thing.

In September of 1860, Blondin and Farini both performed for the last time at Niagara. The Prince of Wales was in attendance, and he watched Blondin carry Colcord across the rope once again. At the end the prince remarked, "Thank God it's all over." Whether he saw Farini or not is a matter of some dispute, but if he did, it was only in passing. The two men packed up their ropes and left town. Blondin was thereafter known as "The Hero of Niagara," and Farini, perhaps in one last attempt to claim superiority, dubbed himself "The Champion of Niagara." Two months later, the American people elected a new president named Abraham Lincoln, and South Carolina promptly announced its secession from the Union.

Lincoln's win was a foregone conclusion in the four-way race, with the divided Democratic party not even voting for the same candidate in North and South. In August 1860, while the aerialists were still cavorting over the Niagara Gorge, *Harper's* ran a cartoon called "The Coming Man's Presidential Career." It showed a buff Blondin in tights crossing his wire with neat steps. His grimly determined face is not Blondin's however; it's Lincoln's. His balancing pole is labeled "Constitution" and on the cliffs behind him, a sign with an arrow reads "To the Whirlpool." On his shoulders, wearing a smile that is half minstrelsy stereotype, half heartrending portrait of hope, is a barefoot black man. The second line of the caption reads: "Motto: Don't Give Up the Ship."

History is frustrating. We can estimate the size of the crowd; we can look at catalogs to surmise what they were wearing, at train timetables to deduce how they got there; maybe we can even find bills of fare to tell us what they ate that day. But what they were thinking remains a mystery. Newspapers tell us the crowds were silent, their wide eyes fixed on Blondin, their faces tight with worry. What lurked behind that mask of expectation? Were the abolitionists among them secretly exulting in this coded rhapsody to freedom and the high-wire act it required? Were the southerners in the crowd hoping the Frenchman would fall? Or did everyone engage in a massive willing suspension of disbelief, agreeing for just two summers to pretend the show was nothing more than the crass, sensational spectacle so many critics denounced it for? As the saying goes, you can't dig up a hole. Unfortunately, history is full of them.

Blondin's manager Harry Colcord went on to narrate his adventures, including the terrifying trip on Blondin's back across the gorge. Not satisfied with the story's inherent excitement, he threw in an attempted sabotage. During their crossing, he claimed, one of the guy lines snapped. This may have happened, but Colcord spiced up the story by claiming that a man was seen yanking on the line and running away. And he added that a visiting group in the audience, the Washington Grays, offered a $10,000 reward for apprehension of the would-be saboteur.

Every subsequent biographer would repeat this tale, though by 1989, biographer Dean Shapiro would have lost its purpose, describing the Washington Grays as a "prominent New York family." They were no such thing. They were the 8th Regiment of New York's militia, dedicated to preservation of the Union. Two years after Blondin's performance, they would swap their gray militia togs for Union blues and go to war for President Lincoln. They would brave the maelstrom; they would not give up the ship.

The Washington Grays did attend one of Blondin's performances—but it was not the one where he carried Colcord across. Blondin's biographers all miss what's interesting about the story: the wily manager clearly wanted to signal his performer's connection with the Union cause.

The next time I'm in Niagara Falls, I go to the public library and look at everything I can find about Blondin again. No writer even mentions the Civil War, let alone the Underground Railroad, except to note that Blondin's 1861 departure from the United States was delayed by war actions. No one who writes about Blondin speculates on the meaning of his performance at all. It's as if his stunts took place in some soundproofed parallel universe, insulated from the hue and cry of the national news.

I wander into the stacks and find Maureen Fennie reshelving boxes in the civil records section.

"Maureen, what do you think of the stunters—the Niagara daredevils?" I ask her.

"Not much," she replies at once. "There's no substance there. It's a few seconds over the Falls. The power, the industry, how they wrecked a beautiful spot; to me that's the real story of Niagara Falls."

That's exactly what I used to think. I ask Maureen if she has ever seen the cartoon with Lincoln as Blondin. Her eyes light up, and the box in her hands goes back onto the metal cart. It's so easy to distract Maureen.

"I don't think I have," she says. We proceed to the flat file of magazine engravings and dig through them unsuccessfully. Then Maureen remembers that there's a separate file for cartoons. She retrieves that and we page through it.

"There it is," she says decisively, pointing at a page.

"No, that's not it," I say, glancing at it.

"But it's Lincoln as Blondin," she says and I look again. Sure enough, it's a *Vanity Fair* cartoon from June 9, 1860, drawn by *Vanity Fair* art director Henry Louis Stephens. It shows Lincoln in tights, crossing the Niagara Gorge on a tightrope so wide it looks like a rotten plank. In his hands, he carries a carpetbag with a doll-sized African-American man inside it. A whiskered fellow behind him is shouting "Don't drop the carpetbag." Whiskers is a caricature of *New York Tribune* editor Horace Greeley, a Lincoln supporter and abolitionist who frequently criticized his president for not freeing the slaves soon enough. The cartoon is far less flattering than the *Harper's* depiction: unlike *Harper's, Vanity Fair* opposed abolition.

When the pirate *Michigan* crashed to its fate, spectators felt an odd sense of satisfaction. Their understanding of the world had been confirmed. As one newspaper put it, "the power of the Almighty was imposingly displayed over the workmanship of mere human hands." Daredevils do the opposite. They defy human limitation. They jump canyons, fall from the sky and ride waterfalls, pitting their puny human bodies against everything the earth can throw at them. As the second season of performances began, *The New York Times* described Blondin on his tightrope as "seeming to defy nature in her very lair, and nature's laws." The writer goes on to describe the Niagara River as a serpent and Blondin as "another St. George," as if his accomplishment drives a sword into the very heart of the landscape. How humiliating for our fearsome Falls serpent, reappearing once more only to be killed, this time not by the Thunder Gods, but by a capering Frenchman in tights! But what the writer is trying to get at is the stunter's spirit of hubris. He is St. George taking on the dragon, David hurling the tiny stone of himself against the Goliath of nature. Of course, American slavery itself was once seen as part of natural law—theories of "natural" racial superiority made it possible to enslave people based on nothing more than skin color. No doubt many in the crowd on those hot summer days of 1860 watched the small figure on his tightrope with a sense—half-articulated in the *Harper's* cartoon— that the whole country was about to climb on Lincoln's back as he attempted to do what had until then seemed humanly impossible. The laws of nature, Blondin's act declared, can be rewritten. The world can go out on a wire. It can be stood on its head.

For black Americans, Niagara's overtones of freedom never died. Encomiums to Niagara Falls turn up in black newspapers and magazines throughout the nineteenth century. And when W. E. B. Du Bois and Mary Talbert decided in 1905 to convene a group of African-American intellectuals and found a civil rights movement to demand suffrage, they first met in Buffalo. Denied a hotel room, they crossed the Niagara River to Fort Erie. There they hashed out a declaration of principles for what they called "The Niagara Movement." The founders had a photograph made of themselves standing before a backdrop depicting the Falls. They frown out gravely, serious yet hopeful. They too were going out on a wire. The Niagara Movement went on to become the NAACP.

They were not the only ones to see themselves as following Blondin. In 1862, with the war going badly, Lincoln chastised his critics: "Gentlemen," he declared, "suppose all the property you were worth was in gold and you put it in the hands of Blondin to carry across the Niagara Falls on a rope. Would you shake the cable, or keep shouting out to him 'Blondin! Stand up a little straighter; Blondin! Stoop a little more; go a little faster; lean a little more to the north; lean a little more to the south?' No, you would hold your breath, as well as your tongue and keep your hands off until he was safely over!"

Redefining the "natural" is never easy. When it's done, it tends to be done by visionaries, individuals who remake the world by pitting their beliefs and bodies against its unshakable order. In the end, that's Blondin's legacy. If he valorized—intentionally or not—the cause of abolition in the process of expanding the limits of the humanly possible, he also diminished the Falls. Many newspapers repeated the sentiment of the small Port Hope *Tri-Weekly Guide*, which declared, "The mighty cataract has ceased to be one of the seven wonders of the world—Blondin reigns in its stead." And Blondin himself, when told by the *Toronto Daily Globe* reporter that he was now as great as the Falls, is said to have laughed and replied, "You can see that I am even greater."

After Blondin, there were more tightrope walkers at the Niagara Gorge. Harry Leslie, the "American Blondin," crossed in 1865, J. F. Jenkins in 1869, Henry Belleni, billed as the "Australian Blondin," in 1873, Maria Spelterini in 1876, Stephen Peer in 1887, Samuel Dixon in 1890, Clifford Calverly in 1892 and 1893, and James Hardy in 1896. And then there were no more, except for one little-known crossing in 1911 by a man named Oscar Williams. What happened?

In 1895, the meaning of Niagara shifted dramatically. After that year, daredevils at the Falls were focused not on tightrope walking, but on going over in barrels or other contraptions. The first person to succeed was a sixty-three-year-old woman from Bay City, Michigan, a fact that has been a perpetual disappointment to history. Even at the time, newspapers reacted to Annie Edson Taylor's 1901 trip over the Horseshoe with unabashed dismay. The *Baltimore American* declared the feat "ought only to excite sorrow and indignation among sensible people"; the *Denver Republican* sneered that poor Annie "seems to be taking a lot of credit that belongs to the barrel," and the *Washington Post* announced that it expected the Falls to write a book one day called "The Fools Who Have Gone Over Me." It's an odd comment, since only one fool at that point had done so and lived.

Annie still disappoints people. One recent author chalks up her success to hydro diversion having "subdued" the waterfall's energy: that a "middle-aged woman" could conquer the brink he declares "an indication of its attenuated power." Pierre Berton in *Niagara* just can't forgive Taylor for robbing some younger, handsomer daredevil's thunder, calling her "a bulky and shapeless woman of sixty-three, with coarse features and a rasping voice." Over the course of ten pages, he brands her "flabby and over-weight," "stout and almost shapeless" and "a lumpy figure with a pudding of a face." I've studied pictures of Annie pretty closely; she looks a bit dour, but she's actually fairly trim for a Victorian matron. Yet Berton is hardly alone in his need to mock her. My favorite date film, *Niagara: Miracles, Myths and Magic*, depicts her as a nagging, kitten-toting old prude, gabbing nonstop even as her assistants row her out into the rapids. "Remember, I'm forty-three!" she keeps insisting. The boatmen roll their eyes and cut her loose. You can still buy obnoxious caricatures of Annie Taylor on Niagara postcards.

Why was Annie so disliked? The answer is simple. Annie's triumph, even more than Blondin's, diminished the Falls. The *Buffalo Express* sums it up:

> We really wanted the great cataract to remain unassailable, unachievable. It is fine to have something at hand which is absolutely master of itself, superior to everything. We thought we had it in Niagara Falls. And now along comes an estimable person—not a mighty athlete, or a wonderful swimmer or anything of that sort, but a quiet, rather matronly fashioned woman—who tucks herself into a barrel and glides over the awful precipice wellnigh as serenely as a decoy duck would bob over a two-foot mill-dam. Could anything—even the impending lectures which the trip has so obviously fitted Mrs. Taylor to deliver—do more to belittle Niagara Falls? The question really becomes serious: Are they any longer worth looking at?

Are the Falls worth looking at? That question would increasingly come to be asked in the early twentieth century. Because the Falls were no longer an unassailable force of nature: in 1895, they were harnessed for electricity. Blondin's upstaging of nature was completed by Nikola Tesla.

The *Buffalo Express* saw Annie's accomplishment as one more win for a technological age: "It is, apparently, an hour in which all the impossible things are getting done," the editors declared. "Here is the great aeronaut, Santos-Dumont, flying around Eiffel Tower as blithely as a swallow around a church spire. . . . Here is Alexander Winton doing ten miles in his automobile at a rate so close to a mile a minute we may as well let it go at that." They didn't mention the conquest of Niagara by power barons, but that surely underlay their feeling that the great cataract had lost its luster.

After Annie, there was a rush on barrel stunts at the Falls. More people rode the rapids. Bobby Leach went over the Horseshoe Falls in a barrel, and in 1910, Lincoln Beachy buzzed under the Upper Steel Arch Bridge in his Curtiss biplane. It continues to this day, but little by little, stunting has dropped off. Today, if Evel

Knievel himself were to show up with a shiny new Cataract-o-cycle, he probably wouldn't get half as many spectators as Blondin did. Stunting on the Niagara River has grown less interesting as the Falls themselves have been increasingly subjected to human control. Today, on the rare occasions when daredevils do attempt to go over the Falls, the New York Power Authority and Ontario Hydro can dial down the water to stop them. Why challenge a waterfall when its masters can turn it off? We are no longer David. The Falls are no longer Goliath.

In the years between the Civil War and the end of the nineteenth century, the Falls would be completely taken in hand, from the arrangement of trees to the creation of viewpoints to the regulation of the waterfall's water. Ironically, it all began with a movement called Free Niagara.

Five

FREE NIAGARA

IN EARLY AUGUST 1869, Frederick Law Olmsted took a stroll around Niagara Falls. After years of civil war, the nation was painfully rebuilding itself, and Niagara, its best-known natural icon, was in need of rescue, a maiden about to be despoiled by nefarious mustache-twirlers. The Falls required a savior, and the eminent landscape architect and planner—already famous for co-designing Central Park with Calvert Vaux—fit the bill.

Fred Olmsted was an enthusiast. Born to a well-off Hartford family who traced their lineage back to Connecticut's original settlers, he spent his youth being supported by his father as he threw himself into different careers. He went to sea and almost died of scurvy. He bought a farm and won a prize for his pears. He rambled around England and wrote a travelogue, *Walks and Talks of an American Farmer in England.* He toured the American South as a correspondent for *The New York Times* and wrote three volumes of essays, collected as *The Cotton Kingdom* and still considered one of the most vivid contemporaneous accounts of slavery. When the Civil War broke out, he founded the U.S. Sanitary Commission, predecessor to the American Red Cross, and ran it with autocratic efficiency. Then he headed for California to oversee an unsuc-

cessful gold mine. While there, he fell in love with the beautiful
Yosemite Valley and lobbied the California legislature to preserve
it for posterity in a state of nature. Now, coming back to his own
side of the country, it made sense he would turn an eye to the
East's great wonder, Niagara. What he saw there appalled him.

The most common photo of Olmsted—the one that appears
on signboards in Niagara Falls State Park—shows a bearded,
heavy-browed grizzly of a man, a tremendous forehead enclosing
the deep thoughts percolating behind it. But a photo in the New
York Public Library gives a better sense of Fred's character. In it,
five young men sit before a table holding an open book. Four
of them—including Frederick's younger brother, John Hull Olmsted—are students at Yale. Frederick was meant to be enrolled there
as well, but was prevented from matriculating when an attack of
poison sumac weakened his eyes. The four Yale students gaze con-
fidently at the camera, no one more so than Charles Loring Brace,
a fervent young man who would go on to become a well-known
humanitarian and founder of the Children's Aid Society. Brace
frowns into the camera with the powerful moral conviction he
held even as an undergraduate. Frederick Law Olmsted, an intense
youth with pretty, almost feminine features, gazes avidly at his
lifelong friend as if hoping to find his own life's mission written
on Brace's stolid face.

By 1869, he had found it. After the Civil War, Olmsted took
up the cause of Reconstruction. Returning to New York from his
nonproducing gold mine, he helped manage a new, idealistic magazine he had co-founded, *The Nation,* while launching the landscape architecture firm of Olmsted & Vaux. Within four years,
the firm had been consulted on parks and campuses in Brooklyn, Boston, Chicago, Buffalo, Philadelphia, Albany, Providence,
Newark, Montreal and the District of Columbia, among others.
For Olmsted, this work was not simply an aesthetic avocation; it
was moral and patriotic.

Olmsted believed avidly in democracy. And like many nineteenth-
century reformers, he believed that democracy required, first and
foremost, the elevation of the moral and spiritual condition of the
"common man." This was the purpose behind his public park designs

no less than behind *The Nation*: true democracy could only happen when everyone, from legislators to laborers, shared a common culture.

In the early nineteenth century, as immigrants swelled the population of the young United States, that task looked difficult. After the Civil War, it looked nearly impossible. The war had exposed the sharp divisions that underlay America, not just between North and South, but between rich and poor, city and country. It magnified the challenges of democracy, especially with the drastic and extremely rapid changes society had been undergoing since the early 1800s. The Industrial Revolution, immigration, urbanization, and now emancipation: how was the reeling nation going to embrace and educate a vastly heterogeneous population? And how were those people going to adapt to the new conditions of life in an industrialized, city-centered world?

These issues furrowed Olmsted's heavy brow as he strolled around Goat Island in 1869, but they galvanized him too. Even with the horrible war still fresh in his memory, he was somehow filled with hope for the future. He shared his ideas with the friends accompanying him: northern New York's district attorney, William Dorsheimer, and prominent architect Henry Hobson Richardson, who was designing a mansion for Dorsheimer in Buffalo. Later that evening, they were joined by a couple more well-heeled gentlemen in Dorsheimer's Buffalo office, and there, according to Olmsted's account, the movement known as Free Niagara was born.

"A lot of people think Free Niagara meant free the Falls from the grip of commercialism," Tom Yots tells me. "It may have meant that, but it also meant the Falls were going to be free to the public."

Tom Yots is the city historian for Niagara Falls, New York. When he was first asked by the mayor to take that position, he said no. He felt he wasn't qualified; he was no historian, but a preservationist. His expertise was helping owners of historic properties get their buildings designated as local or national landmarks. He did this with his own home, a richly detailed Arts and Crafts mansion not far from the public library, built by Union Carbide founder James Marshall. Tom and his wife Louise have turned it into an elegant bed-and-breakfast.

In spite of Tom's reluctance, the mayor persisted, and Tom added the duties of city historian to those of preservation consultant and hotelier, working on books about regional history and answering queries from curious tourists. One of the duties he enjoys now is leading walking tours of Goat Island during which he stops and reads Olmsted quotes to the walkers. He has agreed to give me a private version of this walk.

Tom is a small, impish man with a neatly trimmed, whitish-gray beard. He looks a little like the pictures of Calvert Vaux—thoughtful yet energetic. He speaks and moves with precision. He brings his readings with him for our two-person walk around Goat Island on this cold and windy morning. His black binder, filled with snippets of text taped to pages and sticky notes bearing obscure codes, flaps violently in the wind whenever he brings it out. His black cocker spaniel Ollie looks at us quizzically whenever we stop for one of his readings. She's a creature of habit, and usually the only interruptions to her daily walk are regular stops for treats. Ollie's a bit rotund, and in the interest of slimming her down, her treats have recently been changed to green beans.

To join Tom at our meeting place—the old Schoellkopf Power Plant on the gorge rim below the Falls—I have cut through the parking lot of the Howard Johnson, crossed an entrance ramp, and sloshed my way down the mucky median of the Robert Moses Parkway to skirt a chain-link fence whose only apparent purpose is to keep pedestrians from accessing the Niagara Gorge or its park. The payoff for this indignity is immediate: Tom takes me right to the viewing platform that pokes out into the gorge and begins pointing out parts of the ruined power plant, destroyed by a rockslide in 1956. He identifies an old penstock outfall in the gorge and tells me there's still a wrecked turbine sitting down there. You can scramble over to it from the gorge hiking trails. I make a mental note to use this fact the next time I'm trying to convince Bob to accompany me to Niagara Falls. He loves turbines.

As we begin to walk upstream from the old power plant, Tom tells me the old hydraulic canal that used to run right through town lies directly under the Howard Johnson's indoor pool. This canal was the earliest successful attempt to systematically capitalize on

Niagara's vast power potential. It was begun by Augustus Porter, who worked with civil engineer Peter Emslie to design a hydraulic canal leading from the river above the Falls to the riverbank just below the Falls. Taken over after Porter's death by Horace Day, the 4,400-foot canal came into use in 1861, and an assortment of mills and factories sprang up along it, using its water directly for their waterwheels and then discharging it through tailraces on the riverbank. By 1885, the dense cluster of mills and factories known as the "milling district" was utilizing all of the canal's motive force, about 10,000 horsepower. When the first electrical power plants were built, it made sense to put one on the old canal near the factories, where it remained in operation until the 1956 landslide. Only then were the factories of the milling district razed. Today, the factories have been replaced by a Days Inn, a Howard Johnson, Twist o' the Mist (an ice-cream stand shaped like a giant, soft-serve cone) and, on the site of the old power plant, the Schoellkopf Geological Museum and park.

We're starting in the milling district because it's one of the eyesores Olmsted and his buddies deplored. Olmsted, according to Tom, would have liked to include some of this area in the State Reservation, but he was too much of a realist to think he could talk the state into eliminating the prosperous factories and their ugly tailraces, man-made waterfalls spilling dirty water into the gorge. Instead, Olmsted focused on the district he thought he *could* change, the commercialized area around the waterfall itself and the rapids just above it.

To get to the rapids, we walk upstream along the Niagara Gorge toward the Falls. The little-used asphalt trail we're on dips down and passes under the Rainbow Bridge to Canada, offering a great view of the gorge, the Canadian riverbank, and the bottom of the bridge. Beyond the bridge, the Niagara Reservation, America's first state park, begins. We walk past the visitor center, heading for the bridge to Goat Island. As we walk, Tom tells me about the thinking that underlay Olmsted's park design.

"We have people who would like to go back to honky-tonk and billboards," he says. "They say we're using nineteenth-century design principles. I say Olmsted may have had design principles, but he also had a design philosophy. He believed that all human beings were capable of experiencing what he called the aesthetic impulse. If you took a human being and put him into a natural setting, he would have a reaction to that and be uplifted by that."

When we get to the rapids just above the Falls, Tom stops and flips through his notebook. He finds a picture of the same spot in the 1870s and shows it to me. Along the rushing rapids sits the area Olmsted hated even more than the milling district. There, on the riverbank where Father Hennepin once struggled through dense forest, the booming tourist industry of the post–Erie Canal era gave birth to the Midway's jumble of hotels, attractions, fenced-off views and "Indian bazaars." Every inch of it was crammed with cheap attractions, ramshackle buildings and ugly signs. To Olmsted, the scene suggested nature forced to bow to the demands of crass moneymaking. It was not just an aesthetic loss, but a moral one.

Tom has inherited Olmsted's principled disdain.

"Part of the deal was to remove the amusement park here that was so disgusting," he tells me. "And now"—he gestures toward the skyline across the river in Canada—"look at what's here." The Skylon Tower looms over a thicket of behemoth franchise hotels, and the giant red word "Casino" regards us unapologetically.

Ollie has been waiting patiently at our feet, and a group of tourists coming down the path squeals with delight. The Falls and its rapids are forgotten as the women form a tight circle and begin petting her. Ollie accepts their affection with somewhat dutiful cheer. Every time she behaves pleasantly with strangers, she gets a green bean.

Free Niagara was a well-organized movement led by a group of well-connected public men. What was at stake at Niagara Falls, in their eyes, was not simply landscape, but the future of the United States. People had been complaining about human incursions on Niagara for years. Landscape painter Frederic Edwin Church— a distant Olmsted relative—won great acclaim for his painting of Niagara in 1857, the same year Olmsted and Vaux submitted their plan for Central Park. In his oversized canvas, Church had famously zeroed in on the Falls, giving them monumental stature, but part of why he did so was to edit out the ugliness of the surrounding scenery. Church frequently raised the issue of Niagara's fate at New York's swank Century Club, where Olmsted, Dorsheimer and Richardson were also members. In fact, by many accounts, Free Niagara began not with Olmsted's walk in the woods, but with brandy and cigar-stoked conversations more than 400 miles away.

The Century Club, on 15th Street, was called by Mark Twain "the most unspeakably respectable club in the U.S." Its policy of accepting men based on intellectual, civic or artistic merit as opposed to mere wealth he wryly called "too thundering exclusive." Exclusive it was, but while merit was officially monarch, there was no shortage of the wealthy and powerful within the club's walls. In the Century's parlor, library and billiards room, New York City's rainmakers shared their club chairs with a handpicked coterie of artists and literati. Church joined in 1850, John Jacob Astor in 1856, Olmsted and Vaux in 1859, and J. P. Morgan in 1862. Peter A. Porter, the Colonel, was a member until he died in the Civil War. Among the burled walnut bookcases, tufted leather sofas and Persian rugs, the idea of the State Reservation at Niagara was nursed from infant suggestion to full-grown movement. It was not the only public work to be hatched at the Century—the Metropolitan Museum of Art and the Sanitary Commission also supposedly began in the club's cozy drawing rooms.

The men of Free Niagara came to be called the "reservationists," because they advocated establishing a free public reservation at Niagara. Their strategy for achieving this somewhat unprecedented goal was sophisticated. They worked personal contacts with politicians while attempting to sway the public with a carefully planned series of newspaper articles, pamphlets and lectures bemoaning the rampant greed and bad taste that were ruining the Falls. They funded this campaign by forming a group, the Niagara Falls Association, and soliciting membership dues from prominent citizens nationwide. Eventually, their views were summarized and presented to the governor in 1880 through a special report of the New York State Survey, with a petition signed—thanks to Olmsted and other signature-gatherers—by a Who's Who of leading citizens, including the vice president, the secretary of war, every Supreme Court justice, eight senators, two governors, eight university presidents, an archbishop, and such prominent public figures as Thomas Carlyle, John Ruskin, William Dean Howells, Oliver Wendell Holmes and John Jay. The letter accompanying the petition described the situation at the Falls:

> Their eastern bank was once rich in verdure and overhung with stately trees. In place of the pebbly shore, the graceful ferns and trailing vines of the former days, one now sees a blank stone wall with sewer-like openings through which tail races discharge; some timber crib work bearing in capitals a foot high the inscription "Parker's Hair Balsam"; then further up stream more walls and wing dams. Overlooking this disfigured river brink stands an unsightly rank of buildings in all stages of preservation and decay; small "hotels," mills, carpenter shops, stables, "bazaars," ice-houses, laundries with clothes hanging out to dry, bath houses, large, glaring white hotels, and an indescribable assortment of miscellaneous rookeries, fences and patent medicine signs, which add an element of ruin and confusion to the impression of solid ugliness given by the better class of buildings.

The photographs accompanying the description were labeled things like "Disfigured Banks: Village Shore of Upper American Falls" and "Disfigured Banks: Repulsive Scenery Approaching Goat Island Bridge."

The term "disfigured" comes up again and again in the reservationists' writings, as if Niagara were a body injured—as so many American bodies had just been—in violent battle. Reading their fervent pleas, written when the devastating effects of industry on the environment were only vaguely understood, you can't help but feel the overwhelming urge to heal a nation that had just been torn apart by war. Restoring Niagara was like restoring the innocence and idealism that had been slipping away since the start of the nineteenth century. It was going back, as so many people wanted to do, to the principles and promise that gave birth to the young United States.

For Olmsted, restoring the scenery was critical to recovering that vision. The moral uplift inherent in nature was only inspired by the right kind of landscape. Niagara's scenery was doing the opposite.

Since the Civil War, a new class of tourists had been coming in increasing numbers to the Falls, and Olmsted disapproved of their taste. They were giving the Falls a perfunctory glance—sometimes from a carriage no less—and then indulging in the town's panoply of "degraded" amusements. Chief among these was Prospect Park, at the north end of the American Falls, which Olmsted and the reservationists heaped with scorn. Jonathan Baxter Harrison, hired by the reservationists to write letters to prominent newspapers, called Prospect Park "a poor circus with a cheap celebration of the Fourth of July." Thomas Holder's popular guidebook of the same year sees Prospect Park in a very different light. Holder assures us that at the park "every conceivable aid of science has been used in preparing the means of passing time pleasantly, a handsome Art Gallery and Pavilion, Theater, Ball Rooms, and Restaurants, forming features of the menu, while the beautiful Electric Light, thrown through colored glasses upon dancing fountains of water, give at night a magical effect seldom witnessed elsewhere."

The reservationists disagreed. They hated the theater and art gallery; they thought the restaurants low and tawdry, and the nighttime dancing obscene. They reserved special contempt for the artificial lights. There's more than a whiff of snobbery in all of this, but Olmsted really believed that the nation's future was at stake: he deplored Niagara's little park for its lack of high purpose, not its travesties of wilderness. Much influenced by the Romantic-sentimental view of nature as a kind of living, breathing sermon, Olmsted and Vaux designed parks for nature worship. In a telling essay from the same time called "Public Parks and the Enlargement of Towns," Olmsted claimed that parks were replacing churches as sites of spiritual regeneration. When the Excise Law closed grog shops on Sundays, park attendance went up; church attendance did not.

Olmsted's landscape designs, like his books and his Sanitary Commission, were driven by his zeal for social reform. But he was no revolutionary. His ideals of both behavior and beauty hearkened back to longstanding principles of gentlemanly life. His appreciation for nature was strongest in places where gently rolling hills, open grassy fields and pleasing prospects evoked the pastoral grounds of English country manors. It was an elevated aesthetic taste—those eighteenth-century landscapes had been created, after all, to prettify peasant realities for the landowning English aristocracy. But to Olmsted, who was both a democrat and a snob, the aristocrat's taste was the *right* taste, and ought to be taught to the common man. Just as his friend Charles Loring Brace argued that all children, even those of the lower classes, must be taught to read, Olmsted aimed, as Tom Yots puts it to me at the rapids, "to raise the opportunities for people—no matter who they were—to be in the landscape."

Olmsted's best parks are so naturalistic they are often perceived as nature itself, slices of preserved wilderness, neatened up and made more user-friendly. In fact, they are massive engineering projects, carefully designed, constructed and maintained. Central Park feels like a nicely tended piece of New York's precolonial environment, but it's really New York's largest art object, a monument built from the ground up by 4,000 laborers who blasted out rocks, built watercourses, installed drains and moved 5 million cubic yards of soil to create natural-seeming rolling hills, meadows and woods where there was only flat swampland before.

Based on the theory and practice of earlier English landscape designers, laid out according to eighteenth-century theories of the picturesque and the pastoral, Olmsted's parks are highly artificed works of design expertise. He considered himself an artist; plants and trees were his paints. In fact, he constantly feared that posterity would overlook the extensive work that went into his landscapes. This has certainly happened at Niagara Falls. Widely credited with "preserving" Niagara after the Porters could no longer do the job, Olmsted would more rightly be hailed for having rebuilt it in the picturesque mode.

• • •

"The Canadians originally had their carriage road farther back," Maureen Curry tells me. "Olmsted was the one who convinced them to put it closer to the edge, and his reasoning was that it would keep carriages off Goat Island."

Maureen, a cheery brunette in a Fair Isle cardigan, has driven up from Buffalo to meet with me. She's an environmental educator with the State Parks Office, and the person they nominated when I called and asked for someone to talk to me about the Olmsted legacy at Niagara. I'm sort of expecting Maureen to be a little defensive; just about every single person I've talked to has some criticism for State Parks and how they handle the Niagara Reservation. Complaints about the state's failure to preserve the Olmsted legacy have gotten louder since park concessions were outsourced to global hospitality and food service vendor Delaware North, famous for managing such natural wonders as the Wheeling Island Racetrack and Gaming Center, the Phoenix Park 'n Swap, the Toronto Blue Jays' SkyDome, and the service plazas on the New York Thruway. But to my surprise, as soon as I raise the topic of Olmsted's design philosophy, Maureen launches into a critique of her own.

"Olmsted didn't want there to be statues and monuments in the State Reservation," she tells me. "He said they would be as appropriate as stocking Goat Island with wolves and bears! And yet, here we are today, one hundred years later, filled with monuments and statues." I'm familiar with the wolves-and-bears quote: Tom Yots read it to me as we stood at the giant bronze statue of Nikola Tesla in front of the Cave of the Winds visitor center. Delaware North seems to have heard it too and misinterpreted it: they have stocked the State Reservation with information officers dressed up, for some reason, as big yellow bears.

Maureen enumerates the many ways the current reservation differs from Olmsted's ideal: he didn't want any plantings or gardens—now there's the Great Lakes Garden at the main visitor center, and more landscaping throughout the park. Olmsted didn't want a second bridge marring the view of the upper rapids from the pedestrian bridge; a second bridge has now been added for cars. He wanted to keep concessions off Goat Island; now there's a snack bar at the Cave of the Winds and a giant restaurant and bar at Terrapin Point. Most dramatically, Olmsted only reluctantly agreed that carriages might be allowed on Goat Island, but he insisted on keeping all carriage roads at least 50 feet back from the riverbank. He wanted people to be forced to get out of their carriages and walk to the edge of the Falls. Furthermore, he wanted all of Goat Island threaded with beautiful paths and frequent benches, to encourage leisurely walking and quiet contemplation. There are no walking paths through what remains of those woods today. A trolley circumnavigates the island, dropping tourists at the various viewpoints.

Large parking lots occupy both ends of Goat Island now. It isn't possible—fortunately—to drive around the island and view the Falls from your car, but it is possible to park, run out to the nearby viewing platform, and snap a few pictures before hitting one of the three souvenir shops on the way back to your car. The Niagara Reservation—tourist materials now refer to it as the Niagara Falls State Park—is today one of the top two revenue producers in the New York state park system. I point out to Maureen that this is funny since Free Niagara is in fact a free park.

"Well," she says, for the first time showing a slight amount of hesitation, "the park—ing lots." Those $10 parking fees, it seems, add up. And the Niagara Reservation has a special arrangement inside the New York State Office of Parks, Recreation and Historic Preservation that allows them to keep a percentage of their revenue, instead of having it all go back into the general state parks kitty. Which means, far from encouraging people to walk more, the state park is actually invested in making it easier for them to drive onto the Niagara Reservation. Along with trolley fares and leases to park concessionaires, it's how they make their money.

But that's not as relevant, according to Maureen, as the fact that people simply don't want to be inconvenienced at all when coming to see the Falls. In the basement of the administration building, we hover over a foam-core-mounted aerial view of the entire reservation, and Maureen talks wistfully of Olmsted's visions of slow strolls and quiet reflection in the woods. People were actually upset, she tells me, when State Parks shrank the parking lot at the back end of Goat Island to let more woods grow in.

"We're gradually becoming a society that doesn't understand the outdoors," she tells me. "I think we're a society that has to change our perspective on how to enjoy nature."

How to enjoy nature is exactly what Olmsted was trying to teach the public. Environmental preservation at Niagara is often framed as a return to the values and principles of Olmsted. Like the Porters, he's considered nature's savior. But Olmsted's park designs weren't homages to nature; they were social engineering using nature as medium. He was interested in the landscape mainly for what it could help him do.

In 1883, after much public campaigning and behind-the-scenes string-pulling, the Free Niagara movement finally triumphed. New York governor Grover Cleveland—a Buffalonian who loved fishing on the Niagara River—signed a bill to allow the state to use eminent domain to acquire private lands and create a reservation around the Falls. The lands recommended for purchase by the State Survey—in consultation with Olmsted and the Niagara Falls Association—were Goat Island, Bath Island (now Green Island), the Three Sisters, and a long, thin fillet of land along the river from above the Falls to the Suspension Bridge. Two years and many letters and lectures later, the state legislature made available the actual funds. Olmsted and Vaux were appointed to plan the first state park in the United States. When the reservation opened to the public with great fanfare, the *Niagara Falls Gazette* crowed, "The spirit of the wilderness has come back to Niagara." In helping the state choose nature over industry, Free Niagara had proved that the public right to enjoy nature should trump business's right to despoil it. Or had they?

Within one year of the creation of the State Reservation, a group of businessmen formed the Niagara River Hydraulic Tunnel, Power and Sewer Company and received a state charter to divert water from just above the reservation. One of the directors of this company (later called simply the Niagara Falls Power Company) was Charles Lanier, the treasurer of the reservationists' Niagara Falls Association. The other one, Edward Dean Adams, was the Niagara Falls Association's eighth member. On the power company's list of capital stock subscribers was Thomas V. Welch, a state legislator who helped push through the bill creating the reservation and had then been made superintendent of it. Welch's business partner, Michael Ryan, a former state assemblyman who was also active in Free Niagara, became a vice president of the Niagara Falls Power Company. And one Thomas Evershed was listed as the power company's engineer. In his capacity as state surveyor and engineer, Evershed had been the one to survey the land around Niagara Falls for New York and recommend the boundaries for the state reservation.

Once a young man with big ambitions, Evershed had trained as an engineer and self-trained as an artist. In 1849, he had set out for California to strike it rich in the Gold Rush, but like Olmsted, he saw his gold dreams turn to dust. He returned to New York, married and became a state engineer. He dabbled in art, but his lifelong career was as a loyal public servant, working as an engineer mainly on the Erie Canal. By the time of Free Niagara, the white-whiskered Evershed, a precise, hardworking and modest man, was nearing the end of a long but not particularly distinguished career designing ditches and modifying locks. His life's work, canals, were yesterday's technology, already being replaced by trains. Following the creation of the Niagara Reservation, plans for harnessing Niagara's power were bouncing around in newspapers. It was clearly the big thing to be done. For Evershed, age sixty-nine, it was one last chance to make a mark. In 1886, he published a letter in the *Lockport Union* critiquing another plan. "If the people of Niagara County wish to indulge in a scheme for the management of water-power," he declared in a tone uncharacteristically grandiose, "let me point out one."

Evershed laid out a plan to generate 200,000 horsepower of motive force from the waterfall. It called for blasting out a huge tunnel to divert water from the upper river to a location downstream, away from the beauties of the Falls, channeling it through a number of individual wheel pits to run machinery above. Conveniently, the reservation outlines he had recommended to the state did not include riverfront above the upper rapids, where water would be diverted in his plan, or below the Falls, where the wheel pits for his factories would stand. His power plan was completely compatible with his park.

Evershed's original map is now in the New York State Archives at Albany. One rainy Tuesday, I drive up there to look at it. At the Maoishly named Cultural Education Center, I fill out several pages of paperwork that make the entrance procedures at the American Antiquarian Society feel as loose as air travel in the nineties. After sharing a host of personal information and handing over official ID, I'm handed two single-spaced, double-sided sheets of paper— "Rules of the Research Room Part A" and "Rules of the Research Room Part B." Only after I've made a good show of perusing them am I told that my table awaits.

Evershed's map is exquisite. Every building is labeled with elaborate, curlicued text, every jut and whorl of the riverbank lovingly inked. The Terrapin Rocks are outlined with precision. Even the librarian, all business upon my arrival, has to stop and admire its beauty.

The State Reservation as Evershed mapped it begins in the north just before the Suspension Bridge. It encloses all of Prospect Park, eats up every riverfront lot upstream of the Falls (most are owned by various Porters) and engulfs a hotel, a pulp mill, a machine shop, a silver-plating works, a stable, a gristmill and Tugby's Bazaar, a giant souvenir emporium. It ends at the boundary of a piece of land owned by the Niagara Falls Hydraulic & Manufacturing Canal Company, owners of the original hydraulic canal.

Early historians claim Evershed was motivated by a desire to ensure "protection of the natural beauty of Niagara." But at some point he also began harboring a desire to capture the tremendous amounts of power to be gleaned from the Falls. The map makes it clear that as Evershed planned the state's acquisition of land for scenery's sake, the power developers' interests were, literally, where he drew the line.

Once the reservation was delineated, the men of the Niagara Falls Power Company got to work. But they needed financial backers—preferably those "eastern capitalists" the Porters had unsuccessfully wooed earlier. In 1889, members of the tunnel company met with Edward A. Wickes, an agent for the Vanderbilt family, to form the Cataract Construction Company, a corporation to be the power company's financial arm. The Vanderbilts already had a stake in Niagara: as owners of the Michigan Central Railroad, they had supported the reservationist cause. Now they threw their financial weight behind power development. So did J. P. Morgan, the powerful banker, another member of the Niagara Falls Association.

Evershed's plan laid out a means of producing more power than the nation had ever seen generated from a single hydraulic source. The problem was, who would use it? There weren't enough factories at Niagara Falls to use up that much energy. The minds of the power-brokers quickly turned to transmission—how to get Niagara's power to places like nearby Buffalo, where it could be sold. Engineers came up with fantastic schemes. One called for building a monster steel driveshaft that would extend from Niagara all the way across New York, as if the Empire State were a massive machine and Niagara Falls its piston. Local factories could simply strap a belt to the shaft and go. Another plan suggested connecting New York and Chicago with a giant pneumatic tube that would run through Niagara, where turbines would inject it with compressed air: the Falls pumping away like the nation's heart.

But the way of the future, it seemed clear, was electricity. Getting the waterfall to make electricity was simple: Jacob Schoellkopf had installed a Brush electric generator on the hydro canal in 1881 and used it to power streetlights in Niagara Falls. But no one had transported electricity from one place to another without losing massive amounts of it. The Cataract Construction Company cabled the world's foremost electricity expert, Thomas Edison, in Europe, asking if long-distance electricity transmission was feasible. Edison's reply was confident: "No difficulty transferring unlimited power. Will assist. Sailing today."

Still not convinced, the power brokers kept their options open, even as workers began blasting out 300,000 tons of rock for an 18-by-21-foot tunnel, 160 feet below ground. The Niagara Falls Power Company formed a blue-chip committee of scientific experts, the International Niagara Commission, to canvass the world in search of the best method for generating and transmitting power. Convening at the exclusive Brown's Hotel in London, the five distinguished scientists, chaired by eminent Scottish physicist Lord Kelvin, issued invitations to select groups to "submit projects for the development, transmission and distribution of about 125,000 effective horsepower on the shafts of water motors at the Falls of Niagara." Prizes were offered. Eventually, fifteen European and five American competitors threw their hats into the ring. Eight prizes were awarded, four for pneumatic plans and four for electric ones. Unfortunately, none of the winners was perfect. The power developers still didn't have a plan they could use.

In the end, it wasn't the homegrown Edison who came up with the method for transmitting electricity long distances, but his rival genius, Nikola Tesla. An eccentrically brilliant Croatian with sleek black hair, sparkling black eyes and impeccable sartorial taste, Tesla had invented a motor that used alternating current in 1888. Hoping to secure his future—he had already been bilked out of promised money for some engineering upgrades he had done while working for Edison—Tesla filed a series of patents pertaining to his motor.

George Westinghouse, the tireless inventor and patent mogul, immediately saw the value of Tesla's patents, and bought them all. (Sadly for the perpetually broke Tesla, he paid a fraction of what they were really worth.) Westinghouse had been looking for a way to break Edison's monopoly on electrical innovation, and this was it. He had earlier declined to submit a plan to the International Niagara Commission's contest, but in 1892 he notified the gentlemen of the Cataract Construction Company that he had the answer to their problem. Using Tesla's technology, the Westinghouse scheme "stepped up" electrical impulses, sending high voltages over wires quickly, then stepped them down again when they reached their destination. As a result, much less electricity was lost. Coleman Sellers, president of the Niagara Falls Power Company, visited Westinghouse's factory for a demonstration.

Lord Kelvin still thought using alternating current would be a "giant mistake." But Westinghouse was transmitting power already at smaller operations in Oregon and Colorado, and in 1893 he lit the entire World's Columbian Exposition at Chicago using Tesla's technology. The famous White City at Chicago's World's Fair demonstrated in miniature how transmission at Niagara would work. The directors of the Cataract Construction Company were finally convinced. In November 1896, Tesla's high-voltage AC transmission and polyphase motor brought Niagara Falls power to Buffalo and changed the course of American history.

The giant statue of Nikola Tesla that looms outside the Cave of the Winds visitor center today is as little like Tesla as can be imagined. Dressed in academic robes, the bronze Tesla broods over an open book, although his flesh-and-blood counterpart usually got his ideas while rambling around outdoors in morning coat and spats, or while in the middle of nervous breakdowns. Entire generating apparatuses would appear to him as three-dimensional visions, every detail worked out. Tesla was a quirky, driven, nervous genius; his bronze avatar is ponderous and grave, undisturbed by the children and tourists constantly climbing into his lap to pose for pictures. But even true to life, he'd be exactly the sort of monument Olmsted's plan was designed to avoid.

As the power company was digging its tunnels and casting about for its technology, the "re-naturing" of Niagara's parkland got under way.

One year after the Evershed plan was released, Olmsted & Vaux submitted a plan for improving the Niagara Reservation. In it, Olmsted sneered at the "artificial improvements" that had been made at the Falls previously—things like the flowerbeds, fountains, pavilions, decorative bridges, artificial ruins, "specimens of pseudo-rustic work and of pseudo-wild gardening" to be found in the current Prospect Park. He harped on the artificial illumination of the Falls at night. The public, he sniffed, may clamor for such "decorative detail," but they should be ignored. Ultimately, public taste would improve through "civilized progress," and nothing would be worse than to give in to current low desires and turn the reservation into "an affair of the sumptuous park and flower-garden order."

The plan, according to the heartily approving park commissioners, admitted "nothing of an artificial character not absolutely essential to the proper enjoyment of the Reservation by the people." The word "proper" was significant. All those morally uplifting strolls could damage the grounds, so the plan set out suggestions for keeping people to the walks and not trampling plants, kicking off topsoil, or wearing down rock outcroppings. Olmsted was adamant that all concessions must be banned from the reservation. Even picnicking should be off-limits, allowed only in a special area near the entrance. Picnicking, snacking and drinking were not conducive to serious contemplation. No doubt he would be appalled today to see his own ponderous face emblazoned on an interpretive sign inside the Cave of the Winds snack bar and ice-cream stand.

Olmsted & Vaux's recommendations were meant to keep the landscape pristine, once it had been rebuilt. "We are far from thinking that all that is required to accomplish the designed end is to 'let Nature alone,'" they wrote. In fact, nature might not always get it right: "Inconsistencies, discordancies, disunities and consequent weaknesses of natural scenery may result, even at Niagara, from natural causes." These natural causes included landslides, rockfalls, erosion, even ugly trees. The plan the landscape firm submitted took care to prevent, and when necessary, correct, such blights. Thus, they recommended a host of improvements to nature: sloped viewing platforms, balconies built out from the rock cliffs, "rip-rap walls" of rubble to prevent riverbank erosion, a protective roof over the Cave of the Winds walkway, trees planted in artfully "natural" configurations and gates and turnstiles to control crowds. They added an equal number of recommendations meant to disguise the necessary artificial elements: an elevator to replace the incline railroad, disguised paths to replace stairways, vines and creepers to hide retaining walls and low-profile fences, bridges and walls.

Far from a "return to wilderness," this carefully designed park was devised to create an impression of nature through artificial means. The *New York Tribune* published an editorial praising the choice of Olmsted and Vaux as Niagara's new designers. Their art, it declared, would not hesitate to reshape nature: "If need be it can make a rugged cliff more bold, and shadows deeper and more mysterious as readily as it can add a fresh grace and delicacy to the foliage upon the trees and undershrubs." The landscape architect, no less than the landscape painter, could add a bit here, clean things up there, inject drama or create a unified effect where necessary. Church had eliminated factories and hotels from his famous painting of Niagara; why shouldn't Olmsted disguise his paths and railings?

This was "improvement" to nature, just as the Porter brothers' fish pond and tower had been. It just worked with a new aesthetic: one that banished man. Like his urban parks, Olmsted's plan for the Niagara Reservation focused on hiding all evidence of the human hand, blocking out "unnatural" buildings and roads and obscuring the industrial uses of falling water. The new reservation took the factories and power plants out of the picture, even as it quietly protected the business of what was now a state-backed private industry, the power company. The park design convinced the public that industrial abuse had ended, when in fact it was only getting under way. When the mills were right there, at least you could see and smell what was pouring out of their tailraces. Now the mills on Goat Island were leveled, the diverted water buried in a hidden tunnel. With electrical transmission in place, new factories could be built outside the milling district. And the industries that would soon arrive to take advantage of Niagara's cheap power—the aluminum smelters, electrochemical companies, silicon, chromium, tungsten, molybdenum and carbon-titanium manufacturers that would soon fire up their furnaces—would produce a far more toxic breed of by-product than what had poured out of paper plants and sawmills. The despoiling of the Niagara didn't stop; it just went underground.

With industry moved out of view, the park commissioners began to institute Olmsted's vision. Fences, tollhouses and about 150 buildings were leveled, including mills, shops, bathhouses, homes and a dancing pavilion. Millraces were filled up; the old incline railroad was demolished. But it wasn't just a case of removing the artificial. Things had to be built as well. The commissioners graded and sodded land, drained swamps and planted trees. They added restrooms, lights, elevators, sewers and three and a half miles of macadam roads. The principle behind all of this, according to reservation commissioner and historian Charles Dow, was simple: "Back to Nature."

The early commissioners were true to Olmsted's vision of artificial wildness; they took care not to "gardenize" when they planted flora, and they kept the park free of the memorials and monuments Olmsted deplored. But Dow admits that "sometimes it has happened that the return to nature has, in reality, been an improvement upon nature." The end result was "such charming improvements upon nature as Prospect Point, Hennepin View, Dow View, and the Loop Pond." At all of these places, wooden platforms and stairs were removed, and replaced by artificially elevated landfill and natural-looking rock. "Nature," Dow declares, "has been so admirably simulated that beauties which are in reality the product of human skill seem always to have existed."

As all this nature simulation was proceeding, industrial interest in the Falls spiked. Dow expresses puzzlement at the "remarkable activity" around power development that began in 1886, noting that it would be "interesting to speculate upon the psychological causes of this sudden accession of commercial interest in Niagara." He suggests the Free Niagara movement, by bringing the region into the public eye, may have touched off the stampede of industrialists eager to exploit the Falls. He does not point out that many of those very industrialists were key figures in Free Niagara all along.

In *Walks and Talks of an American Farmer in England*, Olmsted writes of his visit to Eaton Hall, an estate partly shaped by famed English landscape designers Humphrey Repton and Capability Brown. The gorgeous grounds inspire the young Olmsted to effuse rhapsodically on the art of the landscape designer: "What artist so noble," Olmsted muses, "as he, who with far-reaching conception of beauty and designing power, sketches the outline, writes the colours and directs the shadows of a picture so great that Nature shall be employed upon it for generations, before the work he has arranged for her shall realize his intentions."

Nature here is the landscape artist's handmaiden. The artist makes the design, then uses nature to fill it in. Although Olmsted is almost always touted as a devotee of the natural, nature for him was a means and not an end. It was a tool, to be wielded in the service of art and the public good, but a tool nonetheless. In this, he was in agreement with the industrialists who arrived at the Falls at the close of the nineteenth century, eager to exploit its massive motive power. Both were intent on the "designing power" of Nature. But where Olmsted saw a paintbrush, they saw a piston.

The park played into their hands further by helping to create the division of purpose—over here is nature, over there, behind that hedge, is industry—that enabled the full industrial exploitation of the Falls to begin. The hack fares, admission fees and small-time cons that had beleaguered tourists were nothing in comparison with the money to be made now. And the small shop owners, cabdrivers and con men who had made money off the place were chased out of town and replaced by Morgans, Astors and Vanderbilts. Over the next sixty years, industrial incursions on the Falls would increase exponentially, ushering in a new era of rampant energy consumption and industrial pollution. And in keeping with the spirit of Free Niagara, the elaborate disguise of those incursions would keep pace. Olmsted and his companions had inaugurated a new era at Niagara: the era of fake nature, an artificial wilderness designed to hide all evidence of design. Their park, while beautiful, solidified an opposition between "natural" and "man-made" that misrepresents our relationship to nature, obscuring the very real, increasingly critical role we play in the ecosystems of which we are part.

In separating how it looks from how we use it, Olmsted unwittingly made it possible for industry to go to work destroying the environment at Niagara more fully than ever before. As the twentieth century dawned, the power-brokers took over management of Niagara. The massive changes they brought about would bring the Falls completely under human control and would reshape the landscape in more dramatic ways than even the Porters could have imagined. The twentieth century would see Niagara's transformation from nature's masterpiece to ours.

Six

KING OF POWER,
QUEEN OF BEAUTY

IN THE SPRING OF 2006, I go see Niagara Falls get turned on for the tourist season. I drive for seven hours and get there a day early, on March 31. I head straight for the Three Sisters to get close to the river. I want to see what it looks like before they crank it up.

The best thing in New York's Niagara Falls State Park, the Three Sisters form a miniarchipelago off the Canadian side of Goat Island. Sitting in the rapids above the Horseshoe Fall, the three little islands, named after an early settler's daughters, are linked by picturesque stone bridges. I stop on the bridge to the First Sister and look upstream at the Hermit's Cascade, a river ledge depicted on the island's interpretive marker as a surging mini-Niagara. Today it's a few freshets splashing over a flaky slice of rock.

Things perk up on the Second Sister and by the Third, the river's in a frenzy. Even at low water, the Third Sister feels like what it is, a rocky outcropping in the middle of some of the world's roughest rapids. Water rushes and swirls furiously around its edges. It's loud. Just downstream, the river surges over the Horseshoe Fall and disappears. A misty abyss marks the spot.

I am not alone. A middle-aged couple, sneakered and stout, pick their way along the path. They regard the rapids with the dull resignation of people beaten into subjection by miles of Thruway. Dutifully, they take turns posing for snapshots before the man approaches me.

"Do you know where the really big waterfall is?" he asks.

"See that mist over there?" I say, pointing. His face falls.

"The Horseshoe Fall? We saw that." His eyes go to the Canadian skyline. "I thought there was a bigger waterfall."

"Come back tomorrow," I say.

Of course, it's an exaggeration to say Niagara Falls is turned off and on for the tourists. It is actually turned *up* for the tourists. In the Niagara Diversion Treaty of 1950, the United States and Canada agree to go halfsies on one of the world's largest natural sources of hydroelectric power. They promise never to let fewer than 50,000 cubic feet of water per second go over the Falls, and they double that minimum to 100,000 cubic feet per second—about half the natural volume—between 8 A.M. and 10 P.M., April 1 to September 15. This is so that the 20 million or so tourists who flock to Niagara annually, most in the summer, don't all walk away wondering where the big fall went.

But that's unlikely. The man I meet on the Third Sister is unusual; most people are surprised to learn that half to three-quarters of Niagara's water never goes over the Falls. Water diversions for hydropower are enormous, but their effect on the scenery is limited by massive engineering projects that keep everything looking the same. Even as one-half to three-quarters of the Niagara River is drawn off into four hydro tunnels and one canal, the waterfall spreads across basically the same crestline, looks the same depth, and shimmers with the same emerald green. The end result is an environment that elides any conflict between landscape enjoyment and resource expenditure. You see? it cheerfully declares: we can have our lake and use it too.

I imagine the spring increase of water as a kind of local festival: they're turning the Falls back up! I call the New York Power Authority with visions of electrogeeks dialing up the water and watching it rip in a celebratory mood. Maybe champagne would be involved, or pizza. Donuts, at the very least. On the phone, however, Joanne Willmott, regional manager for community relations, assures me there's little fanfare around treaty implementation.

"What if I buy the pizza?" I ask.

There's a moment before her reply. The folks at the Power Authority are all openly suspicious about why I want to talk to them. The Niagara Project is undergoing a relicensing process—their Federal Energy Regulatory Commission license runs out as of 2007—and they appear to be a bit press-shy as a result, even though the press they get is mostly good. The Power Authority is one of the region's economic engines, and in a place as depressed as Niagara County, criticizing an economic engine is like bad-mouthing God. In downtown Niagara Falls, near the bridge to Canada, sits a large square glass building. Formerly the corporate headquarters of Occidental Chemical but now popularly known as "the flashcube," it currently wears a giant sign reading Say NO to NYPA Relicensing. Around town, I keep asking people who put it up. "A crazy guy," they all say, shaking their heads. No one will tell me his name.

About 80 miles east of Buffalo, Niagara power makes an appearance. The giant transmission towers parallel the New York Thruway for miles as you zoom toward the Buffalo-Niagara region, broad-shouldered and narrow-hipped, metal linebackers striding across the Mohawk Valley with high-voltage wires in their stunted arms. By the time you get to outer Buffalo, the towers dominate the view five abreast, every two rows accompanied by a taller one, a Roman decurion marshaling his troops. They march alongside I-190 as you speed toward Niagara Falls, then veer off toward the industrial side of town as you enter the city limits. If you drive away from the Falls toward the city's edge in any direction, you pass under lashings of high-voltage lines, scoring the sky as they take Niagara's bounty to other, more prosperous parts of the world.

The transmission towers accompany me as I drive to their source on March 31. Joanne and I have arranged to meet at the Robert Moses Niagara Power Plant, a monster dam built into the face of the Niagara Gorge four and a half miles downstream from the Falls. The Moses plant collects all of the diverted water on the American side in a huge reservoir and runs it through thirteen turbines in the main plant and twelve more in the supplementary Lewiston Pump-Generating Plant, producing, at top capacity, 2.4 million kilowatts of nonstop electricity. The Power Vista—the Authority's visitor center—is a huge, sunny room suspended over the river at one end of the looming plant. Kids scramble around its maze of displays while their parents try to explain electrons. There's an outside deck, and when you go out onto it, the deep, low whir of turbines fills your ears. The air seems to buzz with voltage. Huge flocks of gulls wheel and scream over the churning water at the dam's base, where fish, alive, dead or stunned from their trip through the turbines, are pushed to the surface on outgoing currents. Across the river, the Canadian dam hulks like an opposing giant. It's impossible not to be awed.

Joanne has the friendly but cautious disposition of a public relations person. She seems especially eager to relieve me of my handbag. She deposits it somewhere mysterious in the back offices, then walks me to the Power Vista's centerpiece, a vast miniature replica of the region highlighting the Authority's intakes, tunnels, generating stations and reservoir. The Falls, in one corner, are represented by an inch-high clear plastic mold. Tiny white lights behind the plastic are meant to produce the illusion of frothy water.

At the side of the miniature landscape, Joanne introduces me to Norm Stessing, supervisor of operations, the man (in my mind) who can dial up Niagara's deluge. He doesn't look like a power king; he looks like a Norm. He's medium height, stocky but trim and tanned, with even teeth and a quick, easy smile. His crisp shirt is tucked in perfectly. Norm grew up in the Niagara Region. In the late fifties, when the turn-of-the-century powerhouse was being replaced by the Robert Moses Power Plant, his parents would bring him to see the massive project underway.

Norm dives into explaining how his power plant works with the vigor of a high school physics teacher who really believes in those kids.

"Our generator capacity is one hundred thousand cubic feet

per second," he tells me, explaining the treaty implementation that starts tomorrow. "But during the day our stream share is about fifty thousand." Before I know it, we've launched into a heady conversation about turbine efficiencies, pump storage, voltage step-ups and price differentials. Luckily, I've read enough to have a basic understanding, because Norm, pointing to the model switchyard and explaining how voltage gets there through a mile of underground tunnels, is like a twelve-year-old boy who has been given a really, really cool toy.

When Westinghouse and Tesla wired Niagara to Buffalo with alternating current, skeptics were convinced it would fail. The switch was thrown in Buffalo in the dead of night, in order to avoid public humiliation. To almost everyone's surprise, it worked.

After that breakthrough, the electrification of America happened quickly. In 1910, 10 percent of American homes were wired for electricity. By 1930, 70 percent were. It's easy to forget how radical a change electrification was. But if there's a main difference between our lives and those lived in Edith Wharton novels, it has less to do with carriages and corsets than it does with turbines and megawatts. Electrification automated industry, deskilled labor, industrialized agriculture, depopulated rural areas, invented suburbs, and enabled a nonliterate mass media. Our fabulous modern lifestyle—Chicken McNuggets to *America's Next Top Model*—all began with electricity.

The change was more than infrastructure; it was a nationwide behavioral modification. And it required reeducation. Americans had to be trained to stop fearing electricity and instead consume it, preferably—at least to the companies who generated and sold kilowatts—in large quantities. Major players General Electric and Westinghouse quickly decided to manufacture demand by inventing a lot of nifty electric appliances: irons, refrigerators, toasters. Just about anything done by hand or with gas, it turned out, could be made electric and sold to consumers as easier. But first they had to get average Americans to adopt what they called the "wedge" product, electric light, because it opened households to everything else. They had to sell the idea of electricity, and in this Niagara was key.

The Falls helped electricity get what marketing consultants

today call "mindshare." Average folks had only a vague notion of what electricity was. But they knew it was deadly; Thomas Edison had proven that. In the 1880s, striving to promote direct current over Tesla's competing technology, Edison had famously staged road shows meant to discredit alternating current by using it to electrocute dogs. This can't have made people eager to wire up their homes, especially those with pets. Nor did it help that New York State quickly saw a good use for high voltage, switching the murder penalty from hanging to electrocution in 1888, and dispatching its first killer in the Auburn electric chair two years later. (This one wasn't Billy Jamieson's chair; a few modifications had to be made by Stickley so the chair would stand up to the current.) Electricity really needed a spokesmodel, and when the Cataract Construction Company signed on to Niagara's power push, the PR campaign had its mascot.

In the 1890s, as the Falls were being harnessed, a flood of articles about Niagara power hit newsstands. *Harper's, Nature, Collier's, McClure's, Blackwood's,* the *Saturday Review* and *Cassier's* all printed articles describing Falls power projects and promoting the image of Niagara as unending bounty. *Popular Science Monthly* declared in September 1894 that "people in general have the idea that the Niagara water power is inexhaustible, and so it probably is, so far as human requirements go." A booklet printed in 1895 to promote real estate speculation in Buffalo claimed that "enough force is contained in the flowing water of the Niagara to run the machinery of the world." By 1903, *Harper's Weekly* could crow that Niagara was turning out, as hoped, to be "an illimitable supply of cheap power."

Niagara, promoters declared, would even free us from dirty coal, already understood to be a resource that would one day run out. Clemens Herschel, hydraulic engineer for the Niagara Power Project, declared in a special Niagara issue of *Cassier's* that "all the coal raised throughout the world would barely suffice to produce the amount of power that continually runs to waste at this one great fall." This was hyperbole. But his enthusiasm was not unwarranted: compared with coal, a hydroelectric turbine was cleaner, safer, more renewable, and easier to understand—a Constable waterwheel writ large. The Buffalo real estate booklet bragged that Niagara created limitless power "without consuming an atom of the world's store of fuel, without destroying in the slightest degree the grandeur of the cataract and its environments." Go ahead and buy that toaster, the message ran; we've discovered a source of endless clean energy. Niagara was America's best-known site of natural splendor. Electricity would simply harness that splendor for man's use.

Brand Niagara launched for real at the 1901 World's Fair, the Pan-American Exposition at Buffalo. The theme was better living through electrification. Visitors were ushered into an electric utopia, featuring electric trolleys, rides, fountains and appliances; a working miniature power plant; and row upon row of electric incubators holding live premature babies, all of it lit by 200,000 incandescent bulbs. At the center was the Electric Tower, a skyscraper featuring a 74-foot artificial waterfall lit by 94 searchlights. On top of the tower was another searchlight, pointing toward the real Niagara Falls.

The famous "Spirit of Niagara" poster for the Pan-American Exposition—called "the most effective advertising poster of all time"—gives us a pretty good idea of how this electric heaven related to nature. With the Buffalo skyline in the distance, the Falls sweep down in a white froth. Emerging from the mist is a lithe nude goddess, head tilted, arms spread wide. Nature as powerful divinity has been supplanted by nature as yielding woman, offering herself for man's use. Little regret was wasted on her subjection. Before the fair, Lord Kelvin was quoted in the *Literary Digest* gleefully predicting the day when men would turn Niagara off and on at will.

Here is what happens. Gravity constantly draws water into hydraulic tunnel intakes located in the river above the Falls. In the tunnels, the water travels underneath the city of Niagara Falls, paralleling the river's course for four-and-a-half miles. But the river drops—not only in the 176-foot Falls, but in the rapids above and below them. By the time the diverted water reaches the power plant's holding pool, or forebay, it is about 300 feet above the lower river. The higher drop means the water spins the turbines with more pressure, generating more power than it would at the brink of the Falls. The process is duplicated on the Canadian side, where power tunnels are supplemented by a canal. The Canadian tunnel intakes and power plants mirror their American counterparts across the river.

At the Moses plant's forebay, the water can flow down through the main penstocks, where it spins the turbines and passes out into the lower Niagara River, or it can be pumped as much as 120 feet up into the 1,900-acre Lewiston Reservoir. The reservoir lets the Power Authority collect water at night, when tourists are sleeping and stream share is greater, and then use it for generation during daytime, when power demand is up. Since electricity deregulation, the reservoir also creates an opportunity to optimize financials. As prices vary throughout the day, the Lewiston plant can pump water into its reservoir during periods of low demand for electricity, then release water through the generator when demand is high. It's a perfect example of buy low, sell high: the Authority spends cheap power to make expensive power.

All this is regulated by the Niagara River Control Center, an arm of the International Joint Commission that manages the Falls. Because rainfall, temperature and even wind direction influence the water level in Lake Erie, and thus how much water flows into Niagara's strait, River Control measures the river hourly. As its volume varies, River Control calculates the amount each nation can draw down, and calls the power facilities—in the United States, the NYPA Energy Control Center in Utica—every hour to dictate their stream shares.

So on April 1, Norm explains, River Control will call Utica at 7 A.M. with a new stream share, reduced by the amount required to let 100,000 cubic feet per second go over the Falls by eight. Utica will call Niagara, and the workers in Norm's control room will sit down at their computers and begin turning off reservoir pumps. Each shutdown decreases the flow of water out of the forebay, thus decreasing the flow of water into the tunnels from the river by 4,000 cubic feet per second. When the water coming into the forebay equals the Authority's stream share, the water going over the Falls should be the amount required by the treaty, and tourists should be oohing and aahing at the sublime power of nature.

"You couldn't really turn off all of Niagara Falls, could you?" I ask Norm, my enthusiasm for the brute strength of it getting the best of me. "If you and the Canadian plant both just sucked as much water as possible out of the river and ran it through your generators at top speed?"

"We don't like to talk about it that way," he says, cracking an involuntary grin, "but in fact, yes, we could."

I pick up photographer Lisa Kereszi at midnight that night at the Buffalo airport. Bleary from a long day, I drive by her twice outside the baggage claim. I've only met her once, but after a barrage of alternately bossy and begging emails, I managed to convince her to fly up to Niagara Falls and meet me for the spring water turn-on.

Niagara power lines swoop above us as we speed out of Buffalo toward Grand Island. As we enter Niagara Falls, the chemical plants are heaving a thick fog into the dark night sky. I slow down so Lisa can get a look at the Power Authority's giant tunnel air intakes. As we glide by the American rapids, I roll down the windows, and the roar fills the car. I love bringing people to Niagara for the first time.

It's after one by the time we head for our rooms in the Howard Johnson motel. We are planning to meet at six-fifteen, so we can get to the Three Sisters early and watch the water rise. Lisa has discussed the best spots to photograph the change with people from the State Park. I set my alarm—or think I do, and collapse.

I wake up at six-thirty with Lisa banging on my door. Fifteen minutes later, we're parking near the Three Sisters. The river volume has already increased dramatically. "Norm told me it wouldn't start until seven!" I wail. We race across the bridge. The Hermit's Cascade has gone from a lacy tablecloth to a billowing comforter, pouring over its small shelf with glee. Rock flats from yesterday are now rushing river, and a cascading minifall between the first and second islands has doubled in size. On the Third Sister, the previous day's boisterous rapids have sprouted jubilant geysers. Everything is louder, faster, greener. Unfazed, Lisa starts taking pictures:

I park myself on a rock. Maybe the water is still rising, I tell myself. I choose a large boulder to stare at. Two Canada geese are holding their ground on top of it. Is the water getting higher? It's hard to say—stare long enough and the volume seems to grow. I imagine pumps shutting down, gates upstream opening. The rapids seem to get more furious. White explosions shoot higher; the white ring around the rock boils harder. The geese turn around, looking perplexed. Geysers erupt around them. Finally one goose, then the other, lifts itself into flight.

The earliest power plants at Niagara quickly became tourist attractions almost as appealing as the Falls themselves. In 1892, the Cataract Construction Company hired the blue-chip firm of McKim, Mead & White, architects of the original Penn Station, to design their two powerhouses and matching transformer building. The resulting structures were architecturally splendid, with clean neoclassical lines, majestic proportions, and noble ornamentation, all clad in stone excavated from the tunnel. Scholar William Irwin calls them "a monument to modern American industrial and technological civilization."

They were also a monument to the marvel of electricity. Once the powerhouses were open, guided tours took visitors inside the plants, where they could observe the cleanliness, order and relative quiet of the operation. The production of hydroelectricity wasn't like the noisy, dirty factories of the Industrial Revolution—far from William Blake's "dark, Satanic mills," this was a sparkling industry for a gleaming new age. Visitors could ogle a scale model of the power project installations and take home explanatory literature. Guidebooks declared the tour a must-see attraction.

Some visitors liked the power plant more than the waterfall. H. G. Wells wrote an article for *Harper's* after his visit in 1906. "The real interest of Niagara for me was not the waterfall, but the human accumulations about it," he declared. "The dynamos and turbines of the Niagara Falls Power Company impressed me far more than the Cave of the Winds." Not only did Wells think the power machinery made for better spectacle; he was unconcerned about its effect on the cataract. He was in agreement with Lord

Kelvin: Niagara Falls would be more of a boon to man if it was turned off. "It seems altogether well," he reported, "that all the froth and hurry of Niagara at last, all of it, dying into hungry canals of intakes, should rise again in light and power."

"I've seen them turn it down to just a trickle," Larry Siegmann tells us cheerfully. "If they get a boat caught in the rapids, they'll lower the river in minutes so the boat grounds on the rocks and people can walk right off." Larry is park manager at the Cave of the Winds attraction, still hugely popular in spite of H. G. Wells's dismissal. Lisa has arranged for him to give us a private, early-morning preview of the newly enlarged waterfall. We meet him at the park office, and he takes us to the elevator that plunges 170 feet down through Goat Island's rock. Two tourists try to get in with us, but he chases them away, explaining that the Cave isn't open yet. This immediately increases my enthusiasm; I'm convinced we're getting something special.

When it was actually a cave—the last dangerous overhangs were dynamited off in the fifties—the Cave of the Winds was reached by means of a long circular staircase. The elevator was built in 1927. At its bottom, the doors open and we walk through a tunnel onto the rocky sliver of riverbank between the Horseshoe and the American Falls. The jewel-green river contrasts with its dull brown banks. The water's edge is rimmed with a dirty white cushion. Larry points to it.

"See all that ice? By Monday that will all be gone," he says. The iceberg is already breaking up. The river level in the Maid of the Mist pool, just below the falls, will rise today by about 11 feet as a result of the treaty's enforcement. The *Maid of the Mist* boats, across the way in Canada, have been pulled aground for winter. With water diversion at its maximum, the river is too low for the *Maid* fleet to sail. They will start up again in May.

Larry supervises the crews who build the Cave of the Winds' decks every year and tear them down at the end of the season. Since the only way down to the gorge is through the surprisingly small elevator, the job has its challenges. Plywood won't fit in the lift, so the decks are built with two-by-fours. The constant wet spray rules out power tools, so everything is done with saws and hammers. All equipment for the job has to be disassembled on Goat Island above, brought down, and reassembled at the river. Larry proudly points out a little forklift he took apart and rebuilt.

"One morning, I came out of the elevator and there was an eight-point buck standing there looking at me," he tells us. "He was all banged up; he'd come over the Falls and survived somehow. The guys made a pet out of him, feeding him apples and stuff." When management got wind of the buck, they told Larry to get him out of there. Larry thought about shooting the buck, but by then, the construction crew considered it their pet and wouldn't let him.

"And there's only one way out," Larry says, indicating the elevator again. "We called the DEP, and they came out and shot him with a tranquilizer gun so we could put him in the elevator and take him up. He's living not far from here now."

He leads us toward the base of the American Falls. Along the railing and the rocky river edge stand thousands of ring-billed gulls. Larry waves an arm, and a few hundred of them rise and form a cloud just over the river's edge, flapping their wings to hold steady in the fierce wind while loudly denouncing the imposition.

People come on the Cave of the Winds tour to get up close and personal with Niagara. And that means getting wet. Larry stops and gestures upward with a grin.

"We get folks who go right under it and dance around, like they're taking a shower." He shakes his head and grins in a way that says *tourists do the darndest things*.

The deck will eventually reach a point about 15 feet in front of the Bridal Veil Falls, the thin waterfall separated from the rest of the American Falls by Luna Island. It doesn't yet reach that far, but the view is still impressive. Although the Bridal Veil is by far the smallest waterfall at Niagara, from this angle it's awe-inspiring. A thick mist rises up from the talus at its base. Larry and his workers will build the decks to zigzag back and forth across the rocks, offering vantage points on the waterfall and spots where freshets of water flow over the tourists' feet. The final platform, buffeted by mist and wind whipped up by falling water, is always called the "Hurricane Deck."

As we walk back, the gulls continue to call us names. Thousands of them eye us warily from their spots on the breaking-up ice pack. Lisa takes photos of them.

"Once all that ice is gone," Larry says, "those gulls will come onto the bank. They lay their eggs here. Then they get really aggressive. They used to lay their eggs on Strawberry Island upstream, but they blocked that off so they can't go there anymore. Now they come here." He's referring to a Power Authority project. Because water fluctuations for power drawdowns interfere with fish-spawning areas and habitats for ground-nesting birds, NYPA covered a number of islands upstream of the Falls with "gull exclusion" devices to help preserve what habitat remains. Larry's normally cheery face falls briefly.

"The more man changes things, the worse they get," he declares.

Niagara is not the tallest waterfall in the world. It's not the tallest waterfall in the United States, or even in New York State. Drive a couple of hours east and you can visit Ithaca's Taughannock Falls, taller by 45 feet: two and a half hours north of New York City, Kaaterskill Falls is about the same height. As for volume, Niagara is sixth in the world, and at least twelve of the world's waterfalls are wider. But stand at the brink of the Horseshoe for a few minutes and you'll hear someone say *That's a lot of water.* Niagara's narrow width accentuates the feeling of volume. One-fifth of the world's fresh water crowds itself into the narrow strait between Lakes Erie and Ontario, rushing—half of it anyway—over 4,000 feet of brink, year in, year out, with little seasonal variation. The impression you get from the resulting hypnotic downrush is less about size than continuity. That's a lot of water, and it just keeps coming.

In our plugged-in modern lifestyle, we like to think of electricity too as continuous. Flip a light switch, plug in a laptop, and a stream of electrons rushes out. Blackouts shock Americans because they undercut the illusion of an unending, ever-ready resource, a waterfall of power right there in the wall. Early hydro promoters played up the connection. "After all is said and done, very few people ever see the falls," declared Thomas Commerford Martin, president of the American Institute of Electrical Engineers in 1896: "Now the useful energy of the cataract is made cheaply and immediately available every day in the year to hundreds and thousands, even millions of people, in an endless variety of ways."

In this view, electricity isn't an imposition on the waterfall; it's the distribution of that natural resource to the general population. Your electrical outlet is your own private Niagara, just waiting to be turned on.

Toward the end of Mack Sennett's 1926 silent Keystone comedy *Wandering Willies*, the bad guy drops a piece of paper. The heroine picks it up, reads it, and gasps in shock. She shows it to the hero. He too is appalled and together they race off after the villain. What did the paper say? According to film lore, the intertitle giving the paper's content was rewritten several times: one version had the heroine crying "He was stealing my diploma as winner of the beauty contest!" Another had her saying "This proves he is the president of the Kidnappers Corporation!" The final intertitle, according to film critics, proved the zany, nonsensical quality of Sennett's Keystone Kops: "Look! A mortgage on Niagara Falls. We must stop him before he shuts off the water!"

But in 1926, the notion of a landgrabbing villain turning off the Falls would not have read as nonsense. Controversy over water diversions raged throughout the early twentieth century, beginning almost immediately after the reservation was established. Between 1886 and 1889, four companies, including the Niagara Falls Power Company, were granted charters to take unlimited water from above the Falls without compensating the state. The park commissioners objected that this was defrauding the public. In giving these monopolistic private companies unlimited rights to river water, they claimed, New York was pouring nature's splendor into the pockets of greedy robber barons.

What made it even worse was that by the turn of the century, a handful of private corporations dominated the power industry. Electricity development is capital-intensive: building hydroplants and coal-fired generators takes cash, and lots of it. The small power companies quickly consolidated in a flurry of corporate mergers.

In an era when vertical integration was becoming an economic byword, power companies offered up a perfect example of such efficiency, controlling the generation, distribution and utilization of electricity. Power was, as magnate Samuel Insull put it, "a natural monopoly."

The park commissioners objected vociferously to giving this monopolistic clique unlimited access to Niagara. The state responded by trying to disband the commissioners and transfer management of the park to the board of fisheries, game and forests. But then the press and high-minded public advocates took up the cause. The federal government got involved, and in 1902, the River and Harbor Appropriation bill included the creation of a six-person International Waterways Commission, to be divided between U.S. and Canadian appointees. In 1905, this commission recommended that the nations grant no new water rights until further study of their effects. President Theodore Roosevelt took a stand, announcing in a message to Congress that "nothing should be allowed to interfere with the preservation of Niagara Falls in all their beauty and majesty. If the State cannot see this, then it is earnestly to be wished that she should be willing to turn it over to the national government." The humor magazine *Puck* ran a cartoon in 1906 titled Save Niagara Falls—From This. It shows a completely dry Niagara, surrounded by factories, snack stands, advertisements and carnival attractions. Visitors are riding a carousel called The Whirlpool, sledding on a luge-like track down the dry Falls and lining up at a stand to buy "Genuine Niagara Water" in jugs.

In Canada at this time, a grassroots movement had arisen demanding public takeover of the power industry. In June 1906, the "Beck Law" came into being, an act creating the Hydro-Electric Power Commission of Ontario, a publicly owned utility charged with managing province water resources. Adam Beck, a leader in the public power movement, was appointed its chair. The birth of Ontario Hydro, although it left American-owned power companies in Canada in private hands, was widely hailed as a victory of the public interest over private capital.

In the United States, where public utilities were increasingly seen as creeping communism, the fight to save Niagara Falls turned instead to limiting the rights of private companies. Representative Theodore Burton introduced a congressional bill limiting diversion in 1906. Hearings were held, with developers testifying that their proposed drawdowns provided far more benefit to the public than a pretty waterfall. General Electric's counsel declared that curtailing their diversion rights would deprive western New Yorkers of jobs: they were just undertaking a huge power and navigation project named, after its originator, Love Canal.

The Burton Act was passed in 1906. A temporary measure to limit diversion, it was replaced in 1909 by the International Boundary Waters Treaty, which granted power plants on the American side 20,000 cubic feet per second, and those on the Canadian side 36,000, little more than was already being diverted. The press hailed the treaty as a guarantee that Niagara's beauty would be preserved. Secretary of War William Howard Taft, concerned that government not infringe on trade, grumbled to Representative Burton that he was "sorry that you had to put in the words 'scenic grandeur.'"

But scenic grandeur was exactly the point. The public outcry had made it clear that, just as with Free Niagara, the public valued beauty. Understanding this, the power companies got right to work. Before the ink was dry on the Burton Act, they wanted more water, but it was clear the public wanted to keep Niagara pretty. To most people, that meant limiting water diversions. Industry spin doctors hatched a sophisticated PR campaign. If they couldn't change people's minds about the importance of scenic grandeur, they would reinterpret what that meant. And so they set out to convince the public that keeping Niagara pretty meant taking more water away.

In 1918, John Lyell Harper, vice president and chief engineer of the Niagara Falls Power Company, wrote *The Suicide of the Horseshoe Fall*, arguing that, because of heavy water flow, the Falls were wearing themselves away into a string of paltry rapids. In 1923, he built an operating scale model of the Falls and used it to demonstrate how natural recession would inevitably ruin the cataract. The Army Corps of Engineers agreed. In 1926, Secretary of Commerce Herbert Hoover told a Chicago audience that Army

Corps surveys proved the Falls were "slowly cutting a deep gash in the rock escarpment and that unless measures are taken the waterfall probably will become a turbulent rapids." Niagara should be preserved, he declared, "if for no other reason, for the sake of the thousands of honeymooners who go there."

The following year, a pamphlet issued by the Buffalo, Niagara & Eastern Power Corporation posed the question "Why is the Horseshoe Fall eating itself to ruin?" The answer, according to power company engineers, was clear: there was too much water! Silly nature. Only bigger drawdowns could save the Falls. Preservation now meant less water, exactly the opposite of what it meant twenty years earlier.

Furthermore, the pamphlet declared, Niagara benefited everyone by providing the cheap, dependable power needed for the "many electro-chemical products which are being manufactured at or near Niagara . . . and bestowed upon mankind." This host of goodies was bestowing something else upon mankind: a cataract of toxic waste. The American power plant's first customer was the Pittsburgh Reduction Company, later the aluminum giant ALCOA. They were soon joined by dozens of other companies that were beginning to use electricity to catalyze chemical reactions, including Carborundum, Mathieson Alkali, Acheson Graphite, Oldbury Electro-Chemical, Roberts Chemical, Hooker Electrochemical, and Union Carbide & Carbon.

By 1925, Niagara Falls was a leading center for the production of abrasives, graphite and graphite derivatives such as electrodes and anodes, dry cell batteries and a wide range of ferro-alloys, metal compounds made by mixing iron with metals such as zirconium, chromium, manganese and silicon. It was also a major producer of sodium hydroxide, a caustic used in everything from soap-making to petroleum-refining. Sodium hydroxide production produces vast amounts of the byproduct chlorine, and new industries sprang up to utilize that waste substance. Niagara Falls became the first municipality in the nation to chlorinate its water, leading to a breakthrough in public health. The number of typhoid, dysentery and cholera cases dropped precipitously. The region also led the way in the invention of chlorinated chemicals:

pesticides, plasticizers, fire retardants, chlorinated solvents and chlorinated organics like PCBs (polychlorinated biphenyls, used in electrical transformers) and mirex, a highly toxic flame retardant and insecticide.

The problem with all of these chlorinated chemicals, of course, was that even as they used up the byproduct chlorine, they created problems of their own. Extremely stable in the environment, chlorinated chemicals are not only toxic, but they're almost impossible to get rid of, especially without proper disposal. With almost no environmental legislation in place, chemical wastes were unceremoniously dumped in the Niagara River, spread on empty lots or poured into wells near the factories.

As industry ramped up and jobs multiplied, public distaste for diversions abated. During the Depression, with jobs scarce, it wasn't unusual to hear repetitions of Lord Kelvin's excitement about turning off the Falls. A reporter for the *Kansas City Star* in 1934 asked the managing editor of the *Niagara Falls Gazette* if honeymooners would keep coming to Niagara forever. The editor declared they would, "that is, if Niagara doesn't dry up." When pressed to explain, the *Gazette* editor declared, "I would rather have the great factories fed by these waters than to have the tourists that the falls bring, and I would be willing to see the falls dry up entirely if it would bring us the wealth and population that a dozen more factories would put in here."

He wasn't the only one. As economic instability grew, interest in the area's natural beauty waned. The preservationists responded by focusing more and more narrowly on the waterfall. A 1931 report of the Special International Niagara Board anatomized its aesthetic value in painstaking detail, calculating how much of its beauty depended on volume, width, height, clarity and color, going so far as to point out that the "actual volume" of the waterfall was not critical to beauty, though the "impression of volume" was. The report estimated how much water could be removed while maintaining the emerald green, the seeming depth and velocity. Charts, graphs and a special set of color chips were adduced. The report concluded by recommending reshaping the riverbed to raise the water level just above the fall, boosting the appearance of volume.

The report was shelved until the 1950 treaty and its subsequent power plant building boom necessitated remediation. But the theoretical transformation of Niagara from sublime natural wonder to engineering feat had begun. Nature would be saved by technology. Or at least the part of it people came to see would.

Why were Niagara preservationists so worried about the waterfall's beauty? They gave the usual reasons: it was an uplifting spectacle, the birthright of every American. It was also, increasingly, a moneymaker. In 1924, New York State consolidated authority over all of its state parks in one body, the State Parks Council, headed up by Robert Moses. Moses (about whom more later) lost no time in driving out the aged park commissioners and quietly undoing Olmsted's vision. Gravel paths were paved. Roads were widened. Parking fees were added. The Tuscarora women who had sold beadwork on Goat Island since the early 1800s were phased out, making way for the state's own souvenir stands. The Niagara Reservation grew more commercial as the cataract shrank.

At the same time, the dark undercurrents of cheap power were beginning to make themselves known. The American riverbank was once again lined with ugly factories. A thick, chemical haze hung over town. Disposing of electrochemical byproducts was an increasing problem. And in 1935, twenty workers filed suit against ALCOA. They were dying of the lung disease silicosis.

At the Power Authority, I asked Norm Stessing how much electricity an average household uses today. About 1,000 watts, he said. There might be stretches of time—when everyone's asleep, or at work, say—when a home is drawing only 100 watts—only the fridge is running, or the air-conditioning. But in the evening, when you add in lights, fans, television, computers, microwave, hot-water heater, dryer, and cell phone chargers, just for starters, that home draws a lot more watts. Averaged out over twenty-four hours, it's an ongoing kilowatt. I asked if that number is on the rise. Norm and Joanne nodded vigorously.

"I remember when it was five hundred watts," Joanne said.

The United States gets about 7 percent of its electricity from hydropower. Most people are surprised by that, because hydro is still the smiling public face of electricity. The Power Authority has visitor centers at several hydro plants. There are no visitor centers at nuclear or coal-burning power plants. The largest nuclear power plants today surpass Niagara's 4½ gigawatt rating (combining the Canadian and U.S. plants), and the largest coal-fired plants are drawing near it. Yet, in the Northeast blackout of 2003, a widely circulated rumor held that the massive loss of power resulted from a lightning strike at Niagara. When he told me this, Norm bristled, as if personally offended. He did not, he declared, lose power for a single second. How much that helped was pretty clear, even in the dark.

It's easy to forget that electricity—70 percent of which in the United States comes from burning fossil fuels—takes an environmental toll, because we don't see the plants that make it. Our power arrives in the socket clean and odorless, and even with recent price hikes, it's still relatively cheap. We may be turning down the heat, and packing extra insulation into attics to lower gas bills. We may be buying hybrid cars faster than Toyota can make them. But conserving electricity seems to have gone the way of macramé and free love. Offices today are air-conditioned to a meat-locker chill. The watt-hungry tech sector is building data centers that push local grids to the limit. And home use is skyrocketing. The *Wall Street Journal* recently ran an article on the supersizing of home appliances, with a picture of a fridge 6 feet wide. My neighbors leave their air conditioner on when they leave town in the summer, so their cats won't get too hot.

What if we had to look at a waterless Niagara as a testament to our greed for watts? Toward the end of the interview, I asked Norm if there were people who say we should turn off the Falls completely. After all, compared to burning coal, hydro is relatively benign. If we can't conserve, shouldn't we maximize power's cleanest sources? Norm and Joanne glanced at each other, and I sensed I had crossed the line into things the Power Authority didn't like to discuss.

"There are some people who say that," he said, "but they're not serious."

What about the reverse, I pressed. Are there people who want the Power Authority to stop diverting water and return the Falls to their natural state?

"Oh sure," he said, shrugging. "There are always people who think that."

"They should let it rip," declares Paul Gromosiak. "If I had my druthers, that's what they'd do." A locally famous Niagara historian and author of such books as *Nature's Niagara, Daring Niagara*, and *Zany Niagara*, Gromosiak is an affable, white-haired man with the face of a Norman Rockwell schoolboy. He has worked as a chemist and taught junior high, but his true calling is as the region's reigning Niagaraphile. He grew up in the town of Niagara Falls, and has been haunting the waterfall and its environs since his age matched his face. Lisa and I meet him, as he suggests, at the visitor center of Niagara Falls State Park on the afternoon of April 1. As we sit down in the café, he opens up a 6-foot-long scale model of the Niagara Gorge showing the area's geology in 3-D detail that would warm the heart of any junior high science teacher. He made it, he tells us, himself. He sits with his back to the park and lovingly points out the spots along the gorge where you can trace the waterfall's historic path.

Outside, the real Niagara rumbles on. It has swelled to full tourist volume, but Gromosiak is not impressed. He liked it better before the treaty.

"I used to go to Goat Island and sit on my favorite log and think," he tells us. Before water diversions ramped up in 1961, the entire island was said to tremble with the force of the pounding water. Gromosiak says he remembers that.

"The ice coming over the Falls would hit the water below with a sound like cannon fire," he says wistfully. Now the Power Authority has installed an ice boom across the mouth of the strait at Buffalo, to keep ice from clogging the hydro intakes.

"They say it's a natural wonder, but they're lying," Gromosiak says, shaking his schoolboy head.

The WPA Guide of 1940 marveled that Niagara Falls was attracting 1.5 million visitors a year. But the town was also full of industry: they report that "the main industrial district borders the river above the falls and from the smokestacks along Buffalo Avenue constantly rise the fumes of industry." With the coming of the war, this booming factory district went into overdrive. The government was buying munitions, metal for airplanes, vehicles and arms, and petroleum and lubricants to keep them running. They were buying leather, fabric, paper, medicines and disinfectants. From 1941 to 1945, Hooker, DuPont, Union Carbide, Olin Mathieson and other local industries focused on providing the building blocks of war. And they added new products to their output: dodecyl mercaptan for making synthetic rubber, hexachloroethane used in smoke screens, arsenic trichloride used to make the war gas lewisite. Hooker operated the Niagara Falls Chemical Warfare Plant, which made, among other things, impregnite, a chemical used to make clothing impervious to chemical warfare.

Disposing of wastes became an almost intractable problem. Landfills popped up everywhere. Some factories paid workers $50 a drum to take waste home with them: what happened to it after that was not the company's concern. Fly-by-night haulers were hired to get rid of barrels as best they could.

"Every old-timer in town will tell you the same stories," Maureen Fennie tells me at the Niagara Falls Public Library. "Unmarked trucks coming in the middle of the night, dumping things in empty lots."

After the war, with troops returning home and housing running short, land for waste disposal got even harder to find. Three chemical companies bought tracts of land along the Niagara River above the Falls and began dumping waste along the riverbank. A 1953 master's thesis noted approvingly that this was not only helping the disposal problem, but "also acts to fill in low land along the river's edge and in time may render the property salable for building purposes, or for future plant expansion."

Far from being seen as a problem, waste was a sign of prosperity. An article in the *Saturday Evening Post* of October 30, 1948, described the "chemical-saturated haze which settles over the city when the air is heavy" at Niagara Falls. This toxic smog, the magazine assures us, "is sniffed happily by the industrially minded. Less materialistic residents move to the outskirts, away from the stench." Rather than trying to cut back on wastes, industries sought to ramp up production. For this, they needed more power. They got their wish in 1950, when the new diversion treaty was signed, raising the U.S. stream share from 20,000 cubic feet per second to 50,000. (The United States somehow convinced the Canadians—in whose country 90 percent of the water plunges over the brink—to divide the stream share equally between the two nations.)

With the new treaty in place, Canada moved quickly to utilize its new water allowances, starting work on the Adam Beck plant seven miles below the Falls. In the United States, progress stalled with a bitter public debate over who would control Niagara power. Private power companies once again tried to commandeer the Falls. They would likely have succeeded, but now they had a new opponent: Robert Moses, the famed "power-broker" who reshaped New York City. Niagara has been transformed throughout its history by powerful, autocratic men determined to leave their mark. Moses was perhaps the pinnacle.

New Yorkers love to hate Robert Moses. In one of the world's best walking cities, he built tunnels and bridges (all the ugly ones are his) to bring in more cars. He uprooted hundreds of thousands of people to build highways but ignored public transportation. He mowed down the corner stores and small buildings of poor communities to build soulless housing projects. He did add nearly 650 parks to the city, but few of them were near poor neighborhoods. He built Jones Beach, a stunningly beautiful spot, but made it inaccessible to public transportation. He built community swimming pools, but fought to keep them segregated. A one-man wrecking crew who held multiple public offices and was known as "Big Bob the Builder," Moses wasn't just autocratic, but vengeful: when community activists and preservationists thwarted his plan to build another bridge between Brooklyn and lower Manhattan's Battery, Moses punished the neighborhood by taking down the Battery Park Aquarium and moving it to Coney Island.

However, compared to what he did at Niagara, Robert Moses was a saint in New York City. He sent the city budgets of Niagara

Pag 19.

The first published image of Niagara Falls was an engraving based on Louis Hennepin's account of seeing the Falls with La Salle in 1678. This one by Pieter vander Leyden appeared in a 1704 Dutch edition of Hennepin. Castellani Art Museum of Niagara University Collection. Generous donation from Dr. Charles Rand Penney, partially funded by the Castellani Purchase Fund, with additional funding from Mr. and Mrs. Thomas A. Lytle, 2006.

5116. The Red Man's Fact, Niagara Falls.

*L*elawala takes the plunge: Though this card is from the early twentieth century, postcards showing the mythical "Maid of the Mist" continue to be a staple of Niagara souvenir stands. From the author's collection.

*L*ooking across the Railway Suspension Bridge. Pedestrians and carriages—and fugitives—passed through the tunnel underneath while trains ran above. J. J. Reilly stereoview, courtesy of the Niagara Falls Public Library.

A nation transfixed by the drama of fugitive slaves couldn't look away as Blondin carried his manager Henry Colcord across the tightrope. Courtesy of the Niagara Falls Public Library.

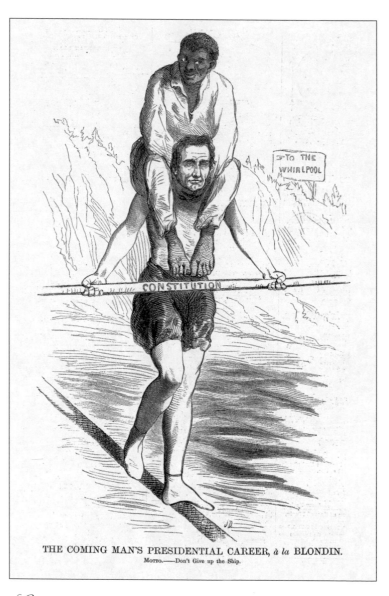

THE COMING MAN'S PRESIDENTIAL CAREER, à la BLONDIN.
Motto.——Don't Give up the Ship.

𝓛incoln goes out on a wire. The *Harper's* cartoon, probably drawn by Jacob Dallas, compares the Republican party's antislavery stand with Blondin's crossing of the Niagara Gorge. *Harper's* Magazine, August 25, 1860.

*W*ith Frederick Church's iconic 1857 painting of Niagara, American landscape painting came of age. The Granger Collection, New York.

*I*n the early 1960s, the Army Corps began remediations to the waterfall that would include filling in and landscaping the American end of the Horseshoe Falls, then excavating the riverbed to ensure an even curtain of waterfall at the brink. The Horseshoe Falls are now entirely in Canada. Courtesy of the Niagara Falls Public Library.

*I*n 1969 the American Falls were literally turned off so the Army Corps of Engineers could perform tests and shore up the rockface. Courtesy of the Niagara Falls Public Library.

*T*he price of cheap power was paid by the poor: one of many homes eventually bulldozed at Love Canal. ©Bettmann/CORBIS.

*P*erilous ground: even as the government resisted evacuating Love Canal, Terrapin Point was entirely rebuilt. Here, a worker puts the final rocks into the neat rock wall that hems in the Horseshoe Falls and keeps water from flowing over the artificial land of Terrapin Point. Photograph by Dennis Enser, *The Buffalo News,* May 25, 1983.

𝒥n Frank Moore's revision of Frederick Church's Niagara, the human can't be painted out of the picture: the mist is laced with chemical compounds, the landscape is framed by plumbing pipe, and it's all caught in the camera's eager iris. Frank Moore, *Niagara*, 1994/95. Collection Albright-Knox Art Gallery. Courtesy of the Gesso Foundation and Sperone Westwater Gallery, New York.

County's towns into a spin by removing the old private power companies from their tax rolls and replacing them with his tax-exempt Authority. He created an artificial boom with his massive project and made no provision for the economic aftershocks when it was done. He drove a knife into the heart of the struggling downtown by ramming a parkway through it, dividing its urban center from the Falls. He reshaped the riverbank, rebuilt Goat Island, tore down homes and relocated churches, all with little regard for what anyone else thought. Could he do it? Yes he could. At least until he ran up against Niagara's Indians.

Robert Moses had first turned his eye to Niagara in 1926, when he began wresting control of the Niagara Reservation from the park commissioners. When he came back in 1956, he had just been appointed commissioner of New York's Power Authority. Authorities—essentially private corporations granted special rights and privileges by the state, but free of state supervision—were Moses's favorite way of getting things done without any pesky taxpayer backtalk. He was head of several, including the Triborough Bridge Authority in New York City. In Niagara, he controlled the two agencies, State Parks and the Power Authority, that together could reshape the entire Niagara frontier.

At the Power Vista, the story of the power plant construction is bathed in the rosy glow of corporate boosterism. The massiveness of the project is the main theme, as if the only bar to its completion was size. In fact, the Power Authority faced obstructions at every turn, and Moses toppled them one by one. His papers include bullying letters to town councils, county boards, lawyers, unions, CEOs, realtors, railroad heads, contractors and editors who were standing in his way or just speaking out against him. "I have been involved in quite a few public enterprises with the usual conventional, outrageous and also comparatively innocent pressures," Moses declared in a public statement in 1958, "but nowhere in my experience has there been so much of this as on the Niagara Frontier."

The first to be removed were the private power companies. Moses wanted the new power plant at Niagara to be built and operated by his Authority. The private power developers were screaming socialism at the thought of a public authority taking over Niagara's water. Moses, as was his style, began a vicious PR campaign, but then, ironically with the help of nature, he won that fight. In 1956, a landslide destroyed the Schoellkopf Power Plant, by then the United States' only operating hydro facility at Niagara; the old McKim, Mead & White powerhouses had been taken out of service in 1926. Nothing better could have happened for Commissioner Moses. Facing a serious power shortage, New York State took less than a year to pass the Niagara Redevelopment Act giving Moses the authority to build his plant.

The next obstructions to be toppled were the local communities that resisted, among other things, the open canals Moses wanted to use to bring the water to the power plant. Moses issued press releases, appeared on radio programs and created glossy brochures. He canceled dinners and official appearances to embarrass local politicians who weren't helping him enough. He continually threatened to stop the whole project and throw several thousand workers off the job. At the same time, behind the scenes, he pulled strings and made threats.

Eventually, Moses would be forced to cover his canals. But the most difficult battle was still to be fought, and it was with a highly unlikely enemy—the Indians. Around 700 Tuscarora Indians lived on a 6,249-acre reservation on the escarpment just above Lewiston, about five miles downstream of the Falls. Moses, seeing a chance to get his hands on some cheap, "unimproved" land that wasn't on the tax rolls, decided to build his power plant's reservoir on the Tuscarora Reservation. He announced his plan to appropriate 1,383 acres of Tuscarora land and began the job of surveying.

The standoff between Robert Moses and the Tuscarora Nation has the feel of Niagara history repeating itself. It was not, in the end, about 1,383 acres. It was about two different ways of viewing the environment. Like the explorer La Salle, Moses arrived at the Niagara frontier with dreams of technological mastery in the service of greater use, and was stopped short by a completely baffling Indian worldview that seemed to have no interest in using the land for profit, and no interest in letting him do so. Like La

Salle, Moses bulldozed his way across this worldview, pretending to be conciliatory while doing exactly what he wanted. He too left his name plastered all over the landscape.

The New York Power Authority's Niagara Power Project is being relicensed as of 2007. As part of the relicensing process, the Authority had to gain support from regional "stakeholders." Every stakeholder group submitted a statement about the project's environmental impact on their community. Most of the statements are written in the dull, bureaucratic language of public documents. The Tuscarora statement is completely different. Swift, pointed and emotional, it makes one thing abundantly clear: the Tuscaroras are still mad.

"One of the things we wanted was an official apology from the Power Authority for what Robert Moses did years ago," Neil Patterson, Jr., a Tuscarora, tells me. They didn't get one. Neil, a compact young man with intense brown eyes, is director of the Tuscarora Environment Program, a community organization designed to help the Tuscaroras form strategies for protecting and restoring their cultural and natural resources. I visit him at the program's office, an addition built onto the side of his house on the Tuscarora Reservation. We sit at a round table that holds a bowl of apples, a quarter of a Wegmans chocolate cake and a bottle of 7-Up. People work at desks a few feet away, and Neil's father walks through occasionally.

"The idea outside," Neil says, meaning not on the reservation, "is power. But you can't control and own everything on your land or even in your house or car. That's a Western idea."

The notion that not everything in the world can be mastered—or bought—is what Robert Moses hit like a wall when he arrived at Niagara Falls ready to commandeer some "unused" land from the Indians. In March 1957, nine months before he even had his official license from the Federal Power Commission, Moses sent surveyors onto the Tuscarora Reservation to "take soil samples." One of them happened to knock on the door of Chief Clinton Rickard, one of the founders of the Indian Defense League. Rickard called a council. Although they were assured there was no question of taking their land, the Tuscaroras smelled a rat. They decided to refuse all access to their reservation.

Unlike most Indian reservations, the Tuscarora Reservation is not land held in trust for the Indians by the federal government, but is owned outright by the Tuscaroras. Originally from North Carolina, the Tuscaroras were forced out after a series of land skirmishes with white settlers in the early 1700s. A man named John Lawson, surveyor general of the colony, sold some Tuscarora land to a group of German settlers. The Tuscaroras captured Lawson and executed him. The colonists of neighboring South Carolina sent aid, a small force of settlers with a large contingent of non-Tuscarora Indian allies, and the Tuscaroras were defeated. They packed up and headed north, where the Oneidas took them in as refugees.

In 1722, the Tuscaroras were officially made the sixth nation of the Haudenosaunee. The Senecas, who became their official protectors, gave them some land near Niagara Falls. The rest they purchased from the Holland Land Company. It was because of this purchase that the Federal Power Commission, in granting a license to develop Niagara power to the Power Authority in January 1958, agreed that Moses had condemnation rights on the reservation. The Tuscaroras retained a lawyer, and asserted that later treaties with the United States guaranteed them the right to keep what land they had.

In February, Moses sent the Tuscaroras an open letter, high-handedly asserting that "the treaties you talk about have nothing to do with your reservation in Niagara County, as you must know." He expressed his desire to proceed with friendly negotiations, but declared, "we must go ahead in any event." Moses offered the Tuscaroras $1,000 an acre. He was offering adjacent Niagara University $50,000 an acre. The Tuscaroras protested that they were not interested in selling at any price. "We will keep our land, and the Power Authority can keep their money," declared Chief Elton Greene, the primary Tuscarora spokesman.

Moses resorted to his usual tactics, beginning with assembling a "dossier" on the Tuscaroras. A January memo to his general manager William Chapin asked, "Do we have the basic facts about the Tuscaroras—for public consumption apart from the rhubarb about condemnation and pre-revolutionary and pre-state rights of the noble red men? I mean acreage they have, living conditions, land, cultivation, how much we take, how much we offer, what they could do with cash, what they work at, etc. I don't want a lot of mawkish sentiment manufactured by the sob sisters and other SOBs. It would be a hell of a thing if we had to move the reservoir to cemetery and taxable farmland."

By April, he was still looking for dirt but he was also trying to come up with cheap ways to get the Tuscaroras to back down. He wrote another memo to Chapin:

> I would like to hire somebody—an authority, of course—to give us briefly some information about the Tuscarora Indians—to wit:
>
> Origin tribe, etc.?
>
> Record—anything destructive?
>
> How long at Lewiston?
>
> What did and do they now—hunting, fishing, farming, weaving and arts?
>
> Would a small Indian museum at Lewiston serve any purpose—attract visitors, sale of Indian stuff or what not? Would Tuscaroras take any pride in it, make or sell anything? Do they have any genuine relics for exhibition?

Clearly unaware of the Tuscaroras' history with surveyors, Moses sent his men back onto the reservation in April 1958. Power Authority surveyors arrived on the reservation and began driving stakes into the ground. The Tuscaroras rolled up in a line of twenty-two cars and—according to a letter Moses sent that day to the superintendent of State Police—lit the stakes on fire. The surveyors left and came back the next day with a drilling rig, 32 sheriff's deputies and 30 state troopers. One hundred and fifty Tuscaroras, men, women and children, formed a blockade in front of the equipment. There was some pushing and shoving, but no serious violence. Nonetheless, three Indians, including Wallace "Mad Bear" Anderson, a young, militant activist, were arrested.

Anderson, a veteran of World War II and Korea, had become intensely interested in issues of Native American justice when he was refused a GI loan to build a home on the Tuscarora Reservation. A round-faced, charismatic man with a stocky physique, Anderson was an activist and a natural leader, taking part in sovereignty actions not just on Tuscarora land, but across the United States and Canada. The Power Authority found his activism unsavory: in their slick, commemorative 1960 book about the project, they pointed out that Anderson "holds no position of authority among the Tuscaroras," and claimed that he "seeks the limelight, travels about the country citing 'injustices' visited upon the Indians by the U.S. government."

Mad Bear Anderson may have been something of a hothead—his grandmother gave him his nickname for being quick to anger as a child—but his approach to the Power Authority was strictly nonviolent. Nonetheless, following Moses's lead, the press treated the Tuscarora actions as if Pontiac's Rebellion was breaking out all over again. "Redskins Go on Warpath!" screamed the *Chicago Tribune.* The next day, in a story titled "Indians Whoop Up Cold War; Halt White Invasion," they called the protest an "Indian uprising, punctuated by prairie fires and pow-wows." *The New York Times* titled its story "Tuscarora Braves Repel Surveyors."

Moses seemed completely incapable of understanding the Tuscarora position. After the first protest, he sent a memo to Chapin.

If the Tuscaroras are proud and want recognition I am for giving them, not substitute land which would be almost impossible to acquire and of no use to them, but the following:

Reservoir name to be "Tuscarora Reservoir."

Bronze Indian Memorial Statue at Reservoir by distinguished sculptor, design to be agreed on.

Indian Museum adjacent to Power House building.

He concluded that he might even go so far as to raise the price per acre to $1,500, "for the benefit of the more mercenary braves."

Throughout the conflict, the commissioner continually expressed his conviction that the Tuscaroras were merely holding out for more money. Everything, in Robert Moses's mind, had a price. What flummoxed him was that the Indians didn't want to sell land they didn't seem to be using. "Much of your land is presently uncultivated and unused," he wrote the Tuscaroras, assuring them they would be much better off with the money, which could be used "for scholarships for your children and for community improvements, or used to acquire and develop other land."

He harped on the notion of use again and again. When the Tuscaroras suggested he replace their acreage with new land, he sneered. "We cannot as a basis for settlement," he declared, "acquire and convey to you other adjacent privately owned land which you do not need and which is needed for other constructive purposes." For Moses, as for nineteenth-century advocates of Indian removal, the Indians' failure to *do* anything with the land proved they didn't deserve it.

The Tuscaroras were unimpressed by offers of statues and symbolic names. They remained so when Moses pulled out plans for a "community center" on the reservation. Even in his plan for the center, Moses expressed his scorn for the Tuscaroras, noting to his chief park designer that the Indians weren't likely to take good care of the building. "No use giving the redskins something they won't take care of," he sniffed.

Moses was impervious to outside intervention. When Eleanor Roosevelt wrote New York governor Averell Harriman to ask about the disparity between Niagara University's settlement and that offered the Indians, she received a stiff reply from Moses. "This is the first time it has been suggested," he huffed, "that in harnessing these waters we have operated on the basis of religious bias or prejudice against a minority." He then fired off a memo to his general counsel declaring that "the Indian counsel and various frontier jackals have apparently steamed up the braves and squaws to believe they can make a killing by reference to University prices." The Indians' lawyers, he guessed, would be thrilled with "a phoney story that Tuscarora land and University land look just alike to them." Never mind that the university land and Tuscarora land *did* look just alike; they were contiguous.

Moses's intolerance for differing views extended from the ex–first lady all the way down to second-graders. When twenty elementary schoolchildren at P.S. 31 in New York City sent him letters protesting the taking of Indian land, he *returned them* with a cold letter to the principal. "Obviously these children were completely misinformed, and no effort was made to tell them what is really going on," he fumed. "This is the way to bring government into contempt and to create a youth problem."

Robert Moses was not a man to brook opposition, even from nature itself. This was the man who filled New York City's marshes with garbage and turned them into parks. He dredged sand from the ocean floor to build beaches and moved the Bronx River 500 feet when it got in the way of his highway. He harnessed the St. Lawrence River, building an artificial lake on the U.S.-Canadian border and stocking it with fish. But even then he wanted more control. In a staff memo on a new fish hatchery, he fired off a series of questions for the engineers: "What kind of fish? Muskies? Located where? How do we keep the bastards from staying on the Canadian side?"

Now the man who wanted to micromanage muskies was harnessing Niagara Falls, and no one was going to stand in the way of his dominion, especially not a group of Indians who, inexplicably, just wanted to coexist with their land. It took him nearly three years, but he won. Instead of a lieutenant with an iron hand, Moses had the Supreme Court. On March 7, 1960, the court voted 6 to 3 to allow condemnation of the Tuscarora land. Justice Hugo Black wrote an eloquent, emotional dissent.

"It may be hard for us to understand why these Indians cling so tenaciously to their lands and traditional tribal way of life," he wrote. "The record does not leave the impression that the lands of their reservation are the most fertile, the landscape the most beautiful or their homes the most splendid specimens of architecture. But this is their home—their ancestral home. There they, their children and their forebears were born. They, too, have their memories and their loves. Some things are worth more than money and the costs of a new enterprise."

Not to Robert Moses. By the time he was done, the Power Authority had excavated almost 10 million cubic yards of earth and more than 24 million cubic yards of rock. The power plant bearing his name came online in 1961, a mere three years after the massive project began. To decorate the powerhouse with sufficient grandeur, Moses commissioned Thomas Hart Benton to paint a 7-foot-high mural showing Father Louis Hennepin being guided to Niagara Falls by Native Americans. The mural hangs over the escalator in the Power Vista today. It looks exactly as Moses imagined it in February 1958. "I don't want any phoney, primitive, abstract or other freak stuff," he wrote in a memo to Chapin. "Maybe we should have T. H. Benton do something about Father Hennepin with assorted Indians (not Tuscaroras)."

Indeed, the Tuscaroras are not in the picture. Today the giant berm of the reservoir cuts across their reservation. It looks like the cold, disinterested back of a sleeping giant. Some of the Tuscaroras climb it to fish in the reservoir.

Robert Moses did not, in the end, take as much land as he originally wanted, he didn't need that much. But according to Neil Patterson, Jr., some of the people who lived through the land acquisition are still so upset they can barely speak of it. I ask him if it's harder for an Indian to be removed from his home than it is for a non-Indian.

"Absolutely," he says, without hesitating. "We don't sit on the land and build a big house. We're tied to the land. We're as important to it as the deer or the trees. This land was fought for, tooth and nail; we gave up land in North Carolina for this land. So it's a double loss." He speaks with a kind of steady calm that only adds to his intensity. "Six thousand two hundred forty-nine acres for an entire nation," he tells me. "A language, a custom, a way of life. The people of the U.S. have millions of acres. People on the outside have all the room in the world and they still encroach on our land. They took about six hundred acres—between nine and ten percent. What's nine or ten percent of the land in the U.S.? That's like the eastern seaboard. It's not right. It's not logical. This is the only place we have."

The Tuscarora Environment Program put together an oral history of the power project and its impact on the community, and submitted it as part of their comments for the FERC relicensing. Nearly forty people were interviewed for about three hours each.

"It's not opposition to the license but an attempt to set the record straight," Neil tells me. "We like the idea of hydropower; it's fairly noninvasive. But there's a responsibility to look at other things: how water-level fluctuations in the river are affecting the reproductive ability of fish, for instance." He also believes the Power Authority should spend more resources looking at other renewable sources of energy.

"We want them to recognize that they're not in the business of providing power so people will use it," he says. "They're in the business of using it responsibly."

In 1959, Robert Moses read a speech by his friend James Duncan, chairman of Ontario Hydro. He sent a copy to Governor Nelson Rockefeller. Moses was trying to convince Rockefeller to let him build a nuclear power plant.

"Throughout the world," Duncan's speech declares, "a high per capita consumption of electricity and a high standard of living go hand in hand." He notes with approval that the citizens of Ontario use more electricity than almost anyone in the world, and explains that this is what keeps rates low. "With direct competition between electricity and natural gas in some areas, however," he warns, "Ontario Hydro and the municipalities must take steps to ensure that they hold on to their customers and maintain a steady rate of growth in consumption."

Encouraging people to consume means making sure they don't see any ill effects resulting from their consumption. But this was exactly what was going to happen at Niagara. According to a report by the International Joint Commission, once all the new power plants were running under the 1950 treaty, the river above the Falls would drop by 4 feet, the flow over the American Falls would shrink to next to nothing, and even the great Horseshoe would dwindle, its flanks going completely dry at times. There were other problems as well: ugly stretches of dewatered flats above Goat Island, riverbanks exposed by lowered water, severe diminishment of the American Falls, and thinning of the Horseshoe near Table Rock. Something had to be done.

As the Robert Moses Niagara Power Plant was being blasted out downstream, the U.S. Army Corps of Engineers and the Hydro-Electric Power Commission of Ontario, working with the Power Authority and State Parks, addressed the waterfall. Two working models of the Falls were built, one by each nation, and plans were drawn up for a massive engineering project to guarantee "a very satisfactory scenic spectacle" during the day, at 100,000 cubic feet per second, and "an impressive scenic spectacle" at night, with water flow reduced by half.

The works undertaken by the Corps of Engineers and Ontario Hydro are still in place today. The most visible is a large International Control Works in the river just above the Falls, a partial dam with eighteen sluice gates that open and close to enable precise changes in water flow over the brink, directing more water to thinning areas and less to those that look good. They also built weirs—submerged dams—upstream to raise the river level above the Falls and at the edges of the Horseshoe, so that water would spread out to the edges and create "an unbroken curtain shore to shore." They excavated 94,000 cubic yards of rock from the flanks of the Horseshoe, lowering the riverbed 4 feet to further encourage an unbroken crestline. While they were at it, the Corps blasted off overhangs, scaled and graded the earth at Prospect Point to make a natural-feeling slope and added the 280-foot-high Prospect Point Observation Tower. They reshaped the American riverbank with excavated earth—generously donated by Robert Moses's power project—and added 8.5 acres of land to Goat Island's eastern end, enough for a helicopter pad, parking lot, concession stand and roadway.

By the time Robert Moses cracked a bottle of champagne on his new power plant in 1961, engineers had completely rebuilt Niagara Falls—and it looked better than ever.

The Canadians too were ramping up efforts to beautify Niagara. They completed a parkway in 1931 that ran the entire length

of the river, using fill and grading to build roadbed. They blasted
off the remains of Table Rock—a jutting ledge that formed a popular but treacherous viewpoint—and reshaped the cliff around it
in 1934. They completed the Oakes Garden amphitheater and
ornamental gardens on the bluff across from the American Falls in
1937. In the fifties, as part of the binational remediation project,
they had 3,000 acres of parkland set aside along the river, 2,000
of which were maintained as formal gardens and parks. Their staff
of 600 summer gardeners operated a conservatory to provide the
park's 200,000 plants. The operation of the International Control
Works beginning in 1957 alleviated their "spray problem" at Table
Rock; too much mist was scaring off visitors to the scenic tunnels
behind the Falls. The control structure redirected water to reduce
spray, and attendance jumped 22 percent.

As the waterfall remediation proceeded, the landscape was being
transformed in additional ways. In 1957, the Niagara Falls Board
of Education had a meeting. Four years earlier, Hooker Chemical had deeded some land to Niagara Falls; the city had built a
school on it and wanted to subdivide the rest. Hooker attorney
Arthur Chambers came to the meeting to stop them. No basements, water lines, or sewers should be built on the site, he told
the school board, because "you're apt to hit something we buried
there." Wesley Kester of the Board of Ed remarked to the *Gazette*,
"There's something fishy someplace."

Indeed there was. The following year, as Robert Moses squared
off with the Tuscaroras, it was reported that some local children
who used the ditch near their school as a playground had been
burned by mysterious substances in what was called "Hooker's
dump" or Love Canal. The never-finished canal had been used
for years as an unofficial landfill. Throughout the forties and fifties, during the massive chemical output of the war effort and
the Cold War that followed, residents had seen trucks, sometimes
dozens in a single day, pull up to the canal and dump mysterious barrels into the ditch. Neighborhood residents watched army
personnel with sidearms and gas masks unloading drums into the
canal. Children who followed the olive-drab trucks were chased

away. Caustic gases sometimes filled the air after dumping, and at night, spontaneous explosions in the canal were common. During this time, locals continued to use Love Canal as a swimming and fishing hole. At least until the fish died and the water began to burn their skin.

In November of 1964, with the Robert Moses Niagara Power Plant up and running, Niagara Falls fire chief Edwin Foster wrote a letter to the city manager. He had seen someone using construction equipment to cover something fuming and noxious at the Love Canal dump. "Upon my arrival at the Hooker dump," he wrote, "the wind was blowing from a westerly direction and the area was permeated by the odor of chemicals and fumes emitting from a pile of chemical wastes." After seeing and smelling the unknown substance, Foster was convinced it "could be a detriment to the health and well-being of residents in this area." He suggested that the "proper authorities be notified and remedial action be taken."

The city declined to take remedial action. The state, when notified, also refused. But in 1966, more remedial action began on the waterfall. A *Niagara Falls Gazette* editor named Cliff Spieler—he would later become the Power Authority's director of public relations—began running a series of articles decrying the imminent "death" of Niagara Falls. Once again, Niagara was threatened by the force of its own water. Spieler lined up political supporters, and within a year Army Corps engineers reduced the flow over the American Falls by three-quarters to "find ways to preserve the scenic splendor of the falls against the ravages of erosion and rock slides." They drilled core samples and inserted miniature cameras into the rockface to examine its interior, and used sandblasting and water jets to map fractures in the rock. In 1969 they turned the American Falls off completely to continue the work. With a cofferdam blocking the water, they installed sensors to detect rock slippage, and an alarm system to alert park police to impending rockfalls. They drove bolts into cracks in the rock and braced up Goat and Luna Islands with dowels, cable tendons and drains to reduce water pressure. In 1973, as more and more residents at Love Canal were fruitlessly complaining about noxious odors and oily sludge leaking into their basements, the International Joint Commission distributed thousands of surveys to tourists asking how the viewing experiences of the Falls might be enhanced. They were offered the options of having the rocky talus removed from the base of the American Falls, having flow increased over the American Falls, or having the water raised in the Maid of the Mist pool to hide the rubble. The fourth option, chosen by only 30 percent of respondents, was to do nothing.

Nothing is what they did at Love Canal, until the situation was desperate. Pesticides, chlorobenzenes and dioxin, among eighty-two identified chemicals, began leaking into nearby basements and surfacing to contaminate playgrounds. Residents developed nervous and blood disorders, and miscarriage and birth defect rates in the neighborhood rose to appalling levels. A baby was born with two rows of teeth, another with three ears. Finally, in 1978 a housewife named Lois Gibbs began a door-to-door survey to prove that residents were sick and to insist the government take action. Her efforts made the plight of the neighborhood's working-class families a national issue, and the environmental justice movement was born.

The story of Love Canal is fairly well known, made famous in 1979 with the airing of the ABC News documentary *The Killing Ground*. The struggle is credited with creating Superfund, a federal program organized to clean up the nation's worst toxic messes and collect costs from polluters afterward. EPA took Love Canal off the National Priorities List in 2004, and now cites the location as a positive example of regulatory-driven cleanup.

What isn't usually discussed is how, throughout the seventies, as complaints about Love Canal reached higher and higher levels, a government that was willing to spend up to $10 million clearing ugly rocks away from the base of the Falls fought tooth and nail against every dollar spent evacuating a neighborhood that was killing its residents. Love Canal was less than a mile from the Niagara River. The toxic brew was leaking into the river and going over the Falls, but it couldn't be seen by the tourists. In 1979, as President Carter finally declared Love Canal a federal disaster area and began evacuating the first of 950 families, a psychic predicted that a rockslide at Terrapin Point would swamp the *Maid of the Mist* as it carried a boatload of deaf children. The area was closed, boreholes were drilled and more meters were installed to give warning of imminent rockfalls. Four years later, the Corps of Engineers blasted 25,000 tons of rock and removed 60 trees from Terrapin Rocks, where walkways once extended out to the Porters' precarious tower. Erecting a diversion dam to push water away from the American end of the Horseshoe Falls, they filled in the sporadically watered flank with made land, carefully shaping and grading it into Terrapin Point. They built an 835-foot retaining wall to keep water off the point and create a new, manufactured American edge for the waterfall. Combined with 100 feet of fill on the Canadian side, these remedial works eliminated 400 feet of the Horseshoe Falls, including all of the waterfall that was in the United States. The iconic Horseshoe now sits entirely in Canada.

They stabilized what was left with rock bolts, and relandscaped the spot. It all happened in less than half the time it took for sick families to be moved from Love Canal.

Paul Gromosiak was there for all of it. He worked for Hooker Chemical as a young man, and later, when Love Canal was making the nightly news, he was teaching at a middle school in that very neighborhood. Children who lived near the canal sometimes asked him if they were doomed to die. But well before Love Canal, the town of Niagara Falls had environmental issues. When Paul was growing up, he tells Lisa and me, his mother, like other Niagara Falls housewives, would go outside every morning and wipe a layer of sooty, greasy scum from the railing of the family's front porch. Everyone knew it came from the chemical and metallurgical plants, but no one really minded. Those plants employed the town's workers.

Toward the end of our interview, I ask Gromosiak how it makes him feel that water is diverted from the Falls. He seems surprised by the question, and takes a moment to think about it.

"Insulted," he says at last. "I'm not getting a chance to see what I should be seeing: the full flow that would cause this natural wonder to do what it should be doing, cut out a gorge. The natural world doesn't stay the same; it changes all the time. Look at us: do we look the same as we did twenty years ago?"

I assure Gromosiak that I do, in fact, look the same as I did twenty years ago. He laughs.

"I like change," he tells me. "Change has natural beauty. It's unpredictable. There could be a big rockfall right now, and I would be so honored to be here for it. Erosion is a bad word to some people. We're so afraid of the natural world. But we're still at nature's mercy. And I hope we always will be."

After we leave Gromosiak, Lisa and I drive east on Buffalo Avenue, the street where many of the chemical factories once stood. Only a few remain: less than a mile from the Falls sprawls the massive complex of the Occidental Chemical Corporation, the folks who bought Hooker. Factory buildings line both sides of the road, storage tanks and pipelines and smokestacks and a couple odd bathyspherelike structures whose purpose I can only guess, all of it threaded with electrical transmission towers. We continue east, with the river on our right. The street numbers go up as the houses grow smaller. An unassuming little marina appears: Niagara Boat Docks. Just beyond it we can see a huge mesa, raised in that telltale landfill form, landscaped, fenced, barbed-wired, and dotted with exhaust pipes. At its edge sits a playground, kid-free. I pull into the small parking lot and park at a fence posted with the address, 9829 Buffalo Ave.

"What is that?" Lisa asks.

"That," I tell her, "is Love Canal." Technically, it's Hooker's 102nd Street landfill, the less-publicized riverbank end of William T. Love's canal. We contemplate it in silence. Like Love Canal, which continues across the expressway, its fake mountain shape ominously suggests a landscape pregnant with monstrosity. How did we end up here? I think of Norm at his power plant, proudly talking about turbine upgrades, and H. G. Wells rapturously describing Niagara dynamos as "human will made visible." I think of my own giddy thrill at the Power Vista, hanging over the edge of the deck to admire the massive penstocks. Who wouldn't be awed by the prospect of harnessing such a giant organic machine?

Niagara full-force is a fantastic natural spectacle. Niagara turned off is another kind of spectacle, just as fantastic, and just as natural, since we too are part of the natural world. Somehow, it's the in-between Niagara, the harnessed waterfall pretending to be untouched, that leads to the landscape we're parked at now. Because if we don't admit that the things we do to make our lifestyle possible even have a cost, how can we ever know when that price has become too high?

In their book *The Bottomless Well*, Peter Huber and Mark Mills argue that increased energy efficiency only leads to increased usage: the fewer watts our appliances use, the more appliances we buy. Wastefulness, they argue, is thus a form of efficiency. Why bother to use energy-saving lightbulbs if it just means you'll turn on more lights? But what Huber and Mills ignore is the fact that we go to great lengths to disguise and ignore our wastefulness. We may ramp up consumption to match what we believe to be supply, but in part that's because we are blind to supply's real cost. We don't conserve, because we don't think we need to. The effects of waste, like so many of history's unsavory scenes, are carefully swept out of sight.

We get out of my car and walk to the playground. The jungle gym is shaped like a ship and topped by an American flag. A light rain is falling, but the flag is flying high, because it's not an actual fabric flag. It's a fake flag, made of stiff plastic so it stands there, always unfurled, always undulating in just the right way. It's pointing in the direction of the Falls.

I think about the painter Thomas Cole, who once called waterfalls "the voice of the landscape." Here, looking at the neatly landscaped dump, it's hard not to think that Niagara's sparkling, carefree roar is an outright lie. Or at least a great big fake. But the Falls landscape, in its funny way, seems to recognize that too: the more toxic it became underneath, the more spectacularly gorgeous its surface grew. From the fifties on, Niagara would not simply grow more artificial: fakery would increasingly become its very theme.

Seven

SENTIMENT IN LIQUID FORM

As ONE OF HER signature songs put it, she started a heatwave by letting her seat wave. In 1952, as the Army Corps engineers were contemplating how they were going to rebuild Niagara Falls with half its water gone, Marilyn Monroe arrived at the General Brock Hotel in Niagara Falls, Ontario, trailing sex in her wake. The Niagara Falls honeymoon industry had been around for over a hundred years, but this was its biggest boost ever. Monroe, on the brink of becoming a superstar, was famously dating retired Yankee Joe DiMaggio. He checked into the Hotel Niagara on the American side, while over in Canada, Monroe got down to work.

Marilyn was playing sultry seductress Rose Loomis in Henry Hathaway's new film, *Niagara*. In the film, Rose and her husband George, recently released from an army mental hospital, visit the Falls. But things aren't going great between them, what with Rose vamping around town and George flying off into rages about it. She's up to something, and he knows it. The Loomises are contrasted with the wholesome, happy Cutlers, Ray and Polly, who stay at the same motel and get drawn into the other couple's marital misery.

Niagara turned Falls honeymoon fever into an epidemic, even though neither couple in the film is really honeymooning. The Cutlers, we soon learn, are on a delayed honeymoon, presumably because the Korean War intervened. And George Loomis, also a veteran, is deeply depressed. He and Rose honeymooned at Niagara before the war, and Rose has brought him back, ostensibly to cheer him up. But secretly, she is plotting with her hunky lover to kill poor George and throw him into the Niagara River. Since George has been acting depressed all over town, it will look like suicide.

Marilyn Monroe assumed her position as icon of American femininity with the release of *Niagara*. Her performance was much admired. An inordinate amount of attention, both then and since, landed on one particular scene. It takes place after Rose's young lover is supposed to have killed her husband. Rose has just been shown George's unclaimed shoes at Table Rock House. The police clearly believe he has committed suicide. She, of course, knows better.

"Why is everyone standing around? Do something! Look for him! Find him!" she cries, giving a great performance as hysterical wife. Everyone falls for it. The Cutlers are enlisted to take her home. She's a picture of nerves as they approach the car. But when she hears the bell tower playing her favorite song—the signal her lover was going to use if the murder went off without a hitch—she suddenly stops.

"You've been very kind, but thanks, I'd rather walk," she says. The baffled Cutlers watch as Marilyn, in a shiny black pencil skirt, shimmies toward the Falls. From her front, we see her smile—which the Cutlers can't see—and then we see her from their point of view. The camera lingers on her retreating behind for an astonishing sixteen seconds. It became known as "the longest walk in film history."

"Many an actress has walked into stardom," writes Pierre Berton in *Niagara*, "but, as has been said, she succeeded by walking *away* from it."

Much of the interest in the "Marilyn walk" focused on the question of whether it was real. A minicontroversy—the kind that perpetually swirled around Marilyn—arose over the seemingly trivial question of how her hip-swinging, eye-catching wriggle of a walk came to be. Natasha Lytess, who had coached Monroe in acting, took credit for it. Emmeline Snively, once Monroe's modeling boss, claimed it was the result of weak ankles. Arthur Miller, later her husband, protested that the swivel-hipped shimmy was natural. Typically enigmatic, Marilyn would only say, "I learned to walk as a baby and I haven't had a lesson since."

The controversy reflected what biographer Sarah Churchwell calls "the central anxiety in Marilyn's story: Was she natural or manufactured? Scripted or real?" In the fifties, with the iconic landscape being given a facelift, this question was settling on Niagara Falls too. Marilyn's 116-foot walk strode right to the heart of an issue that was playing out on many fronts in American life. What is real, and what fake? If something is artificial, do we admire its beauty less? How much are we willing to be hoodwinked?

What Marilyn came to embody, as Churchwell points out, was the anxiety about realness as it related to femininity. Even as so-called "natural" gender roles were promoted and valorized by the culture, the nagging possibility arose that they weren't "natural" at all, but just an act. Marilyn was almost always cast as a gold-digger, a woman trying to leverage her sexuality to better her position in the world. Rose Loomis, Lorelei Lee, Marilyn herself: they were all women on the make, and at the same time icons of the feminine. The mid-century wife was meant to be a paradigm of selflessness, devoted to husband, children and home. But what if that selflessness was just a mask for pure, unadulterated self-interest?

I find myself thinking of Marilyn on April 21, 2006. I have just arrived at Niagara, and so has spring. The Falls have been turned up for the tourist season and they look spectacular; like Marilyn sewn into one of her dresses, they've been girdled and boosted into the shape the audience wants. The town on the Canadian side is strutting its stuff. The parks are lined with daffodils and the Korean teens who wade in them. The Hard Rock Cafe is blasting *Burning Down the House* loud enough to drown out any number of waterfalls, and "Samuel Jackson" and "Sarah Jessica Parker" are ready for their close-ups at the entrance to Louis Tussaud's Wax

Museum. Souvenir shops are stuffed with hockey tunics, moose cups, edible insects, and Native American dreamcatchers.

Like Marilyn, this town is over the top. And the 920 older women pouring into it are trying to outdo it in campy fun. Dressed in head-to-toe purple, topped with outlandishly decorated red hats, and accessorized for Mardi Gras by way of Kmart, the members of the Red Hat Society swarm through Niagara. The viewing platforms at Table Rock are dotted with red hats. The lines at the Secret Garden Restaurant have a distinctly lavender tone. The Falls are always artificially lit in the evening, and in honor of the purple posse, on Thursday night, they too glow a luminous, lurid violet.

The occasion for the raid is "Barrels of Fun," the Red Hat Society's thirteenth convention and first national-chapter event outside the United States. I'm standing at the Sheraton's Starbucks counter, hoping a double-shot latte will stave off a mounting flight impulse. The hotel lobby has become a near-riot of purple outfits donned by fifty-plus women shouting hellos, introducing friends, and bursting spontaneously into song. There is voguing; there are secret handshakes. Buses keep pulling up and disgorging hatted ladies. A Japanese man in a New Zealand All-Blacks jersey is sitting on the couch, shaking his head with a speechless grin. Two older British women in line with me seem vaguely nervous. They keep glancing at the garish Red Hatters.

"Something for us to consider—when we're older," one of them says, half-joking to the other.

Not me, I stop myself from saying. *Never me.* I'm struck by the force of my own feeling. We all lose our charms in the end. Is being old really that bad?

Men age into power, but women age into invisibility. This is a truism by now, and it's what the Red Hat Society claims to correct: the club slogan is "Red Hatters Matter." Officially formed to promote "fun and friendship for women after fifty," the Red Hat Society has built a marketing empire out of a feeling of disenfranchisement among postmenopausal women. Taking their inspiration from a poem by Jenny Joseph declaring that old age will free her to "wear purple with a red hat which doesn't go and doesn't suit me," the society has grown to more than 41,000 chapters in 30 countries, all of them dedicated to fifty-plus frivolity: luncheons, tea parties, sleepovers and outings. Members call these events "playdates." The society has built a Web site and a retail store in downtown Fullerton, California, and has made licensing agreements with thirty-three companies, including deals on travel services, trading cards, shoes, calendars, books and a bimonthly magazine called *Lifestyle*. Metris recently launched a Red Hat Society Platinum MasterCard, billed as the group's "official sporting equipment." The two founders have done all of this, if we buy their story, without ever having intended to make a dime.

I have to admit, I'm skeptical. Like most not-yet-facing-fifty women I know, the Red Hat Society kind of gives me the creeps. Playdates? Tea parties? Platinum cards? This doesn't feel like empowerment to me. It feels like admitting that older women matter to the culture only as consumers. I was prepared to ignore them with mild scorn, but then they showed up on the brink of my waterfall.

The Red Hatters' choice of Niagara Falls as a meeting destination fascinates me, because it both makes sense and doesn't quite. These are women throwing off the chains of age, and what better place to celebrate escaping the rigidity of the "natural" than Niagara Falls, that partly engineered natural wonder, that force of nature that is in fact completely controlled? Even the attractions that have mushroomed around the Falls seem calculated to celebrate artifice of every kind. On Clifton Hill, you can buy a picture of yourself on a tightrope above the Falls, or in a barrel bouncing over the brink. You can visit a wax museum and take a picture of yourself with Ozzy Osbourne, Austin Powers or President Bush. You can go to the Criminals Hall of Fame and admire a re-creation of the Lincoln assassination. You can go to Dinosaur Park Miniature Golf and tee off amid fake dinosaurs, or visit one of the area's haunted houses and be chased by actors playing ghouls and monsters.

But the thing is, Niagara has traditionally been linked with two female types: the desperate suicide and the blushing bride. The Red Hatters are neither. At an age when suicide rates increase, they are laying claim to joie de vivre. And they're certainly not blushing brides. But maybe they can be seen as honeymooners. If the honeymoon is a sort of epilogue to the romance plot, which ends at marriage—lit-crit types love saying stories hit "deadlock" when they arrive at wedlock—perhaps the Red Hatters can be seen as making space for life's honeymoon, a fantasyland of fun and frolic that comes after the work of job and family has ended. And where would you have a honeymoon if not Niagara?

Like so many marriage "traditions"—diamond engagement rings, white dresses, Jordan almonds in little net bags—honeymooning is relatively new. In early-nineteenth-century England, it became common for newly married upper-class couples to take a "bridal tour," often in the company of friends or family, visiting far-flung relatives who couldn't attend the wedding. The point of these Victorian wedding trips wasn't to "get away from it all" and have a lot of sex. They were demonstrations of a couple's new status.

Bridal tours arrived at Niagara when all the other tourists did: in 1825, the year the Erie Canal completed its journey to Tonawanda. The famous Northern Tour also became the honeymoon tour. It was well established by 1841, when a popular song called "Niagara Falls" made gentle fun of newlyweds:

> To see the Falls they took a ride
> On the steamship 'Maid o' the Mist';
> She forgot the Falls she was so busy
> Being hugged and kissed.

After the Civil War, American tourism increased, becoming a patriotic demonstration as well as a pleasure. But people in search of the sublime were skipping the Falls and heading west, to the vast canyons and craggy mountains now seen as the iconic American landscape. Niagara was still a tourist destination, but it was even less about nature and more about social interaction than before. In the uneasy Reconstruction years, newlyweds at Niagara were a comforting sign that this nation really did have a unified national culture. Popular periodicals such as *Frank Leslie's Illustrated News-*

paper and *Harper's Weekly* ran pictures of honeymooning couples at the Falls throughout the 1870s and 1880s.

The Niagara honeymoon in the nineteenth century was a social trip, even though it was subtly acknowledged to have more private implications. Being a honeymooner meant taking part in what the era called "married love." Isabel March, the new bride in William Dean Howells' 1871 novel *Their Wedding Journey*, is determined not to hold her husband's hand in public or rest her head on his shoulder, because she will be embarrassed to be recognized as a newlywed. "My one horror in life," she declares, "is an evident bride."

But Isabel is not simply ashamed to be newly married. She's also keenly aware that her husband has "been there before" as they visit the sites. In the nineteenth century, single men traveled; single women did not. Introducing the bride to the landscape was simply the more public of the husband's postwedding introductions. Isabel insists on approaching Niagara through Buffalo, because that's how her new husband arrived there the first time he went.

The journey to the Falls thus came to represent something that could only be talked about in metaphor. Oscar Wilde took advantage of the double language to make what is one of the most quoted—and misquoted—quips about the Falls. "Every American bride is taken there," he wrote upon returning from his own visit to Niagara, "and the sight of the stupendous waterfall must certainly be one of the earliest, if not the keenest, disappointments in American married life."

As I'm trying to find the third-floor registration area, I notice that some of the Red Hatters have decorated their doors, which gives me scary flashbacks to cheerleading camp. I'm still processing this when I come upon a sort of shrine, a huge flat-screen monitor hanging on a purple-velvet-draped stand and lit by two theatrical spotlights. A video is playing footage of other Red Hat conventions—they've been held in New Orleans, Dallas, Las Vegas and Disneyland, among other places—intercut with snippets of Mike Harline, the society's official "Troubador," in black Western gear and a purple shirt, strumming a guitar and singing.

At the registration area, I collect my press pass and meet the Red Hatters' director of marketing, Carol Castelli. She's wearing a name tag that reads Baroness of the Brand. Everyone at Hatquarters, the organization's office, has a faux-royal title, as do members. Chapter heads call themselves Queen Mothers. The group's founder, Sue Ellen Cooper, is known as the Exalted Queen Mother. Her best friend and cofounder, Linda Murphy, is the Esteemed Vice Mother.

Baroness Carol is a petite, smiley woman with perfectly layered and highlighted blond hair. She's wearing the regalia required of women under fifty: lavender outfit and pink hat.

"This started out as grassroots; it was never meant to be a business," Carol tells me right off, sounding a theme I will hear often in the coming three days. Then, with no trace of irony, she takes me to see the Red Hat store. Set up in four adjoining conference rooms on the fifth floor—8,000 square feet according to the convention press release—the store is a potpourri of Red Hat merchandise: purple dresses, sweatshirts, T-shirts, pajamas, gloves, Red Hat jewelry, tea sets, teddy bears, license-plate holders, stationery and of course, hats, red, pink and even purple, because in their birthday month, Red Hatters are "authorized" to reverse their colors.

"These hats are all customizable," Carol tells me. "They get them like this but then they decorate them. You won't see two that are alike." She holds up a wide-brimmed, bright red sun hat, and I think *someone's been doing her marketing research*. Anyone who reads trend analysis—or the "Consumed" column in *The New York Times*—knows that customizability is highly valued by today's consumer market.

Not far from the hats, a life-size cardboard effigy of Mike Harline is flashing a come-hither look next to a stack of CDs titled *I'm in Love with a Red Hat Girl*.

Carol has to get back to overseeing registration, so she lets me wander around on my own for a while. The store is already filled with ladies in vibrant purple and red outfits. Some of their hats are indeed outrageously decorated. After a few minutes, I realize everyone is glancing at me: in my tan corduroy jacket and jeans, I look like a Padres fan at a Cardinals home game.

I drift into the room featuring tea sets. On the windowsill there's a poster for a new RHS book, *Designer Scrapbooks the Red Hat Society Way*. Behind it, in the spring sunlight, I am almost surprised to see the Falls, thundering down in their habitual froth of white. They seem so understated.

In the Jazz Age, sex came out of the closet. Freud's *Three Essays on the Theory of Sexuality* had made the rounds. Havelock Ellis, the English sexologist, had issued six of his seven *Studies in the Psychology of Sex* declaring that "sex lies at the root of life." Victorian prudery disappeared and everyone, it seemed, had a one-track mind. Nowhere was this more evident than at Niagara. The Falls, formerly the metaphor for awkward devirginization, became a code word for "sex marathon." Popular depictions of the Niagara honeymoon focused on the new, sexier meaning of the trip by depicting the bride as a flapper.

The flapper was recognized by her signature look: short, baggy dress, dancing shoes, turban hat, bobbed hair. But she was more than just a style. Empowered by the vote, disillusioned by the Great War, and mobilized by the ascendancy of the automobile, the flapper embodied modernity. As a flapper named Jane explained to a *New Republic* writer: "Women have come down off the pedestal lately. They are tired of this mysterious-feminine-charm stuff. Maybe it goes with independence, earning your own living and voting and all that."

An article in the *Niagara Falls Gazette* from 1927 relates the story of a couple found sleeping on Goat Island. When questioned, they tell the reporter they have just eloped. The groom's father, they explain, wanted him to marry an old-fashioned "Gibson Girl . . . who wore trailing skirts." But young James "preferred the flapper type, with rolled stockings, bobbed hair, and whatnot." He apparently found it in Edith, who, according to the reporter, wore a two-piece suit, a turban, two rings, and a "boyish bob."

Things had changed—even the institution of marriage. In 1926, reporter Allan Harding visited Niagara to explore how. His *American Magazine* article declares, "The Honeymoon Trail Still Leads to Niagara Falls." Harding describes a few days he spent hanging around the Falls, observing flapper brides and their grooms and talking to tourist industry experts like the head porter at the Cataract House. They tell him how honeymooning at Niagara has changed—it's not such an upscale affair anymore and the honeymooners don't stay as long. More importantly, as one guide puts it, "Young people today ain't ashamed of being married!" In other words, they aren't so embarrassed about sex. They're happy to discuss their newlywed status, and unembarrassed in their new role as lovers.

In fact, they're even willing to study up for it. In King Vidor's 1928 film *The Crowd*, a typical young American man named John Sims takes a Niagara honeymoon. On the train there, he's preparing for bed in the dressing room when he leans over and a book falls out of his pocket: *What a Young Husband Ought to Know* by Sylvanus Stall. Two older men watching through the open door laughingly return it.

Karen Dubinsky, in her history of Niagara honeymoons, points out that the first few decades of the twentieth century saw an explosion of newly detailed "marriage manuals" teaching couples how to succeed in bed. Influenced by the new science of sex, these guides were still prim in their explanations of "normal" sexuality, but they were an improvement on the previous century's repressive attitudes: they even acknowledged the existence of the female orgasm, and gave explicit tips for achieving it. Unlike their Victorian predecessors, who might be happy to lie back and think of England, modern women had come to expect that "erotic fulfillment was an integral part of a successful alliance."

You might say that a market need had been established for sexual fulfillment. But how do you sell that? Selling sex manuals was one way. Selling honeymoons would quickly become another.

At the first night's dinner, the effort of feeding 920 women has the Sheraton staff frazzled. Carol is answering nonstop questions. The turbulent sea of purple is punctuated by bursts of camera flash. Troubador Mike jams away on the flat screen. Waitresses swivel through the crowd with cakes held aloft. The hats have gotten crazier: fake fur, explosions of feathers, tulle, long ostrich plumes, sequins. No one is out of uniform; the women stick to the dress code with the avidity of junior high school girls wearing the right jeans. It's the kind of mass trend adoption that makes VPs of sales and marketing hyperventilate at PowerPoint presentations.

I try to imagine the scene with 920 men. It's hard, because first of all, I can't imagine men standing in a buffet line. Somehow it just seems obvious that 920 men would be served sitting down. Then there's the silliness. You can't imagine large numbers of men dressing up in goofy getups unless perhaps they were sports fans of some sort. I envision 920 men in All-Blacks jerseys and face paint, spontaneously breaking into a haka. All I can think is that if I encountered such a scene I would be inclined to go to my room and bolt the door.

The problem is, I can't imagine men wanting to hang out together just by virtue of being men, or even men of a certain age. Sure, there are secret societies and power men's groups like Bohemian Grove, where the Manhattan Project purportedly got its start, but they're covert, with no need to advertise their connection. Is it a function of powerlessness, this urge to band together in a public way? Something about the women in their bright colors and sparkly fake jewelry makes me think of vibrant tropical fish, surviving in rainbow-hued glory in part because they've evolved the protective mechanism of schooling together.

The Hatters have sorted themselves out and found places to sit with their buffet spoils when Sue Ellen and Linda make their entrance. Lights low, they proceed in to the tune of "Roll Out the Barrel," escorted by a member of the Royal Canadian Mounted Police. The Mountie, a strapping Ken doll of a man, wields the Maple Leaf with taut formality as they make their way to the stage. There, standing in front of a projected image of Niagara Falls bedecked with the American and Canadian flags, Sue Ellen and Linda welcome everyone to "our first truly international conference." They go through a long process of recognizing the thirty-three states and several provinces that have sent attendees. Four large video monitors display maps of the United States and Canada. Special visitors are called out: "Gutsy Gals" who come alone, mother-daughter combinations, ladies with April birthdays, the person from farthest away, and a group of seven sisters who reunited here. The exalted leaders lead the crowd in a special pledge—*Oh Canada! I am ready to roll and have barrels of fun . . .* —and then, as they are getting down to the duller business of telling everyone to wear their lanyards, the video monitor camera zooms in on the Mountie, standing stiff at attention, and the room erupts in rowdy catcalls.

Eliminate one pen stroke and one letter from Niagara and you get Viagra, the pharmaceutical miracle by which older men are reclaiming their mojo. In the few short years it's been around, Viagra has opened the tap on a veritable cataract of sales: impotence drugs are now a $2.5 billion market. The pill's Niagara association is no mistake: as a symbol for potency—size, power, force—the Falls are unsurpassed, even before you throw in the honeymooners. When Cary Grant tells Grace Kelly in 1955's *To Catch a Thief* that what she needs is "two weeks with a good man at Niagara Falls," no one thinks he's talking about boat rides.

Throughout the thirties and forties, the Falls were sex's Hollywood stand-in. The absurd idea of two people taking a "just friends" trip there is the premise of 1940's *Lucky Partners*, starring Ginger Rogers. Two people who hate each other are locked in a Niagara hotel room in producer Hal Roach's 1941 *Niagara Falls*, with the predictable result that they are married by breakfast. Upright prosecuting attorney Fred MacMurray falls for shoplifter Barbara Stanwyck in 1940's *Remember the Night*, but can't bring himself to say so until they happen to pass through Niagara. "You know I love you," he blurts as they stand at Table Rock. They stroll the promenade, and as they pass behind a bank of lights pointed at the waterfall, she tries to talk sense into him. But once Niagara is in view again, the magic returns and they fall into a clinch. "You know where we're going for our honeymoon?" he tells her. "Niagara Falls."

"But darling," she replies after a sultry Stanwyckian pause. "We're already there."

That's the power of the waterfall. But it's also the power of advertising.

Hollywood product placement was just one angle. In 1928, the New York State Scenic Trails Association, joining forces with the Niagara Falls Chamber of Commerce, renamed the highway from Rochester to Niagara "The Honeymoon Trail." Ten fifty-foot billboards were erected along the road, each bearing the Honeymoon Trail logo: two hearts, pierced by an arrow.

In 1934, *Bride's* magazine was launched. The commodification of the American wedding and honeymoon was under way. Throughout the 1930s and '40s, as Dubinsky puts it, "travel, privacy, service industry hospitality, consumption, romance, and sex were all becoming an integral part of the honeymoon, and these were exactly the ingredients that tourist entrepreneurs began to commodify and promote." But they did more than just sell honeymoons as packages. Admen realized it wasn't enough to bring sexy back. They went a step further, implying that in buying a sexually gratifying honeymoon, you were buying long-term marital bliss.

In 1941, the Niagara Falls (N.Y.) Chamber of Commerce organized the Niagara Falls Honeymoon Club for alumni honeymooners. Newspapers across the country announced that the longest-married couple joining the club would receive an all-expenses-paid return visit. Mr. and Mrs. Albert B. Praul of Philadelphia won the prize, having honeymooned at the Falls sixty-five years earlier. Their media-friendly return to the Falls included stays at the Cataract House in Canada and the Hotel Niagara in New York, a show of "old-time Niagara" lantern slides, a dance, a ceremony at Old Fort Niagara and a ride in the carriage President McKinley took to his fateful date with assassination at the 1901 Pan-American Exposition. They were also given the task of christening the new Rainbow Bridge's walkway the "Honeymooners' Promenade" and choosing the best spot on it for admiring the Falls. Two cupids were erected there so future honeymooners would know exactly where to stand. The trip ended with a gala premiere of the film *Niagara Falls*. Quite a whirlwind schedule for a couple who were eighty-nine and eighty-seven.

In seizing on an older couple to promote the Falls honeymoon, the tourism promoters hit the jackpot. They equated sex with a long-married couple. Now, in buying a honeymoon, you no longer got something to do. You got something to be.

• • •

The Prauls would probably have enjoyed the opening night fes-
tivities at "Barrels of Fun." Like them, the Hatters seem ready to
party. Music has come on, and the conventioneers are on their
feet. Near me, a woman who must be eighty grabs one of the
few men around, a twenty-something Hatquarters employee, and
shows him her hips don't lie. The poor Mountie is still standing
at attention onstage under sweltering klieg lights: Sue Ellen has
announced his availability for photo ops, and the line to get a
snapshot at his side goes halfway around the thousand-seat room.
Carol, at my side in her fuzzy lavender hat, is keeping me informed
on the party's progress: "They're starting the conga line." "We've
got one taking off her clothes." After a few jazzy songs, "I Love the
Nightlife" by Alicia Bridges comes on and everyone dances and
sings along.

One of the things you might hope for from a powerful coali-
tion of fun-loving older women is that they might wrench sexuality from the hot little hands of youth. Can the Red Hats take a
cue from Rene Russo and Susan Sarandon and make being over
fifty sexy, even for women without personal trainers and great
bone structure? That's what I want to see on opening night, but
somehow it's not what seems to be going on here. What's happening here looks like license. The women are in a big group, and it
gives them freedom to misbehave, which is what acting sexual is
for women who aren't young. In fact, the older the woman, the
more willing she seems to act out. I expect at any moment to see
a granny hook a waiter with her cane, or the Mountie emerge
bedraggled from a scrum of purple velour and feather boas. Like
the dressing up, it's over the top, and in that way, it feels compen-
satory. It's like the names the Red Hat chapters give themselves:
Ravishing Redhats, Beautiful Outstanding Babes, Red Hat Gang
of Purple Persuasion, Babes of Joyland. It feels like an act. Men
take Viagra so they can continue to have sex. The Red Hatters'
game of dress-up feels almost calculated to avoid it.

All in all, it's giving me an overwhelming urge to make time
with the bartender. I find him in the corner of the giant room. He
has shiny dark eyes, brown hair that curls at the ends and a tenta-
tive demeanor. His name is Gary. Gary grew up in St. Catharines,

nearby, and he thinks the ladies are "fun." I down a glass of wine and press Gary on his comment, asking if he can imagine such a group for men.

"There is a group of older men who have their convention here," he says. "They're called the Jesters. They're all millionaires and it's supposed to be a big debauchery. They take a whole floor and drink expensive booze and have lots of single women walking around like a men's club."

"That's just my point!" I say, but Gary is taking one of the purple tickets the ladies must exchange for glasses of cheap pinot grigio and doesn't hear me.

The Queen Mother of a Pennsylvania chapter approaches in elbow-length red lace gloves. "Aren't they floozy?" she says with delight when I admire them. The bar, it turns out, is a good place to chat with Hatters. Charming Gary seems willing to overlook my lack of purple tickets, so I'm still there drinking about two hours later, when the Mountie is finally released from photographic servitude. I see him striding my way, flag aloft, and trot out to intercept him. He's hot and sweaty and seems almost frightened when I show him my "press" ID and ask him how he feels after his ordeal.

"Well, I do this for a living," he manages to say. "I *am* a constable." Before he can elaborate (a constable?) a couple of ladies materialize to drag him off for a belated photo. I figure that's the end of him and return to my post as Gary's chief barfly, but a few minutes later I see him steaming toward me in a determined beeline.

"People don't usually have contact with the police unless something has gone wrong," he begins, and then launches into a high-speed, full-sentence articulation of the importance of public relations for law enforcement even if it requires him to spend three hours under hot lights in full dress uniform with his arms around an endless stream of garish grannies. When he's done, he hands me his card, and, in a move that stops every conversation within 40 feet, strips down to his T-shirt and jodhpurs.

No one goes near him after that. Sans the getup, he's a living, breathing man.

• • •

After World War II, Niagara's honeymoon promoters aimed to leverage the postwar travel boom. Magazines dedicated to tourism sprang up, like *Holiday*, which declared in June 1946 that "Niagara Falls is still America's honeymoon capital." The Niagara Falls, Ontario, Chamber of Commerce began issuing "honeymoon certificates" in 1949, handing out more than 42,000 of them in ten years. The auto industry was on board as comarketer. A magazine called *Friends*, published by General Motors and handed out by Chevrolet dealers, ran a piece in June 1950 called "Here's Why They Honeymoon at Niagara." In it, a variety of couples give their reasons for choosing the Falls. Andrew and Mary DiCicco of Detroit, for instance, chose the Falls "partly because of its romance and partly because it was conveniently close to Detroit—motorists can drive from there to Niagara Falls in less than six hours."

The postwar Niagara honeymoon was now promoted as an American tradition: a slew of articles about Falls honeymoon history appeared. Honeymooning at the Falls was every American's birthright. The *Niagara Falls Gazette* ran a 1946 feature titled "Lore and Sentiment Behind Niagara's Fame as Nation's Honeymoon Capital." Referring to the waterfall as "sentiment in liquid form," they recounted the results of an informal survey of visiting couples about why they came to Niagara. "Eleven couples queried in succession," the paper reports, said, "Our parents came here. We could have gone anywhere, but somehow, this just seemed right." And why not? The Falls were an American icon, the Canadians our allies, and a trip to Niagara a way to touch the American past. Returning soldiers, many articles declared, had seen enough of Europe. They'd rather enjoy the sights of their own nation now.

A visit to Niagara was, like much of postwar culture, a reassuring encounter with what the nation had just been fighting for: the American way of life. What did that mean? It went beyond democracy and freedom to embrace a host of lifestyle ideals valorized as simply the way things should be: the wholesome family life of *Leave It to Beaver* and *Father Knows Best*, the small-town community values of Norman Rockwell and *Life* magazine, the modernity and progress represented by the torrent of household consumer goods Americans adopted en masse: refrigerators, televisions, cars. And of course, the "traditional" gender roles of *I Love Lucy, The Honeymooners, Marjorie Morningstar*, and the era's fashions: tiny waists, full feminine skirts and high heels for women; gray flannel suits for men. The marriage manuals of the era affirmed the natural order: the man was to dominate and the woman was to let him.

Marilyn's star turn as Rose Loomis turned this stereotype over and examined its seamy underside. Her foil, Polly Cutler, played by Jean Peters, is a mid-century vision of the perfect helpmeet: pretty, impeccably dressed and sensible. She has a bombshell body but doesn't show it off; her husband Ray has to teach her how to pose in a bikini. Rose, on the other hand, is a wife gone bad. Like the Falls, she's a feminine force, with the emphasis shifted from beauty to power. The movie publicity made the connection explicit: "Marilyn Monroe and Niagara," crowed the poster, "a raging torrent of emotion that even nature can't control!"

But that too was an act. Nature may not have been able to control the Falls, but man now could. Having been harnessed for half a century, the post-treaty Falls were completely taken in hand. So too Rose Loomis, who for all her sultry attempts at running wild, ends up strangled and left sprawled on the floor of a bell tower. She may be a raging torrent, but only until the man in charge stops her for good.

The "realness" of Rose Loomis—and by implication of Marilyn—is questioned several times in *Niagara*, even before anyone suspects her of plotting to kill her husband. In one instance, early on in the film, she emerges from her cabin during an evening soiree in a slinky, low-cut, hot-pink dress. As she leans against the wall, the camera caressing her form, Ray Cutler nudges his wife Polly and demands, "Why don't you ever get a dress like that?" Polly, her eyes lit up with admiration for the other woman, responds, "Listen, for a dress like that, you've gotta start laying plans when you're about thirteen!" The line gets its laugh, but what does it mean, really? What is it Rose Loomis is supposed to have laid plans for? Her figure? It's the sort of suspicion that settles on sexy older women today—think Demi Moore. A body like that must be manufactured.

Nunnally Johnson, who wrote *How to Marry a Millionaire*, called Marilyn "a phenomenon of nature . . . like Niagara Falls and the Grand Canyon." In contrast, Billy Wilder, who directed her in *Some Like It Hot*, called her a "DuPont product." Ironically, DuPont owned one of Niagara's many flourishing chemical plants in the fifties; they were one of the industrial clients whose need for cheap power was causing the Falls to face a realness crisis of their own. Wilder was right, but so was Johnson. Marilyn *was* Niagara: natural and artificial, her beauty belying a toxic underside. She was an icon, a victim, a marvel. Like the Falls, she defies description: all her films include moments when onlookers are struck speechless at the sight of her.

Marilyn, on location for *Niagara*, toured several of Niagara's factories. She had the body. She had the act. And she knew how much machinery was behind it all.

On Saturday, I wake with a headache. Cheap wine and cute bartenders: a lethal combination. I get dressed, but I don't need to: Saturday's first event is a pajama bingo breakfast.

When I get to the conference center, Hatters are pouring into the Great Room in purple pj's, fuzzy bathrobes, slippers, nightcaps, muumuus. One group sports shortie nightgowns and red fishnets. Some carry teddy bears or dolls. Carol seats me at a table with the Red Hat Poppers from Nazareth, Pennsylvania, who are all wearing hats made out of red bras decorated with spangles, feathers and sequins. The stiff cups create a sort of turban effect: half flapper, half alien.

"You know what you have to look forward to," one of them tells me. "When you get older, you can be as nutsy as you wanna be!" And I was hoping for *gravitas*.

There are two other ladies at the table, from a chapter in Portland, Oregon. "I love to travel and my husband doesn't," explains an Oregon lady named Clara, who looks a little like the mother on *Golden Girls*. "He figures the Red Hat Society gets him off the hook." The Oregon ladies seem abashed by the amount of attention the Nazareth bra ladies are getting. Clara keeps trying to show them her shoe, a flip-flop she decorated with a purple plastic scrubbie. But Hatters are arriving at the table in a steady stream, requesting photo ops with the bras. Clara clutches her flip-flop under the table, waiting for her moment to jump in. Each time she starts to pull it out, another camera-toting bra fan turns up. Finally there's a lull and she brings out her prize. The Nazareth ladies look only vaguely interested. Her face falls. Immediately, they dial up their enthusiasm. They get out their cameras and take pictures of her creation.

The room quiets instantly when the bingo session begins. Cards and markers are distributed, and special games are announced (the T, the Cross, the Box—who knew there were so many bingo variations?). Concentration is as intense as an SAT sitting at Andover. When someone wins, her table gives a jubilant cheer. There's a break after game seven, so everyone can decompress. The ladies are encouraged to stand. Latonya, an employee from Hatquarters, gets on stage and sings a plucky rendition of "Love Will Keep Us Together." The Hatters dance and sing along. Some stand on chairs. I'm surprised to find myself touched. Maybe it's the hangover. But whose heart wouldn't melt at the sight of 900 pajamaed grannies getting down?

"This is recess," Red Hat Society founder Sue Ellen Cooper tells me. We're in her corner suite on the Sheraton's twentieth floor on Saturday afternoon. She's lying on the bed fully dressed when I arrive. I like her instantly. She and Linda are taking turns having their makeup done by a young Goth girl. Framed in the picture window is a perfect view of the Falls.

Sue Ellen has had one of those colorful fits-and-starts careers not unusual among upper-middle-class wives and mothers— part-time graphic artist, painter of murals, writer of cute books, inventor of "That Earring Thing," an earring-holder marketed to teens, and now, driving force behind a woman's social group. She has an edge I didn't expect, a vaguely sarcastic yet down-to-earth canniness. She doesn't smile as easily as Linda. When I ask her questions, her sharp eyes pin me for a moment, and then she answers, unguardedly but thoughtfully. "We really didn't know where we were going with this," she tells me at several points, in a voice that betrays a suspicion I won't believe her. She returns regularly, like any good CEO, to the core message of her brand: that Hatters are women who have earned a well-deserved break for fun.

In their communications, the society always foregrounds this idea: "now it's time for us." But women who turned fifty in the last five years were born between 1950 and 1955. They belong to the Baby Boomer cohort: raised during the sixties, they came of age in the years between the summer of love and the end of Vietnam. A cynic might claim it's no surprise that the "Me Generation" would turn menopause into a festival of self-celebration. Following a rash of cultural critics, starting with David Brooks, who have derided Boomers as materialistic revolutionary sellouts, a cynic might see the Red Hatters as yet another example of how Boomer idealism has been co-opted by corporate culture. The kids who were going to remake the world—end the war, liberate women, launch a sexual revolution and save the planet—have become instead a marketer's dream: an army of affluent, educated luxury-lovers enamored of their own pop-cultural past. The Red Hat Web site declares their goal is "world domination," but they're about as countercultural as a $300 ticket to a Rolling Stones concert. It's just another instance (our friendly cynic might say) of bending the language of revolution to the cause of fun: hanging out, dressing up, listening to seventies music. And shopping. *Newsweek* called the Hatters a "red and purple buying machine."

All this has gone through my head. In fact, I arrived at Sue Ellen's room envisioning myself as Joan Didion, asking the hard questions. But Sue Ellen's unabashed openness takes me by surprise. It's clear that she believes in what she's doing. She tells me how celebrities refuse to be associated with the society, and how a company came to them wanting to market Red Hat coffins. She turned them down. "We're not going just anywhere with this," she declares, looking as fierce as a woman in purple sequins can look, which is pretty fierce. "People could just ruin it." I raise the topic of the society's purpose, and she returns to her core message.

"We all kind of know that we have been expected to take care of everybody and that's okay," she tells me, "but that's not what this is about."

I think of a bumper sticker I saw in the Red Hat store: It's All About Me.

Soft-pedaling, I ask Sue Ellen about the Baby Boomers who would be joining up now, pointing out that they are not a cohort particularly known for self-sacrifice. She gets it immediately.

"I hadn't thought of that," she says, shrugging. "Maybe they won't need us as much."

That, I can't help thinking, was exactly the right thing to say.

I walk with Sue Ellen and Linda to the next event, the "Royal Canadian MounTEA Party." Hatters stop us all along the hall, asking for pictures or just ogling the women with starstruck glee. The queens extract themselves kindly and head for the stage. Carol finds a seat for me next to two ladies from Ohio. They have a bear named Lucille that sings "I Wanna Be Loved by You." Whenever they feel ignored, they make the bear sing.

Over the course of the twentieth century, weddings—and honeymoons—evolved from practical, family-based events into commodified products for the mass market. Everyone went to the same places and did the same things. You might expect a revolt against this sameness, and indeed there was one. But instead of taking back the right to live, rather than buy, life experiences, consumers turned weddings and honeymoons into the lavish orgies of conspicuous consumption that now drive the multibillion-dollar wedding industry. Today, you can distinguish your wedding by how much you spend on it, and your honeymoon by how exotic and distant your destination. And it's important to do so, because in the culture of "you are what you buy," your honeymoon tells the world—and maybe you—who you are. Honeymoons are not even talked about in terms of "getting to know" each other or spending time together as a married couple; they are, in the words of one popular contemporary guide, "a well-deserved break from the stresses of getting married, a delightful interlude in which you decompress after the hubbub of your wedding." Having just spent nearly an entire book telling you how to assemble a huge, overblown affair, the authors tell you with no trace of irony that another expensive purchase will be required to help you recover from it.

Niagara Falls fell out of fashion in this world. It's no longer exclusive enough or expensive enough to make a splash in what one critic calls the "wedding-industrial complex." Canadian Niagara is a family-fun park, packed to the gills with franchise restaurants and kid-friendly attractions. The Brock Plaza—called the General Brock Hotel when Marilyn stayed there during the filming of *Niagara*—now features indoor connections to the Fallsview Water-park, Marvel Superheroes Adventure City, the Rainforest Café, and the MGM Studios Plaza. As for American Niagara, it's shabby and decrepit. Joe DiMaggio's glamorous Hotel Niagara is now a grubby, unrenovated Ramada Inn with a nightly $11 all-you-can-eat Indian buffet. I've eaten it and it's not bad, but still. You can't imagine today's newlyweds, having just shelled out $23,000—the average cost of an American wedding—decompressing from the hubbub with some romantic Spiderman trivia, followed by eleven dollars' worth of lukewarm curry on a styrofoam plate.

To be fair, Niagara honeymoons started going out of fashion before the affluenza epidemic hit America in the 1980s. By the seventies, reporters were declaring the Niagara wedding trip dead. In the sexual revolution, the honeymoon was repackaged as a Playboy-mansion-style sex romp, and the Poconos became the hot place to go. In 1977, 10 percent of honeymooners were heading there to indulge in the exotic decor, in-room pools, specialty cocktails, and planned activities devised by the honeymoon resort industry. Forget about remote Fijian islands with spas in grass huts: Niagara couldn't even compete with champagne-glass-shaped whirlpool tubs.

Still, Niagara's honeymoon industry is continually reinventing itself and being reinvented by others. Today, gay marriage might rewrite the honeymoon script. Responding to Canadian prime minister Jean Chrétien's June 2003 announcement that Canada would seek to legalize same-sex marriages, CNN columnist Bill Schneider announced that "Niagara Falls, the honeymoon destination that straddles the U.S.-Canadian border, has taken on a whole new meaning." And so it had. Niagara, true to form, lost no time in repackaging itself. Many Ontario hotels quickly added a "Same-Sex Weddings" section to their Web sites. Sheraton, hosts of the Hatter convention, declared themselves "proud to host many same-sex marriage ceremonies, receptions and honeymoons." People seemed to love the image of gay couples flooding the Falls. The *Village Voice* began an article on Canada's legalization with the story of two men so eager to wed they jumped in their car and headed for Niagara, only calling Lambda Legal for advice from the road. The Web site Gay Niagara optimistically declared: "Niagara Falls has been the honeymoon capital of the world for decades. Now it's becoming the gay and lesbian marriage capital of the world!"

Gay-marriage-haters also frequently invoked Niagara Falls. A writer in the *National Review* envisioned a "stream of American same-sex couples shuffling off to the Canadian side of Niagara Falls for their marriage licenses." With Massachusetts's legalization of gay marriage, opponents raised the specter of a certain town in the state becoming a "gay Niagara Falls." Provincetown's tourism director joyfully took up the banner.

The tone of these statements evinces an odd protectiveness toward the Falls. But why? Ken Connor of the Family Research Council summed it up for CNN. "Same-sex marriage devalues the real thing," huffed Mr. Connor, "in the same way that counterfeits devalue the authentic."

The artificial rears its head again. Postmodern theorists love to talk about how the things we consider "natural" are in fact constructed: gender, sexuality, so-called "normative" behavior. Marilyn Monroe provoked the anxiety that femininity might be an act in the 1950s; by the 1980s, the age of Madonna, Prince, and RuPaul, the "performativity of gender" was being celebrated, at least by literary theorists and self-proclaimed gender outlaws. Femininity—and masculinity too—were now understood as performances, behaviors shaped to fit made-up codes established less by nature than by culture.

After all, if there's a unifying theme to Niagara Falls attractions—wax museums, miniature towns, water parks—it's that the world can be endlessly remade. Maybe postcamp appropriation of the commodified Niagara honeymoon will wrench it back from the hands of corporate culture. Gay couples taking part in Niagara honeymoons are rewriting an American tradition, opening it to new kinds of lived experience.

And what of the Red Hat ladies? Are they too getting inside a tradition and busting it open, making more possibilities for life lived outside the narrow strictures of manufactured market needs? Or are they buying into yet another one of late capitalism's cheap tricks—the marketing of life experiences—and putting it on their Red Hat platinum cards? I came to Niagara thinking I knew the answer to that, but by Sunday, I'm not so sure.

The last event of the "Barrels of Fun" convention is the Sunday breakfast talent show. The tables outside the Great Room are stocked with brochures about a Red Hat cruise. Sue Ellen and Linda introduce the show with pitches for upcoming events: a Chicago convention, a new cookbook, a traveling musical called *Hats*. As a parting gift, Carol gives me a press packet, an impressively sophisticated folder with clippings, newsletters, a copy of *Lifestyle*, and a four-color summary of the society's history and mission. There's no doubt that this organization is a marketing juggernaut. And its market is growing fast.

And then the talent show begins. I'm standing at the side of the room, toward the front, so I can get a good view. There's Flaming Agnes, a former dancer who shimmies fabulously through moves last seen in pre-Castro Cuba. There's Bertha Rose Parks, a gray-haired little lady in a purple cowgirl dress who tap dances her heart out to "Grandma's Feather Bed." There's Karen Oke (Carol describes her as a "shy church secretary") who wears a ruffled dress and fishnets and sings a song she wrote herself. There's the Red Happy Tappers, a group of eight ladies in red cowgirl minidresses, who shuffle off to Buffalo to the tune of "It Doesn't Get Countrier Than This." And there's the Steppin' Out Red Hatters, a group of five ladies dressed as Marilyn—white low-cut dresses, blond wigs, elbow-length gloves, heels, and a rainbow of feather boas—lip-synching "I Wanna be Loved by You" and "Diamonds Are a Girl's Best Friend."

The audience is hooked from the opening line.

The Marilyns are of assorted heights. Their makeup is a little garish. Some of them look perfectly at home in their dresses and vamp it up with their boas; others clutch at the mass of feathers as if it's a fluffy security blanket. The group's choreographed dance moves are simple, and sometimes the Marilyns are in sync, sometimes not. A couple of them watch the others, like nervous kindergarteners in the school play. But nobody cares. By the time they're through, the crowd is on its feet cheering and so, remarkably, am I.

I'm reminded of a conversation I had with the ladies at my pajama-breakfast table the previous morning. When I asked them whether they were enjoying the convention's Niagara locale, they all nodded eagerly. The bra hats bobbed up and down.

"It's a good place for dreaming," one of them said.

Of course, dreamland has a dark side. The more Niagara transformed itself into fantasyland, the harder it became to keep the dream from morphing into a nightmare.

Eight

THE BOMB AND
TOM BROKAW'S DESK

WHAT HIGH SCHOOL PRINCIPAL checks out his football field—
with a geiger counter? That's what I'm pondering late one sunny
afternoon as I stand outside the fence of Niagara Catholic High
School's gridiron. Having read EPA reports, I know the answer: a
high school principal in Niagara Falls. A principal whose school lies
about two miles west of Love Canal. Whose parking lot, according
to the EPA, occasionally yields up mysterious waste drums. Who
watches his team, the Niagara Catholic Patriots, play atop a field
that doubles as a Superfund site. Whose town—even as its natural wonder was being rebuilt by the Army Corps of Engineers and
publicized by Marilyn Monroe—was quietly playing a key role in
developing, and disposing of waste from, America's atomic arsenal.

For most communities, radioactive 50-yard lines and barrels
of chemicals bobbing up in school parking lots would be bizarre
anomalies; in Niagara Falls, they're unpleasantly familiar. The
town has had a hazardous waste problem ever since its waterfall
was harnessed for power. Today the Environmental Protection
Agency lists ten active Superfund sites in the city of Niagara Falls,

three on the National Priorities List, meaning they are dangerous enough to be eligible for long-term remediation. The New York State Department of Environmental Protection lists 649 hazardous waste "areas of concern" in Erie and Niagara Counties, and designates about half the downtown of Niagara Falls as brownfields, former industrial sites where redevelopment is complicated by toxic contamination. And the Army Corps of Engineers' environmental cleanup program for former nuclear weapons plants, the Formerly Utilized Sites Remedial Action Program, or FUSRAP, has more locations on the Niagara frontier than anywhere else in the nation: seven radioactively contaminated sites within ten miles of America's waterfall.

Many of these sites were little-known until 2000, when *USA Today* published a multipart series detailing the extensive nuclear contamination of people and communities by government contractors during the Manhattan Project and the Cold War. Even now, few people outside the region are aware of Niagara's key role in the nuclear weapons complex. This is typical of the area's environmental legacy. Like the toxic brew in the landfills, the history of both the Manhattan Project and its aftermath is covered over and hard to access, but bits of it burble to the surface from time to time. Cesium-137 in Love Canal. A silo full of radium in Lewiston. Radioactive sludge in the groundwater at Tonawanda. Roads and driveways throughout the region with gamma readings above background levels. Those are the things I learn about not from talking to activists, but from reading official government documents. Love Canal became a national byword for ecological disaster in the late 1970s, but few people in the nation realized what many Niagara locals knew in their hearts: that ditch full of toxic chemicals was not the end of the story; it was the tip of the iceberg.

The chemical industry began the practice of treating Niagara Falls, or at least its margins, as a dump. Throughout the forties and fifties, as dumping went on unabated, residents complained of noxious fumes emanating from sewers, mysterious barrels in vacant lots and substances that caused coughing or headaches or burns.

What they didn't know was that a new danger had been added to the mix: radiation.

When most of us think of the Manhattan Project's race to build the atomic bomb, we think of physicists scribbling equations at Columbia and mushroom clouds in the New Mexico desert. The National Park Service recently proposed three locations for a national park commemorating America's atomic legacy: the national laboratory at Oak Ridge, Tennessee; the testing grounds at Los Alamos, New Mexico; and the plutonium production reservation at Hanford, Washington. But there were important sites all across the nation. The original offices of the Manhattan Engineer District, the army branch that oversaw the project, were in Lower Manhattan at 270 Broadway—two blocks from where I live. I like to walk by and imagine poker-faced generals inside, using code words to discuss the big shipment of uranium that was stored in a 20th Street warehouse, now home to trendy art galleries. The building at 270 Broadway, a state office complex, was converted to luxury condominiums a few years ago—four-bedroom units started at $4.6 million. I doubt many buyers realized they were buying a piece of atomic history along with their Sub-Zero refrigerators and Philippe Starck soaking tubs.

In the same way, few people think "Niagara" when they think of the Bomb. "When the TV specials speak of radiation problems," local activist Don Finch wrote in an opinion column for the *Tonawanda News* in 1998, "you will hear the names Los Alamos, Hanford, and Oak Ridge mentioned time after time. Yet, Tonawanda is NEVER mentioned." Nor is Lockport, or Buffalo, or Niagara Falls. But the factories of the Niagara frontier played a key role in making Fat Man, Little Boy, and all the unnamed bombs that came after those first entrants in the nuclear arms race. In 2000, the Department of Energy released a list of 336 facilities that had government nuclear contracts and would be covered under the new Energy Employees Occupational Illness Compensation Act, which guaranteed medical expenses to laborers made sick by their work on atomic weapons. Eight sites were in Tennessee, and two were in Washington. New Mexico had ten, Nevada four. New York State had thirty-six. Thirteen were on the Niagara frontier.

Why was Niagara so central?

"Several things were going on," Timothy Karpin tells me by phone. "Most of the existing sophisticated chemical plants were in the Northeast. They had the labs and facilities in place to be able to take these materials. The other thing was that General Groves and others were looking at people they knew personally; a lot of business at that time happened through personal contacts." General Leslie Groves, military director of the Manhattan Engineer District, was the manager of America's atomic effort.

"They were worried about keeping secrets," adds Jim Maroncelli. "And if they knew each other, they trusted each other. The people in charge of the companies may have been aware of what the projects were about, though the workers were not."

Timothy and Jim are the authors of *The Traveler's Guide to Nuclear Weapons*, available on CD-ROM, a must-have for anyone who likes road trips, American history and A-bombs, and really, who doesn't? In addition to giving handy overviews of America's nuclear timeline and the weapons production process, the book maps out the U.S. nuclear weapons complex, chapter by chapter, in order of production stage.

A nuclear bomb requires fissionable materials: enriched uranium or plutonium. Plutonium was created in nuclear reactors; uranium was mined and then processed and refined. There's also a need for simple metal components, triggers, and fuels. Weapons must be fabricated and assembled. Physicist Niels Bohr told Edward Teller in 1939 that just separating the uranium for a bomb would require turning the whole country into a factory, and General Groves and his associates did just that: Colorado mined uranium, Rust Belt states like New York, Michigan and Ohio milled it, and Tennessee enriched it. Washington created plutonium, Ohio built polonium triggers, New Mexico fabricated the weapons, Pennsylvania conducted implosion tests, Utah and California test-dropped dummy bombs, and New Mexico, of course, saw the first detonation. And that's just a sampling. Thousands of industrial sites were utilized, particularly in the years before the Atomic Energy Commission consolidated production at its own facilities. By the time the first nuclear device was exploded in New

Mexico, locations in more than thirty-nine states as well as mines in Canada and Africa were involved, and more than two hundred private contractors, many of whom hired subcontractors of their own, had been recruited to the cause. Timothy and Jim's book catalogs these sites, and includes handy tips on visiting them: how to get there, where to park, how to get the best view and whether you will need special clearance. It outdoes my hydroinfrastructure road trip by a long shot.

In the Niagara region, Linde Air Products, a division of Union Carbide in Tonawanda, was one of the most important sites. Linde scientists were already working with uranium to produce dyes before the war (that nifty orange vintage Fiestaware is slightly radioactive), and they brought this experience to bear turning the uranium oxide in mined ores into uranium dioxide, used in nuclear fuel, and uranium tetrachloride, a stepping-stone to making uranium metal. They also experimented with enrichment of uranium hexafluoride by gaseous diffusion, the method ultimately used to make the nuclear fuel for the bomb dropped on Hiroshima.

Linde was perhaps the most critical Niagara region site for the project, and the reason the Manhattan Engineer District put one of its six field offices in Tonawanda, but many other local factories were involved. Electro-Metallurgical in Niagara Falls turned Linde's uranium tetrachloride into metal ingots that could be used in reactors. Simonds Saw & Steel, a few miles inland at Lockport, rolled uranium fuel rods. Local metallurgical specialists, like Bethlehem Steel in Lackawanna, outside Buffalo, and U.S. Vanadium in Niagara Falls, developed ways of processing and reprocessing uranium. Hooker made additives necessary for uranium refining. All of it happened in secret.

"The people at Fernald (a plant in Ohio) would make a metal part and send it a few miles away to Ashtabula. The plant there would then cut it and ship it to South Carolina," Jim tells me. "When we were talking with the people who worked at all these different facilities and laboratories, in many cases they did not know how they themselves fit into the overall operation."

Only a small group of scientists understood the big picture, and they carried technology from one industrial corporation to another. Workers almost never knew what they were working on. Men who handled uranium were rarely told they were handling radioactive material. Drivers trucking uranium ore from one plant to another weren't told what their cargo was. At Simonds Saw & Steel in Lockport, workers who were rolling uranium and thorium rods to be used in nuclear reactors were visited by federal agents and warned not to discuss their work—but they weren't told what it was. Even the train engineers who brought uranium ores to the Linde Air Products plant at Tonawanda didn't know what their train was carrying. The engineer had to stop the train at the factory gates and get off. A Linde employee would come out and steer the train into the plant for unloading. I imagine the guy pacing back and forth outside the gate, maybe having a smoke, waiting to get his train back.

"During that time period," Timothy says, "it was perhaps easier to tell people to shut up and do your job and don't ask questions."

Timothy and Jim are atomic geeks, and I mean that in the best way. They talk with an almost breathless enthusiasm about the nuclear weapons complex; it's clear they're impressed by the scale and speed of the operation. Both of them work as environmental consultants, helping remediate the kinds of sites they list in their book. As scientists, their approach is superrational. At one point, Jim refers to America's stockpile of waste plutonium as a "national treasure." They seem slightly bemused by my focus on Niagara, as if contaminating America's most famous natural wonder is no different from contaminating a strip of untraveled desert in Nevada. And they're right, it really isn't. Such carelessness with human life would be appalling wherever it happened. Timothy and Jim agree, but they point out there was a reason behind it.

"They were saving the world," Timothy says.

They were so busy saving the world, in fact, that they didn't care what they left behind.

"You're not chicken, are you?" Ralph Krieger asks me. "Don't be chicken. Remember one thing: Railroad tracks are federal property. And they can't chase you off them unless they're railroad people."

Ralph has promised to give me a tour of the Linde Air Products plant at Tonawanda. Now the sprawling Praxair complex, the former Linde plant is infamous today for the amount of radioactive contamination left behind. The most egregious, and unfixable, mess came about after the plant dumped 37 million gallons of radioactive uranium-laced sludge into shallow wells on its property in the forties. Radioactive isotopes eventually found their way into local creeks, and ultimately, the nearby Niagara River, which means that uranium from building the Bomb went over Niagara Falls. Linde chose this method of disposal because, as they wrote in a letter to the Manhattan Engineer District field office, "our Law Department advises us that it is considered impossible to determine the course of subterranean streams and, therefore, the responsibility for any contamination could not be fixed." In other words, this stuff will make a big mess, but no one can trace it back to us.

Liquid effluent was only part of the contamination at Linde. The Army Corps of Engineers began remediating the site under FUSRAP in 2000, and work continues to this day. Ralph, who worked at Linde for thirty-four years, can't take me onto the property, but he says there's a good view from the railroad tracks.

But first he has some stuff to unload. We meet on Third Street outside the Seneca Niagara Casino, and Ralph promptly goes to the back of his black Chevy pickup and drops the gate. There are two white file boxes in the back, overflowing with booklets and papers.

"I've brought some materials," he says. "I was up late last night, making copies for you."

Ralph is a stocky man, with salt and pepper hair on a squarish head. He wears black jeans, a checked shirt and a black sweatshirt, and he stands solidly but bent slightly forward, the posture of a man with a lifetime of physical labor behind him. At Linde, he was president of Local 8215 of the Oil, Chemical and Atomic Workers Union (now part of United Steelworkers) for thirty years.

"I'm still vice president of Amalgamated Groups," he tells me proudly. "I got eight companies." I begin to see why Seneca Niagara security guards keep walking by the truck, casting dark glances our way.

"I got thrown out of there," Ralph says, waving a hand toward the casino after two guards stalk by.

"What'd you do?" I ask him.

"Tried to organize the workers," he says. "I handed the bartender a tip with my card folded inside it." Ralph has brown, almond-shaped eyes that he fixes on yours when he talks, waiting to make sure you're getting it. After a moment, he laughs fondly at the memory. When he laughs, his face cracks with a kind of relief.

Ralph opens the first box and pulls out a photocopied news article. Under the headline "Praxair Concerned with Cleanup Efforts," there's an aerial photo of the Linde plant.

"This is the infamous processing building," he tells me, pointing. "You see it? That's Building 30. That was the main processing building. And then over here is the roadway. Building 38 was right there, 27 was there, but we tore that down. That was radioactive and we tore it down."

From 1940 to 1948, the years of its contracts with the Manhattan Engineer District, Linde processed 28,000 tons of radioactive ore from mines in Colorado, Canada and Africa.

"The richest ore came from Africa," Ralph tells me. "That was the richest ore in uranium; it was twenty percent. That was great. But the bad part was, it was radium too."

Actually, African ores, mined in what was then the Belgian Congo, could be as much as 65 percent uranium. When the ore came into Linde on railcars, stored in burlap bags, workers would unload it by hand. They were never told to treat it differently from any other ore. The burlap bags that had held the uranium ore were stacked up in the storage area, and workers used them as an informal place to sit and rest or eat lunch. The bags were eventually incinerated in the late 1950s.

According to the Advisory Board on Radiation and Worker Health, workers in only one building at Linde were required to wear dosimeters, badges to track their radiation exposure. But all workers were required to pass through a monitor when leaving the plant. If they didn't clear the monitor, they were told to go scrub off in the shower and try again, until they could clear it. Workers were never told what exactly they were being monitored for.

Ralph didn't work in the plant during the Manhattan Project years, but his father, who was union president for thirty years, did. I ask Ralph if the men at Linde then knew they were helping their country build a nuclear bomb.

"They had no idea, as far as I know," he says.

Ralph spends two hours taking me through the documents that tell the story of Linde. Then we get in my car and drive to Tonawanda. He frowns at my Toyota Prius. When we zip through the E-ZPass tollgate on the Grand Island Bridge, he tells me that for every E-ZPass, a toll collector somewhere has lost his job.

We park at a vacant warehouse adjacent to the Praxair property and walk down the railroad tracks, toward the plant complex. Over our heads, high-voltage transmission wires buzz faintly. It's a beautiful fall afternoon. Crickets chirp all along the Praxair fence, two rows of razor-wire-topped chain link posted with bright yellow radiation hazard signs. Ralph tells me he was walking there one day when some kids came along the tracks with their dog.

"I told them, 'Look at these signs. What do you think that means? It's all contaminated here.' I told them, 'Don't be coming down here anymore, especially with your dog, if you want him to live.' They asked 'What's it from?' and I said, 'This is where we used to make the atomic bomb.'" There's a hint of pride in his voice.

Ralph points out every building as we walk. The Linde cleanup is still very much underway. Building 30 has been taken down and removed, but near where it used to be, a steam shovel is chewing up ground and depositing it, a shovelful at a time, into trucks. According to a 2004 press release from the Corps of Engineers, five buildings and more than 200,000 tons of material will eventually be removed from the site and sent for recycling and disposal at hazardous waste facilities outside of New York State. Some of that material awaits transport now; just inside the inner fence, stacked railroad containers bear signs saying Do Not Hump. I ask Ralph what that means.

"They can't bang the car; they have to hook it," he tells me. "Most of the time, when they're switching tracks for going wherever they're going, they'll let the car roll down the hill and hit the next car. They can't do that." He stops and we both stand there, watching the shovel scrape away at the contaminated earth.

Ralph started working at Linde in 1964. Back then, only a few workers knew about the plant's Manhattan Project legacy. But they did know that the plant had radiation issues. One worker there was nicknamed "Nuclear Eddie," because he had the official geiger counter. Every now and then, Nuclear Eddie would be called to check something out. In the late 1970s, Linde decided to put new ventilators on the roof of Building 30. The old ones had been there since Manhattan Project days. Ralph's maintenance crew was brought in to remove the old ventilators. They got them down, but when Ralph went to take them to the scrap pile, his supervisors stopped him.

"They came over," he says, "and said, uh, no, don't do that." The supervisor told Ralph to take the ventilators into another building, where some plastic sheeting had been laid out. Two men were told to wire-brush them.

"They didn't have white suits on; they didn't have breathing masks. They had just regular paper masks," he says. "They would wire-brush it, and then it would sit there for a couple of days. And Nuclear Eddie would come over with the geiger counter and read it, the whole thing: 'No guys, wire-brush it some more.' By hand! Not electric! This was a hand wire brush. They wanted it so they could just throw it out in the scrap. So after about three or four times, they finally got it down to where they thought it was okay, and they collapsed it and threw it out on the scrap pile for the scrap dealer to pick up. They did five of them like that. They took weeks to wire-brush them, read them, wire-brush them. Those were the exhausters that were exhausting uranium dust out of there."

Ralph's thick eyebrows draw together. "One of the guys is already dead," he tells me. "Died at a very young age. Tommy Wheeler—he was probably in his late forties. Very good welder. Excellent welder-fabricator. But he happened to be working in maintenance and that was one of the jobs he got."

Tommy Wheeler is only one of the cancer victims Ralph tells me about as we're looking at the Linde site. He tells me about Bobby, who died of bladder cancer at fifty-six; Charley, who worked in the room with the African ore; Sam, who died of lymphatic cancer; and Eddie, who's dying of cancer now. Whenever he starts talking about one of his former fellow workers, his fuzzy eyebrows draw together and his eyes soften. Then he looks at the plant and starts speculating about the cleanup some more. At the end of the day, he tells me that every one of his work partners has died of cancer, as has his brother, who also worked at Linde. Ralph's personal experience, of course, does not constitute an epidemiological study. But Linde is one of the two private contracting sites where the federal government did do a worker health study. Carried out in the early eighties and reported in the *USA Today* series, the study found elevated incidences of cancers and respiratory ills among workers.

"Listen. It was horrific," Ralph says as we're heading back to the car, and at first I don't know what he means. "But they wouldn't surrender. They were told to surrender and they didn't want to surrender. Do you want to sacrifice two million men in a fight like we got today? 'Cause that's what it would have been. They would have fought to the death. Or do you drop a couple of bombs and convince them maybe we got a few more of them?"

Clearly, Ralph Krieger is no antiwar activist. I think of Timothy Karpin's comment: *They were saving the world.* I ask Ralph what should have happened that didn't happen. He stops walking and fixes me with that look.

"What should have happened here and at all the sites," he says, "is they should not have been left knowing—and they knew—what the long-term effects are. They should have at least tried to clean it up better than they did, but they didn't want to do it. And the reason was money."

When I get back to my hotel room that night, my face has a line down the center. The right half is glowing red. I stare at myself in the mirror. For a minute, I panic. *I never should have gone to that radioactive factory!* And then I realize it's just a sunburn. It's only on one side because I stood there with Ralph, not moving for several hours, listening as he slowly unfurled his tale.

They wouldn't surrender. The story we all learn about the Bomb is that it was a horrible thing to do to Japanese civilians, but we had to do it. What that story usually leaves out is that the Manhattan Project was also a horrible thing to do to many unwitting Americans. Would the calculus of acceptable collateral damage change if people were aware of how far that damage reached?

Pictures of General Leslie Groves show a portly man with a thumb-shaped head. In contrast to the natty, European-looking scientists whose knowledge of nuclear physics built his bomb, Groves looks like what he was: a manager, a company man who worked fourteen-hour days and never let on to his wife what he was doing. Coordinating supply chains, land acquisition, labor and manufacturing as well as the ongoing theory behind it all, Groves spent $2.2 billion dollars of the taxpayers' money without Congress ever knowing the project existed. He convinced hundreds of corporate contractors to assist in a project they never fully understood. He hired hundreds of thousands of workers without ever revealing to most of them what they were doing.

On July 17, 1945, General Groves stood behind a cement and earth wall seventeen miles from the Trinity test site and saw the results of his effort light up the mountains around Alamogordo, an effect he later described as beautiful. Seven miles closer to the blast, Los Alamos lab director J. Robert Oppenheimer hunched in a bunker with test director Kenneth Bainbridge. "It worked," Oppenheimer reportedly said, and Bainbridge declared, "Now we are all sons of bitches." Three weeks later, a B-29 took off from Tinian Island in the Marianas with the bomb called Little Boy aboard.

History holds that a line was crossed at Hiroshima. But what was it exactly? The line between military and civilian targets had already been crossed in the long and awful war—German schoolgirls boiled to death in water tanks during the firebombing of Dresden; Londoners died in their beds during the Blitz. But the flights of the *Enola Gay* and the *Bockscar* still spawn a special feeling of horror, in part because of the seeming disparity between effort and result. One small bomb—Little Boy was 6 feet long— one quick flight, manned by eleven jolly-looking men, one opening of the bomb-bay doors. At Nagasaki, the target was clouded over, but then a small break in the cover gave Captain James Van

Pelt a window to slip through. So much hung on so little. Or so it seemed, because the extraordinary effort behind that bomb was covered up.

Shortly after Hiroshima, 6 million leaflets were dropped on Japan, along with Japanese newspaper stories showing the destruction. "To the Japanese People:" the leaflets began, "America asks that you take immediate heed of what we say on this leaflet. We are in possession of the most destructive explosive ever devised by man." *We are in possession*—as if it somehow fell into our hands. More than any other product of human effort, there's a powerful ambivalence about having built the atom bomb. The White House press release after Hiroshima called the world's first nuclear bombing "the greatest achievement of organized science in history," but taking credit for the thing was never uncomplicated. Even General Groves, in a Trinity memo he and his deputy Thomas Farrell drafted for the secretary of war, described a feeling of having usurped power that didn't belong to humanity. The sound of the explosion, they wrote, was a "strong, sustained awesome roar which warned of doomsday and made us feel that we puny things were blasphemous to dare tamper with the forces heretofore reserved for the Almighty." Here, once more, was the sublime, resurrected by the awful metaphysics of the mushroom cloud.

One historian later described that same blast as "a Niagara of white light."

After the war, the government canceled many of its contracts, but the nuclear ones lived on; America needed an atomic arsenal. With the Soviet Union's test of a nuclear device in 1949, the Cold War was officially on. The United States, ignoring the objections of Oppenheimer and some of the other Manhattan Project scientists, moved to develop thermonuclear weapons, with thousands of times the destructive power of the first generation of nuclear bombs. The government would eventually shift production to its own facilities at places like Oak Ridge National Laboratory, but many of the Niagara region factories continued to process uranium well into the fifties.

In the meantime, the long-term effects of radiation were

becoming clear. The massive production effort of the Manhattan Project was accompanied by the collection of health data. Workers were tested, usually anonymously. Huge animal studies were done: scientists at the University of Rochester injected dogs, cats, rabbits and mice with plutonium and exposed them to plutonium dust in specially built gas chambers. They even injected eleven unknowing human subjects with plutonium in 1945 and 1946, a gruesome experiment that, along with other experiments on humans, was first made widely public in 1994, prompting a government inquiry and an apology from President Clinton's energy secretary, Hazel O'Leary.

Human experiments on unwitting subjects bespeak a callous disregard for human life, but in an odd way, they also testify to a growing concern for worker safety. Scientists were beginning to fear the effects radiation would have both in the short and the long term. It's hard to say how much they knew and when. In the immediate aftermath of Hiroshima and Nagasaki, General Groves seemed genuinely baffled by reports detailing the grisly effects of radiation sickness. Some scientists insisted the Japanese were simply suffering the aftereffects of regular burns, and in an attempt to calm the public's anxieties, Groves, Oppenheimer and a few others were photographed standing at Trinity's ground zero to prove there was no dangerous radioactivity lingering there. Of course, they were wearing special booties to keep from tracking radioactive sand off the site.

In the years after the war, the effects of both high and low doses of radiation were becoming increasingly clear. The newly formed Atomic Energy Commission, charged with maintaining weapons production, became increasingly concerned about issues of worker safety and waste disposal. But when they tried to issue guidelines and enforce standards, their contractors resisted on the grounds that safety standards would create fear and slow things down. According to Jim Maroncelli and Timothy Karpin, the atomic travelers, this was because of two things: patriotism and profit.

It's a dangerous combination—the greater good and the bottom line. During the Cold War, military and civilian contractors alike were driven by what Timothy calls "piles of money and an almost religious desire to kill communists." Love of country merged with love of cash to maintain the frantic pace of production.

"Under this combination of the national mission and pure profit," Timothy tells me, "Atomic Energy Commission managers and corporate leaders decided that workers' health and lives were not as important. And since the drum of patriotism was incessant, workers also accepted and often trusted the decisions of management as part of their duty to their country. And besides, the other choice, unemployment, was not an acceptable alternative."

Ralph Krieger gives me the phone number of a man named Harry Wiest. I meet Harry on a Sunday at the Goodyear plant where he works. He's standing at the gatehouse when I pull into the parking lot, a tall, good-looking man with a neatly trimmed mustache that forms an upside-down U around his mouth. He's friendly and quick to smile, even in his hardhat and clutching a sheaf of blueprints: as union vice president, he's doing fire inspections today. Harry is going to introduce me to his father Dan, and it's easiest to meet here because, even on Sunday, Harry is working a double shift. Dan drives up within two minutes of my arrival. Together, we go through the security gate and into the Goodyear factory to find a quiet place to chat.

Inside, the plant looks like a college campus, spotless and immaculately landscaped. Metal tanks gleam and the sidewalks are so clean you could eat off them. Above us, framed against the brilliant sky, steam pipes and electrical lines in square metal exoskeletons connect buildings. A huge smokestack blinks down at us. We go into the empty lunchroom—also spotless—and sit down at a cafeteria table to talk.

Dan Wiest is one of the many Niagara workers who was unknowingly touched by the Cold War arms race. In 1950, he came from Pennsylvania, where he had been laid off from turnpike construction, and got a job at Linde.

"I had a friend on the turnpike who said 'Let's go to Niagara Falls; I hear there's a lot of jobs up there,'" he tells me. "You coulda went to any plant in Niagara Falls and got a job back then."

Dan is a striking older man, small, with a deeply lined face harboring electric-blue eyes. His thick white hair rears up in tufts that stick out in many different directions from his head. He has prostate cancer and has submitted a claim under the Energy Employees Occupational Illness Compensation Act. It's still being processed.

After two months on the job at Linde, he was drafted for the Korean War. He came back to the Falls in 1952 and got his job back. He moved into Griffon Manor, the housing project built near Love Canal by the federal government. His children were born there, including Harry, who chips in that he remembers riding his bike around the neighborhood. It was a nice neighborhood; they liked living there.

Dan's case illustrates one of the many problems with the Energy Employees Compensation Act: how to assign blame. In the fifties, he worked on and off at Linde, but whenever production slowed, he was laid off. Then he would go to other plants. He worked at U.S. Vanadium, also an Atomic Energy Commission contractor, at the New York Power Authority project, and at GM's Harrison Radiator Division. He picked apples for a season in Ransomville, below the escarpment. He worked briefly at Olin Mathieson, another nuclear contractor.

"I was only there a month or so," he says, "and I broke out in boils all over my body from the chemicals. They made me leave."

Dan's claim is against Union Carbide, Linde's parent company at the time. One of his jobs there was to feed ore into a big crusher. I ask him what it was, but he doesn't know.

"There was one place—I was trying to think of the name of it—where they had this smelly stuff," he says. "It was part of Union Carbide."

"Was it Electromet, Pop?" Harry offers.

"That's it. Union Carbide Electro-Metallurgical. The last guy I knew that worked there died two years ago."

ElectroMet was one of the earliest factories to begin producing uranium metal. In the first year of production, workers there made 1,000 tons of uranium ingots, most of which became fuel for Hanford's nuclear reactors. The building in which all of this was done was demolished in 1958.

At Linde, Dan worked in Building 6, which has since been demolished by the Corps of Engineers cleanup, and in Building 8, the powerhouse. Its fate is uncertain.

I ask Dan if he knew Linde had handled uranium—supposedly the plant's uranium processing went on standby in 1949—or that the place he worked made bombs for the Cold War. He shakes his head cheerfully.

"Nope," he says. "Back then we had no idea."

Dan seems a little surprised that anyone would want to talk about his experiences. Like many men of his generation, he's a man of few words. The conversation proceeds in mild fits and starts, and when there's silence, Dan glances at his son, his face lit with quiet pride.

"You're looking real official there, with your hat, Harry," he finally can't help saying. Harry opens up the blueprints and shows his dad the spots he's inspecting today.

"I work here eighty, a hundred hours a week," Harry tells me. "We're short-staffed. Us manufacturing people, we're dinosaurs."

Harry has been fighting bladder cancer himself. The Goodyear plant has had a mini-epidemic: thirty-nine cases. In 1989, the union brought in the National Institute for Occupational Safety and Health to investigate; they traced the cancers to the chemical ortho-toluidine used in making Wingstay, an antioxidant that prevents tires from cracking. When the epidemic was first noticed, Goodyear claimed they had no idea what could be causing it. But attorneys for the sick workers found documents showing that DuPont, previous manufacturers of ortho-toluidine, gave Goodyear a written warning in 1977—the year Harry started working there—stating that the chemical caused cancer in rats and mice. DuPont recommended giving workers protective gear. Goodyear did not. Today, after union intervention, they do.

Listening to Harry discuss his cancer, so many years after the Manhattan Project, I can see why workers would have gone to work in factories that gave them boils and rashes, why men would have crushed strange metals without asking what might be airborne in the resulting dust, why the workers at Linde would have made jokes about "Nuclear Eddie" and gone on scrubbing a radioactive vent. Harry is grateful for his job at Goodyear. It's a good job. He's a unionized worker with a good hourly wage and medical benefits. After five years of working there, he got vested in his pension plan, so even if he's laid off, he won't lose it all, as workers used to do. Harry was laid off once for fourteen months, and he applied for other jobs, but when they asked him if he would go back to Goodyear if recalled, he was honest and said yes. He has seniority there.

"I want to retire out of this plant," he tells me. He even met his wife on the job; she worked in the Goodyear lab. He's not happy about the bladder cancer, but he credits Goodyear with putting a screening program in place, and offering the protective gear. He insists they acted quickly, and I don't ask him about the 1977 DuPont memo. As a union officer in his local, he's sending out letters to all workers, even retired ones, making sure they come in for screenings. His own cancer was caught early, though not by the factory's screening.

"Goodyear has been good to me," he says.

Dan Wiest, Harry's father, still knows so little about what happened to him. The more people I talk to about the Bomb and Niagara, the more it begins to seem like the problem—just as much as ores and isotopes—is talk. Or rather, lack of it. For years, talk about the project was suppressed, and even today, darkness shrouds the activities of the government contractors. The radiological legacy they left behind is far less known than the legacy of government sites like Hanford or Oak Ridge. That, more than anything, is the line that was crossed with the Manhattan Project: the line between a knowable world and one based on secrets and lies.

"After spending more than $5.8 trillion," write Timothy and Jim on their Web site atomictraveler.com, "the American public is still in the dark."

One effect of darkness is rumors. Niagara County abounds in them: giant rabbits, glow-in-the-dark deer, plutonium in the drinking water, radioactive bowling alleys, driveways where geiger counters peg. Some of the rumors have clear groundings in fact; others point more toward emotion than logic. In the early eighties, just after Love Canal, the region saw an outburst of alleged sightings of a Bigfoot creature in the Lewiston area and a Loch Ness–like sea serpent was reported to be lurking in the Niagara River. Clearly, something monstrous was afoot.

Niagara's role in the nuclear weapons complex was not unusual for an industrial region. Other Rust Belt communities today face the same legacy: the Corps of Engineers is currently cleaning up twenty-two sites in nine states, including sites in St. Louis, Philadelphia, Cleveland, and Middlesex, New Jersey. But what happened after the Cold War at Niagara does stand out. In spite of its fame as a natural wonder, the Niagara Falls region became the dumping site for chemical and radiological waste not only from its own factories, but from those of other states as well.

Seven miles below the Falls, just east of the Lewiston crossing where slaves rowed to freedom, and just north of the reservation where the Tuscaroras took on Robert Moses, is Model City. Little more than a zip code today, Model City was originally meant to be a new, utopian metropolis at the other end of Love Canal. On the flat plain that stretches from the Niagara Escarpment to the south shore of Lake Ontario, "the most appealing and beautiful town site in existence," William T. Love intended to build a workers' paradise. Powered by electricity generated with the canal, Model City would eventually grow into a metropolis of 700,000, "the new manufacturing center of America." Love got title to the land from the state, but his canal never made it that far. What's now called Love Canal is the abandoned intake end of the canal. The never-built outfall is Model City.

The area, a bucolic plain of orchards and small towns, was sparsely populated before World War II. In 1942, a large chunk of it was commandeered by the federal government and turned into a TNT factory known as the Lake Ontario Ordnance Works (LOOW). Today this flat rectangle of land is still called by that name, and it's the site of a household sanitary landfill and the Northeast's only operating hazardous waste dump, Chemical Waste Management's Model City facility. When Tom Brokaw's desk was contaminated by anthrax mailed in September 2001 to senators and news media, hazmat crews removed it, sprayed it with bleach, pulverized it, and sent it to Chemical Waste Management for disposal. Mr. Brokaw's desk was only the latest entrant in a long list of things dumped at the Lake Ontario Ordnance Works, including high-level nuclear materials stored in the part of it called the Niagara Falls Storage Site.

"This area here is all of the Lake Ontario Ordnance Works site, seventy-five hundred acres bought in 1942 by the U.S. government," Vince Agnello tells me, unfolding a map. "By eminent domain, they told everybody, we're buying this."

We're sitting in the Village Diner, a homey place on the quaint single block that constitutes the main drag in Youngstown. Youngstown is the northernmost of the Niagara River towns, the site of Fort Niagara and a pretty marina that hosts a regatta every year. Like its one-stoplight town, the Village Diner is classic. The room we're in is painted the same minty green as the Underground Railroad exhibit at the Castellani Art Museum, and it has anchors and ship's wheels on the walls. Outside the picture windows, a thicket of bobbing masts can be seen in the windy, gray morning.

Vince is a brown-eyed man with a thick head of salt and pepper hair. He wears a neat gray sweater with blue and purple stripes. Somehow, I'm surprised when I see him. He looks like a law professor, which he is, rather than an environmental activist. But he's president of a local group called Residents for Responsible Government, and as he unfolds his map of the Lake Ontario Ordnance Works with all of its current owners' land shaded in different tones before I can even get a cup of coffee, it quickly becomes clear that he's definitely an activist too.

Vince sketches out the history of the site—what's known of it. The Army Corps engineers, currently charged with the cleanup, readily admit they don't know everything that went on there. Their site history document is 339 pages long, with 46 figures and 14 tables. The story it tells is pretty much the same one Vince maps out for me over eggs and toast.

Lake Ontario Ordnance Works was one of hundreds of similar sites across the nation bought and hastily converted to TNT production after Pearl Harbor. The cookie-cutter factories quickly produced so much TNT that, by the middle of 1943, the War Department found itself with too much of the stuff. They ordered the plants to stop production.

Of LOOW's 7,500 acres (about 14 square miles), 2,500 acres in the center were developed for the TNT plant and its attendant buildings: storage igloos, dining hall, hospital, security building and USO hall. The surrounding area was considered a security buffer zone. After TNT production ceased in 1943, the War Department did a rudimentary cleanup, then sold the buffer zone land back to private owners. The original TNT plant was taken over by the Manhattan Engineer District.

"All the other sites were being cleaned up," Vince tells me. "This site was the repository for all the radioactive waste and other waste being shipped by rail."

Beginning in 1944, the Manhattan Engineer District began to dump radioactive sludge from the Linde plant into a concrete reservoir at the Lake Ontario Ordnance Works. Over 10,000 tons of the sludge, containing radium and uranium, were trucked over from Tonawanda, accompanied by an unmarked vehicle watching for leaks. Although the Manhattan Engineer District originally intended to clean up the site, by 1948 the Atomic Energy Commission—their successor—declared that the site was too contaminated to be used for anything other than waste. The Niagara region thus became the site of one of the nation's earliest nuclear dumps.

Contaminated soils and building rubble from wartime plants in St. Louis, Cleveland, Wilmington, Delaware, and Canonsburg, Pennsylvania, were shipped in. LOOW received radioactive wastes from fission reactions at Knolls Atomic Power Laboratory, uranium rods and billets rolled at Bethlehem Steel in Lackawanna and Simonds Saw & Steel in Lockport, and 1,400 barrels of radium-bearing sludge from Middlesex, New Jersey. These dangerous materials were shoved into existing warehouses, poured into cement reservoirs or piled up wherever space could be found. Drums and barrels were left standing along railroad tracks. Nearly half the radioactive waste was out in the open.

In 1949, K-65 residues, uranium ore remaining after most of
the uranium has been separated from it, were brought from St.
Louis and stored first outdoors, then in an open silo on the 182
acres that became known as the Niagara Falls Storage Site. These
ores had little uranium left, but they were still very high in radioactive radium and thorium. The silo where they were stored, built
as a cooling tower, leaked radon into the surrounding countryside
for years.

The scientists at the University of Rochester sent over an
especially macabre shipment: several hundred thousand animal
corpses—dogs, cats, rabbits, guinea pigs and mice—that had been
injected with plutonium or exposed to plutonium dust. There was
also unspecified medical waste from the secret plutonium exposure research on humans. All of it was buried at Model City.

According to the Corps of Engineers site history, shipping of
radioactive wastes to LOOW ceased in 1953. But throughout the
fifties and sixties, as Robert Moses was building his power plant
and the Corps was carefully reconstructing Niagara's natural wonder, the land in Model City was parceled up and used for all sorts
of projects nobody else wanted. The air force got some land and
contracted with Bell Aircraft Corporation to develop rockets, mis-
siles and lasers there. The navy, and later the air force, used part
of it to develop high-energy fuels with Olin Mathieson. The army
built a Nike missile base at one end. The Chemical Warfare Service was given a plot to store incendiary bombs; later the National
Guard used the same plot for weekend training sessions. The
Atomic Energy Commission contracted with Hooker to build and
operate an isotope separation plant on the site for boron-10, a
neutron absorber used as a radiation shield in nuclear reactors.

"After the contracts ended," Vince says, "everybody just walked
away. Whatever was there was there. They just left it all."

The land was considered a total loss. The various government
agencies and their private contractors had carried out their activities without any concern for environmental contamination and
had adhered to no standards for safe waste disposal. The place was
a minefield of waste drums, many of them unmarked, contaminated soils, toxic surface water and combustibles stored in wooden

crates. In 1972, a large chunk of the site was purchased by Chem-Trol, later SCA Services, a waste disposal company acquired by Chemical Waste Management (a subsidiary of garbage giant Waste Management) in 1984.

One of the ground rules of waste disposal is that you don't site a hazardous waste landfill on previously contaminated land. The reason is so that if something local shows signs of contamination, you know where it's coming from. Furthermore, the digging and disturbance of earth on a landfill can spread toxins around. These rules didn't apply in 1972: government regulation of landfills didn't begin until 1976, with the passage of the Resource Conservation and Recovery Act. Under RCRA, the owners of the Model City landfill applied for a hazardous waste permit. It was granted in 1980. The thinking was that the land was already so fouled it was useless for anything else.

Today, Chemical Waste Management has identified a number of contaminated sites on its property that it believes are the responsibility of the Department of Defense. In other words, they want the government to clean its mess off their hazardous waste dump.

After breakfast, Vince drives me out to look at the Lake Ontario Ordnance Works. The houses grow more widely spaced as we move from Youngstown to Model City. Residents have decorated for the holidays; there are bows, wreaths, plastic Santas and inflatable snowmen. At the end of each driveway is a blue plastic recycling crate. As we get to the western edge of LOOW, we pass the Lewiston-Porter schools—primary, middle, high school—all built on donated land in the buffer zone. Vince pulls into the school parking lot and indicates a scrubby woods on the other side of a football field.

"All that land behind the playing field, they can't use," he tells me. "They own it, but it's not safe." I have the map in my hand, so I know what's less than two miles beyond that line of trees: the Niagara Falls Storage Site.

We leave the school and turn down Pletcher Road. We pass a KOA campground and slow down to turn near a giant greenhouse.

"What's in the greenhouse?" I ask.

"Hydroponic tomatoes," Vince says. He turns into a gravel drive and pulls up to a padlocked gate. The gate and chain-link fence are posted with signs: No Trespassing—U.S. Government. There's no guard or camera. To the right of the gate, a neat red Army Corps of Engineers sign says Niagara Falls Storage Site. To the north and east of this little area sprawls the rest of the LOOW site.

I climb out of the car and walk up to the gate. About one football field away looms what looks like an outsized barn, with huge exhausters on top and three silos marching down its side. This is Building 401, formerly the TNT plant's boiler building, later a boron-10 production building, after which its history is unknown. The building looks like a barn for a reason: from the air it was supposed to look like just another farm, albeit one on steroids. To the left of the hulking barn is a mound, a small one for Niagara County, but ominous all the same—it's the landfill where the radioactive wastes were consolidated. In 1984, after high levels of radioactivity were detected in the area, the K-65 ores were taken out of the silo and encapsulated in the basement of a demolished building on the site. The silo was taken apart and put in there as well, along with anything else around known to be radioactive. The one-acre landfill was covered and capped. It was meant to be a temporary solution. Now, even if the Corps of Engineers dug up the wastes inside, they wouldn't have anywhere to put them. No place in the nation would take them.

I stand at the fence and stare at the grassy rise. Why did they name it the Niagara Falls Storage Site? Why not Lewiston, or Model City, or Porter, the next town over? Why not Devil's Hole? Devil's Hole is only a couple of miles away, at the top of the escarpment. The Falls are about eight miles away, up the Robert Moses Parkway. But for some reason the army saw fit to name their ugly cache after America's iconic falls.

Here, on the town site where William T. Love planned a city of dreams powered by the mastered waterfall, the real outcome of that mastery cycles through its decay chain under the earth. The atomic bomb could not have been built without Niagara. It wasn't just cheap electricity and industrial know-how. At the waterfall, Americans embraced their power to remake nature. Leslie Groves claimed later that when the bomb exploded at Trinity, he thought of Blondin crossing Niagara Falls. He had gone out on a wire. Like Blondin, he had upstaged nature. But he had gone one step further: he had made the elements into a seemingly all-powerful tool. That process was begun by Niagara power, nature's most awesome force now wielded by humans. *We are in possession* . . . The international coterie of scientists who built the Bomb are the direct descendants of the International Niagara Commission, convening at Brown's Hotel to harness the Falls. Oppenheimer split the atom, but Tesla split the world.

It's a gray, wet, windy morning when I drive to visit the Army Corps of Engineers at their district office in Buffalo. The Canadian skyline hunches miserably under a dark cloud bank, and even the Seneca Niagara looks subdued, flashing bleakly in the dull morning. I follow the Niagara River upstream: the Corps offices sit right on the riverfront at Black Rock—now a sprawling industrial warehouse district and working-class neighborhood on Buffalo's west side.

Peter Porter would be appalled to know that his beloved Black Rock is now incorporated into its hated rival, but no doubt his entrepreneurial heart would be warmed by the sight of the big lock the Corps of Engineers built there to guide ships through Black Rock's treacherous narrows, and the railway bridge connecting it to Canada. (He would probably also approve of the Border Patrol SUV parked at the bridge, keeping fugitives out now, instead of in.) I'm a little early for my appointment, and I'm sure the Army Corps engineers are sticklers for the schedule, so I drive to the foot of Breckenridge Street, where the old Porter depot was. The architecture along the river is still heavily industrial, and many of the buildings are gorgeous, with old hand-painted signs: Great Lakes Pressed Steel, Bison Storage & Warehouse, S. A. Day Manufacturing, Hohl Machine & Conveyor. Many have For Lease signs stuck on their sides. Breckenridge Street, named after Porter's slave-owning Kentucky relatives, is still a brick road. It ends before the water at a scrubby fence, because Interstate 90 plows right through this part of town, cutting off the warehouses from the river. A toll plaza stands on the very spot where the Porter depot must have been. My favorite Niagara region sign is posted at the dead end: No Dumping. I back up and turn right to ease down a brick alley littered with strips of metal and discarded tires.

At the Corps security booth, Bill Kowalewski, project manager for the Lake Ontario Ordnance Works, is waiting for me. A neat, sandy-haired man who rarely smiles, Bill has a slightly worried air about him. He takes me to a conference room overlooking the Black Rock lock and introduces me to Judy Leithner, project manager for the Niagara Falls Storage Site. The Niagara Falls Storage Site is inside LOOW, but unlike the rest of the site, it's still owned by the federal government, so it's dealt with as a separate project. Joan Morrissey, a community outreach specialist, is also there, and Bruce Sanders, a public relations officer, pops in occasionally with a digital camera, getting snapshots for his monthly newsletter.

Bruce is an affable, happy-go-lucky guy, and Joan Morrissey is as chatty as you would expect of someone whose title includes the word "outreach." She has a way of talking herself into an increasingly excited state, but Bill and Judy both have the careful, thoughtful attitude of engineers. There's a short flurry of introductions and coffee-getting, and then they slide into their chairs at the conference table with the resigned air of schoolkids sitting down in the principal's office.

Many community activists hold Bill and Judy personally responsible for what happens—or fails to happen—at the LOOW site. The Corps is the only agency currently taking any action there—they are, as Bill puts it, "the only game in town," and they're thus the focus of the community's frustration and ire. Much of the anger is really about Chemical Waste Management, the current operators of the hazardous waste dump on the site, who are seeking to expand their landfill. Many in the community are suspicious of Chemical Waste Management, though as Lewiston's economic engine, they have their supporters too. But everyone seems to mistrust the Army Corps, which moves at a glacial pace.

Add to that the history of Love Canal, in which the community was fed lies and misinformation for years, and you have the makings of a pretty dysfunctional relationship.

"The legacy so overshadows anything we can say technically," Bill tells me.

"I worked for Oxy during the Love Canal," Judy adds, referring to Occidental, which bought Hooker Chemical, "and believe me, this is like going through it again. Nowhere near the hazard, but the perception of the hazard is there."

"Why is it nowhere near the hazard?" I ask.

"The radiation that is currently present is confined," she says immediately.

If the radiation is in fact confined—and if so it only became so in 1984, when it was moved out of the silo and into the ground—the Army Corps has not done a good job of helping people understand that. In fact, they seem pessimistic about getting the community to understand much.

"Some of the problem," Judy tells me, "is a few people who don't have a technical background but truly believe that if only we did our job right the property would have zero radiation. To try and get it across that there is no place on earth that there is no radiation—that there's naturally occurring material—they think that's a story."

"People are incapable of understanding the concept of background radiation?" I ask, and she nods. "Some of them are."

I think about the people I've talked to—Dan Wiest, for instance, or Ralph Krieger. I'm pretty sure that, even if they came to a conversation without an understanding of background radiation, it wouldn't be that hard to explain it to them. The thing that the Corps of Engineers might find harder to accept is that the public might not believe it coming from them. They are, after all, the same organization that secretly brought what they like to call "rad" to Niagara in the first place. Nor would residents necessarily agree to whatever the army decided was a safe level of radiation to live with. It was the army, after all, who let Linde pour their uranium sludge into underground streams, who figured it was fine to stick radium in a silo and see what happened.

Corps press releases declare that "restoring the environment is the Army Corps of Engineers' ultimate goal." In truth, their mission in the region is not defined as broadly as those words suggest: they are there to clean up potentially harmful sites that were the direct result of War Department contracts. To this end, they have produced a working history of the site; the binders full of paper they've generated in their investigations fill a wall of bookshelves at the Lewiston Public Library, their official public repository for this project. But they readily admit this doesn't mean they know everything; piecing together the history is a process of historical sleuthing that often leads to dead ends. And even if they did know everything that was wrong with the site, they wouldn't try to fix all of it, but only the part that was the direct result of War Department activities. Local community activists characterize this attitude as passing the buck, leaving Niagara County burdened with a mess they didn't make. The Corps of Engineers points out that they can only do as much as Congress authorizes—and budgets—them to do.

"We're a federal presence," Joan tells me. "It doesn't matter that we're one agency with no regulatory authority. . . . When you try to explain that, it sort of sounds like 'That's not our job.'"

The Corps gained responsibility for the site in 1998, when Congress took the Formerly Utilized Sites Remedial Action Program away from the Department of Energy and reassigned it to the Corps. Like any bureaucrats, the engineers in the Corps have a strict protocol, which they follow to the letter. They move slowly and deliberately, and they throw up a lot of paper as they do; it's their idea of transparency. They also talk to the community regularly, but that doesn't always seem to go so well. On top of it all, the cleanup itself is hardly straightforward.

"I've been told it's one of the most complex environmental cleanup projects historically for the army," Bill tells me. "And the challenge is that the site did so many things, was so big and was then broken up into so many parcels that it's like this huge three-dimensional jigsaw puzzle that we have to put together."

He hops up several times as we're talking to get charts or reports. At one point he brings in a giant, laminated flow chart of the United States Nuclear Weapons Complex. It's colorful and packed with information, and when I'm enthusiastic about it, he couldn't be happier.

"You can keep it!" he says with delight. Later he gets me a giant rubber band to keep it rolled.

We go over the history of the site: the war work, the postwar waste, the sale of the lands to private owners, the arrival of waste disposal companies. For all their mistrust of one another, the Corps and the community activists basically agree on what happened at LOOW in the forties and fifties. Their opinions diverge when it comes to what's still there now.

I ask about the infamous "Rochester burial," the creepy cache of plutonium-laced guinea pigs and radioactive mice. The Corps spent $100,000 digging a huge trench looking for the site of the burial.

"We had maps that showed where it should be," Judy tells me. "We dug the whole area, huge trenches looking; there was nothing in there except one remaining animal bone which somebody called a 'bunny bone.' We also found some laboratory waste—petri dishes, vials with samples in them and so on, very few, fit in a garbage pail."

If it's not there, I ask, where did it go?

"The records show, although the public doesn't believe it, that it went to the Argonne National Labs area," Judy says. "It's somewhere in Oak Ridge. They had a couple of spots where they disposed of it, but the records say it went to Oak Ridge; I can't say what the facility is exactly."

For some activists, that's not enough of an explanation. They insist the Rochester burial is probably still there, possibly hidden beneath one of Chemical Waste Management's toxic lagoons. One of the problems for engineers and activists alike is that ongoing hazardous waste dumping makes it impossible to search the whole site. The Corps specifically excludes from their cleanup those areas that have been made "inaccessible" by "subsequent activities by the present owner." This includes the landfill's soil piles, drum storage buildings, lagoons and roadways.

It's hard to prove something is *not* somewhere. One of the results of the secrecy with which the Manhattan Project and Cold

War arms buildup were conducted is that it spawned rumors that are impossible to prove or disprove. During a radiological survey in 1970, the Atomic Energy Commission found signs warning that phosgene, World War I–era mustard gas, was buried on the site. The Corps of Engineers hasn't found any phosgene, or any government documents referring to it. They admit it could have been brought there later by a private owner, but then it wouldn't be their problem. The exact location of this supposed phosgene is now unknown. There are other rumors: one railcar was allegedly brought to the site and buried whole because its cargo was so dangerous. The Corps did geophysical analysis looking for metal; they never found it. They have aerial photographs showing mysterious circular white marks, but they don't understand those either.

"We suspect they might have been burning waste out there," Bill says, pointing at the marks on the photos. "But we went in and sampled and there's nothing there now. Unfortunately, I can't close the book on it, but I can tell you that there's no risk to anybody now and that's really our mission, to determine if there's a risk to anyone now or in the future."

For the Army Corp engineers, not finding a threat means it was probably never there. For the community, it means it must still be there.

I ask Bill and Judy about the things that they do know about the site. They're just as horrified as anyone else at the lax safety precautions and disregard for the environment that happened long ago. Judy tells me about interviewing a ninety-one-year-old man who worked on the Niagara Falls Storage Site. She asked him how he handled the K-65 ores when they came in.

"He said when the drums came in, they had a conveyer, and the drums would go on the conveyer, but they still spilled K-65, so he shoveled it up," she tells me, shaking her head. "He lived to ninety-one, but most of [the workers] died in their thirties and forties."

"I'm amazed at the science and technology and production that occurred to get a bomb delivered within five years," Bill says. "And yet the health concerns and the handling of it—that end of the situation is so crude. It just wasn't a priority or it wasn't known."

"Some of it wasn't known, and I think some of it was, you know, 'For my country,'" Judy says. "You know, the old patriotism. I've taken risks for my country that I wouldn't take for myself. And so have you."

Bill, an air force reservist, nods.

"Well, they were saving the world, right?" I say.

"Yeah," agrees Bill. "Well, they were, frankly."

"Actually," Judy says, "they did."

For my country. Like Bill, my father was an air force reservist when I was growing up. My uncle Howard, an air base commander, used to spoil family holidays by showing a film called *The Price of Peace and Freedom* to all of us kids. It detailed the imminent danger posed to us personally, right there in rural Michigan, by the evil Russians. My uncle Howard was twenty years older than my father, who was my grandparents' late-in-life surprise baby, and we younger cousins used to think he was wacky, a throwback to a Cold War that had already fizzled out. We'd sit giggling through the satellite photos and stolen footage of troop maneuvers and then race outside to brandish my grandfather's broken rifle and lock each other in the barn. But I always felt oddly impressed by my uncle's clarity of vision. It was all so simple—good and evil, right and wrong. My cousins and I, a scrubby bunch of post-Vietnam, post-Watergate slackers and punks, would never be able to see the world that way.

In the same way, I like engineers. I often find myself envying people who can think so rationally about the world. Rationality, I'm convinced, is much needed these days. The Army Corps engineers seem like nice people. When I leave, in addition to the laminated Nuclear Weapons Complex chart, they give me an Army Corps of Engineers lapel pin and a board-mounted aerial photograph of Niagara Falls. I go away convinced—by their genuineness, not by the swag—that they really believe in their mission. They want to do what's best for the public. But, walking to my car

in the sleety rain, I feel like I'm picking my way along the edge of a
giant abyss that slowly yawned wide as we talked. It's the gulf that
opens up when governments lie to their citizens.

Those radioactive lab animals obsess the community not just
because the image is so gruesome, but because they seem like a
symbol somehow. The Niagara region was itself, in many ways,
a guinea pig. Its factories were commandeered for a project the
public never even knew about, let alone condoned; its workers'
health was endangered without their knowledge or consent, and
its ground was contaminated with materials the community—and
even the contaminators themselves—could barely understand.
Now the land lies ruined and discarded with no one even sure
what happened to it.

It's not that the community is naturally mistrustful or rancor-
ous. They were poisoned by the bitter pill they unknowingly swal-
lowed in the midst of their own war feast.

We all want the place we live to be spotlessly clean, exuberantly
healthful, and beautiful besides. The people in the Niagara region
feel doubly betrayed, because they had so much of that beauty—
still do, if you look beyond the landfills and ignore what you can't
see. Which is exactly what tourists do. Locals don't have that luxury. When I talk to Lou Ricciuti, one of the angriest of the local
activists, he tells me with simple conviction how much he used to
love the Niagara region. Lou used to work in the tourist industry;
now he blogs under the name "Nuclear Lou" and datelines his
emails "Los Alamos East."

"It was a place of opportunity," he tells me over the phone.
"To me it was Eden. Before I found this stuff out, to me there
couldn't have been a more beautiful place in the country . . . vast
open water in the Great Lakes and little tiny lakes where you
could go out and teach your kid to fish. To find out this stuff
just changes your perspective entirely, from seeing it as Eden
to seeing it as a place where everything that happened was for a
profit motive."

In 2001, Lou and another activist named Geoff Kelly published a seven-part series on the area's radiological contamination

in a local Buffalo magazine called *Artvoice*. Titled "The Bomb That Fell on Niagara," the piece is angry, heartfelt, exhaustive, and at times, paranoid. Ricciuti and Kelly outline the history of the Manhattan Project and what's known about waste disposal at LOOW. They mention the Rochester burial, the rumored railcar, the possible phosgene. They talk about ex-Nazi scientists working for local companies. They even speculate that there might be sinister motives behind the Corps of Engineers' 1969 dewatering of the American Falls. Were they searching for contamination? They admit that such a suggestion is "wild speculation," but ask, "What else can one do but speculate when it is so difficult to pry information from those who have it?"

What else indeed? The history of lies and cover-ups has made it all but impossible for the two camps in Niagara County to talk to each other. Even the environmental activists are divided among themselves, sniping at each other on Web bulletin boards and protecting their sources of information. I once read through a long list of posts and replies, complete with pictures, in which two locals were arguing over whose geiger counter was better.

Geographer Patrick McGreevy once suggested that for Canada, Niagara Falls acted as a front door. Thus, they landscaped and decorated it, the way you do your front walk, so that arriving guests get a good impression. In contrast, for the United States, McGreevy proposed, Niagara Falls was a backyard: the place where you park your old bicycles, pasture your broken-down couch, and stick your trash. It's a nice, neat theory. But of course, America, no less than Canada, sees Niagara as an emblem for itself. It's why we have spent so much effort "remediating" it, disguising the effects of our use and abuse of the waterfall and its landscape.

"Niagara was treated in a very unusual way," Lou tells me. "There was no reverence for this place." It does seem odd. And yet I'm not sure reverence is the answer to Niagara's—or nature's—ills. Reverence is standing apart. We need to put ourselves back into the landscape—not to harness it or preserve it, but to live in and with it. Moving forward means opening our eyes to a world that is always complex.

Unfortunately, that's becoming harder and harder to do. Niagara Falls today needs help, environmentally and, on the American side, economically. But from the sixties to the present day, the movement to save Niagara has focused on tourism development. The future of Niagara may hang on whether tourism can offer a clear vision, or whether it will just produce one more counterfeit myth.

Nine

BOULEVARD OF BROKEN DREAMS

WHENEVER I'M IN NIAGARA FALLS, I like to jog around Goat Island when I wake up. The rapids are louder in the quiet of morning, and the Falls rainbow is brighter with the sun at your back. Sometimes it reaches all the way from the Canadian Horseshoe to the American bank in an unbroken pastel arch, the Falls grinding away in the mist behind it as if their only purpose is to keep it suspended there. I'm a wimpy runner, so after one lame, iPod-driven circuit of the island's main road, I head to the Cave of the Winds Snack Bar for my reward: a cup of coffee with nondairy creamer.

If I stay at the once-glamorous, now-decrepit Hotel Niagara, which recently sold for $4.6 million (the starting price of a four-bedroom condo in the former Manhattan Project headquarters), I jog down Rainbow Boulevard. I pass between the boarded-up Art Deco United Office Building and the boarded-up Turtle, a bankrupt Native American cultural center. I cut through the parking lot of the nondescript Comfort Inn, cross four lanes of traffic on the Robert Moses Parkway, and enter the Niagara Reservation.

More often, I stay at the Howard Johnson Closest to the Falls, which recently changed its name to the Howard Johnson Closest to the Falls and Casino. From there, I run down Main Street, crossing in front of the toll booths on the Rainbow Bridge. I continue past the derelict Rainbow Centre Mall and its titanic parking ramp, together devouring a whole block to my left. I dodge sections of missing sidewalk as I pass the former Occidental headquarters building known as the Flashcube. Having sat empty for years, it is now emblazoned with a hasty banner: Hot Food—Internet—Gifts—Souvenirs. I pass the tethered passenger balloon that goes up and down from a vacant lot, ignoring the blaring heavy metal music played by its high-school-aged operators, and make a right at Smokin Joes Family Fun Center, a garish, makeshift arcade squatting in the derelict Wintergarden arboretum. I trot past the haunted house (for sale), the putt-putt golf course (closed), and the random assortment of low-end souvenir shops (Dutch Candy Factory! T-Shirts! Beer to Go!).

This is the landscape that greets visitors when they arrive in Niagara Falls, New York. Most tourists know Niagara will be tacky, but they don't expect it to be seedy. Luckily, it's easy to make for the border, because all the main roads in Niagara Falls funnel you toward the Rainbow Bridge, as if the mortified little town wants to hurry you right on through to Canada before you notice anything else.

People who hear that I'm on my way to or from Niagara say either "Oh, I've never been there," or "I can't believe how much better it is in Canada!" When I confess that I actually prefer to stay on the American side, I get blank stares. For one thing, I point out, it's cheaper. That's because instead of looking out your hotel window at the Falls, slowly changing colors like a lava lamp, you're looking out at the back of a bar called Kold Ones, or at a construction site, or a couple of abandoned shopping carts, stuck together as if mating. If you're lucky, the well-known local panhandler known as Birdman will pedal by with his macaw, Sundance, on his shoulder. Sometimes, I explain how I got the big gash on the side of my car when I was driving down a street in Niagara Falls and had to pull into a dirt parking lot to gawk at a mural on the side of a boarded-up bar. It was of the genre known to art historians as "dogs playing pool," though there are variants, the best known being "dogs playing poker." The Niagara variant may be *sui generis*: instead of aiming for the eight ball or grimly inspecting their hands, the dogs are sitting morosely at a bar while another dog—a yellow lab maybe—is pole dancing. The pole-dancing dog is wearing a G-string stuffed with bills. I was so taken by the mural the first time I saw it that I backed around a post and scraped off a long carrot-peel of paint.

There's something downright impressive about the desolation of downtown Niagara Falls, New York. If city planners had set out to lay waste to a town, they couldn't have done a better job.

One day in the Local History section at the Niagara Falls Public Library, I ask Maureen Fennie for all the town's development plans. At first, she just laughs. Then, as she often does when I'm there, she sighs and goes away. A little while later, she comes back pushing a library cart laden with boxes. She parks it next to my table and throws me a look that says *Good luck*.

The boxes overflow with scrapped plans: manifestos for progress, maps of strategic areas, schedules of phased transitions. There are wonky plans with bar graphs, dull plans with page after page of maps, vivid plans with soaring architectural renditions set off by curlicues of greenery. One strategic plan from the early eighties has squiggly little drawings and is written in the style of a bad picture book. "The metaphor for Niagara Falls is obvious," it enthuses. "It's the rainbow! The rainbow is a natural phenomenon that only happens with the Falls." Whatever else these consultants were, they weren't meteorologists.

The stack of binders is overwhelming. More things, it seems, have failed to happen at Niagara Falls than have happened. If you could somehow gather the collective effort and brainpower spent on dashed illusions and turn it toward remaking the town, Niagara would be a showplace. And why shouldn't it be? It sits at the brink of a world-famous natural wonder. At least 8 million people a year visit the American side (more than double that descend on Canada). In one shiny presentation book after another, consultants, city planners, architects and developers all profess themselves flummoxed by Niagara's failure to live up to its potential. After several hours going through it all, I'm surprised the little town hasn't packed itself into a barrel and thrown itself over the Falls.

The failure was not thinking small, that much is clear. The history of planning at the Falls, beginning with the Porter brothers' dreams of waterwheels and international resorts, has aimed at nothing less than heaven on earth. With the waterfall's harnessing in the 1890s, utopia began to look literally in reach. With nature subject to human will, the world could be remade in our image. William T. Love was not the only one with visions of a futuristic supercity at Niagara, powered by electricity and heralding a brave new world of productivity, cleanliness and man-made beauty. King Gillette—inventor of the safety razor—dreamed up a scheme even more far-fetched. His city, Metropolis, described in his 1894 book *The Human Drift*, was meant to house the entire nation—with the exception of a few farmers and miners. Living in giant, climate-controlled apartment blocks, connected to their workspaces with glass-enclosed walkways, the citizens of Metropolis would no longer fear the whims of nature. In fact, nature too would be perfected—carefully landscaped parks and gardens would offer up a more regulated beauty, with no end other than human pleasure.

One planned utopia was actually built, and still remains in Niagara Falls. The model workers' town Echota, built at the turn of the century, was meant to prove that harnessing the waterfall for humanity would not only benefit the power-brokers, but would lead to a workers' paradise too. As nightmarish, coal-driven factories gave way to cleaner, modern, electric facilities, so too the roiling chaos of industrial cities would be replaced by sparkling, wholesome planned communities.

Romantically declared to mean "town of refuge" in Cherokee, Echota was designed by McKim, Mead & White in 1891. The Niagara Falls Power Company set aside 84 acres off Buffalo Avenue, walking distance from the factories. They hired civil engineers to lay out roads and utilities. The engineers designed a tile drainage system for the swampy land and built dikes to protect the residential area from regular flooding at nearby Gill Creek. They drew up a neat neighborhood of tree-lined sidewalks and electric-lit streets. At its center was a wide boulevard, with room for two electric rail lines connecting it to downtown Niagara Falls and Buffalo. There was a school, a firehouse, a store, a community center, and the first install-ment of dwellings: sixty-seven attractive Shingle-style homes drawn up by star architect Stanford White. In single, duplex and triplex arrangements, White's yellow and white homes had attractive Geor-gian elements: gambrel rooflines, bay windows, columned porches. Every house was equipped with central heat, water and gas, as well as what the *Ladies' Home Journal* enthused were "the best modern appliances for household convenience."

For a few years, Echota gleamed. More homes were built. The neighborhood was held up as an emblem of a new and improved society, moral reform inspired by architecture, what theologian Reinhold Niebuhr dismissed as "the doctrine of salvation by bricks." He was in the minority. Most people loved the idea; mag-azine articles profiled the town and its planners; reporters turned up to document its milestones: the first family moving in, the first baby to be born there. "How fortunate," crowed the *Daily Cata-ract*, a Niagara newspaper, "is the dweller in this charming corner of the earth!"

It didn't stay charming for long. The power company decided to resign as landlord in 1910, and put all the homes on the mar-ket. The Depression caused the housing stock to deteriorate. Absent the eyes of the world, the infrastructure was allowed to decline. In 1958, Robert Moses and his Power Authority decided that one of their water conduits needed to traverse the area. Sev-enty-four homes were picked up and moved to a new develop-ment called Veteran Heights. After the conduit was finished, new Echota homes were built to replace them, tiny, postwar boxes that reflected the neighborhood's fallen value. Workers with good jobs were now moving to the up and coming neighborhood of LaSalle, with its newer homes, schools and parks. Echota was undesir-able; the very proximity to the factories originally considered an asset was now a drawback. Smokestacks belched pollution over

the area, and outfall pipes dumped sludge into Gill Creek. The
trees died and the water turned toxic. Housing prices dropped,
and the neighborhood lost its identity. Eventually, people driving
by saw only some run-down houses on potholed streets, against a
backdrop of chemical plants and power lines. It couldn't be further
from utopia.

One day downstairs at the public library, waiting for the Local
History department to open, I flip idly through a book of current
real estate listings. One of the Stanford White homes is up for sale.
The price is $12,000.

Echota was based on a sweeping social vision that began with
industry. Throughout the first half of the twentieth century, city
planning for Niagara Falls proceeded on the understanding that
the factories were customer number one. As one planner put it,
"while the tourist interests of Niagara Falls should be more carefully served, the industrial interests are of even greater consider-
ation." Industry needs workers, which meant that city planning
focused on making Niagara Falls a nice place to live.

Once the factories began to leave and jobs grew scarce, keeping workers happy became less important. That began happening
even in the postwar boom years. Some factories headed out West,
where the federal government was building dams on the Columbia River, making even cheaper power than Niagara's. Others were
simply looking for places with lower wages and lighter state tax
regulations. Many downsized after they lost their wartime contracts. The 1956 landslide that destroyed the Schoellkopf Power
Plant was the last straw. Alcoa, Hooker, Union Carbide, International Paper, DuPont and Bell Aerospace closed local factories and
laid off workers. Between 1956 and 1963, the city of Niagara Falls
lost nearly 12,000 manufacturing jobs.

The sense of urgency that set in drove the Power Authority
project. But even as they knocked themselves out trying to get
manufacturers back, it was becoming clear to local city planners
that industry alone was not going to keep Niagara Falls afloat
anymore. The forward-thinking were already turning their eyes
away from industry—and the community that supported it—and

toward visitors. Throughout the power project, they continually wrote letters to Robert Moses, asking for clarification about his plans for the city of Niagara Falls. Was he planning for an increase in visitors?

Moses regularly assured them that his improvements would benefit tourism. But his focus was on arterial transportation. Moses, for all his brilliance, was a shortsighted man. For him, getting visitors to come to town meant building roads they could come on. It was partly the mania of the automobile age, and partly Moses's personal blindness to quality-of-life issues beyond infrastructure. He thus planned and executed only one major "improvement" to the city of Niagara Falls: the Robert Moses Parkway, an expressway sweeping through the city center and past the Falls, following the gorge rim to the new international bridge at Lewiston. With the opening of the parkway, the Niagara Reservation, for which Olmsted and his cronies fought so hard, was separated from the downtown by four lanes of high-speed traffic. The park could now be accessed only by a pedestrian bridge.

Even had they foreseen the devastating effect the Robert Moses Parkway would have on their city center, the people of Niagara Falls probably could not have stopped it. Robert Moses was, after all, the man who declared of New York City that "you have to hack your way through with a meat axe." And Niagara Falls had its own meat-axe wielder, Mayor E. Dent Lackey.

Lackey was elected in 1963, the year the first sections of the Robert Moses Parkway opened. An ex–Methodist minister with a habit of referring to his enemies as "those goddamn sons of bitches," he had a foul mouth and an intuitive understanding of spectacle: he was known for leading city parades on a white horse. Lackey was determined to remake Niagara as a tourist mecca. He helped form Niagara Falls Urban Renewal, a public agency authorized to issue tax-exempt, limited-liability bonds and to acquire land by eminent domain.

Niagara Falls Urban Renewal unveiled its master plan in 1965. Most of the city center—a mish-mash of nineteenth- and early-twentieth-century stores, motels, restaurants, factories and theaters—was slated for demolition. In its place was the Rainbow

Center: a completely new downtown anchored by a $40 million, 130,000-square-foot convention center intended to make Niagara Falls "the trade show center of the world." The convention center would be linked to the state park by the Falls Street Mall, a park-like pedestrian walkway lined with brand-new shops, restaurants, clubs and entertainment spots. Behind the convention center was a sprawling "International Garden," and more gardens were planned for Goat Island, which would be extended all the way to the Grand Island Bridge with fill from the power plant.

"The city that walked on one leg—industry," declared Mayor Lackey, "will now walk on two—industry and tourism."

The Rainbow Center plan included offices, educational facilities, libraries and affordable housing. But after the federal government, which had agreed to foot half the $26 million bill, held up groundbreaking by asking for clarification on a number of points, an amended plan was issued. In it, the downtown became more focused on the commercial and civic center. Residents were taken out of the picture.

There were only glimmers of dissent. A French architect and city planner called the renewal scheme "a crime." And a *Niagara Falls Gazette* staff writer named Marthe Lane Stumpo wrote an impassioned plea for preserving at least some of the city's historic architecture, as had been done successfully in cities such as New Haven, Philadelphia and San Francisco. Stumpo pointed out that renovating old buildings was cheaper than building new ones. Furthermore, it gave a town character, and reminded tourists of its historic past. It would be tragic to tear down Niagara's Victorian buildings, she declared, only to discover "they were a priceless asset to our community." Her piece was printed in the "Family" section.

Just four years earlier, in 1961, Jane Jacobs published *The Death and Life of Great American Cities*. A devastating critique of the dominant orthodoxy of city planning, the book declared that what was called the rebuilding of cities was in fact "the sacking of cities." At the root of the problem, according to Jacobs, were the utopian dreams of city planners. The most influential city planning movements, from Ebenezer Howard's turn-of-the-century "Garden City" to the soaring high-rise metropolises of Le Corbusier, depended on sorting and separating urban people and functions. And the sorting was based not on an understanding of how cities were actually used, but ideals of how they ought to be used. Paternalistic and moralizing, such utopians favored community centers over bars, game rooms over street gatherings, families strolling in parks over spontaneous dance parties. Like Olmsted's park layouts, their development plans aimed to control how people—especially poor people—lived their lives. In prescribing "correct" activities, they were blind to lived experience as it was already being lived. Life follows life, Jacobs declared, and to plow it under and attempt to replace it with a sanitized ideal was nothing less than murder.

Jacobs's book neatly identifies every single thing wrong with the Rainbow Center development scheme. She promoted mixed-use districts, preferably with more than two functions, to ensure the presence of people at different times of day. The revised Rainbow Center focused on visitors and their schedules only. Jacobs demanded that districts mingle new buildings with old; Rainbow Center began by razing everything old. She dispensed scornfully with the notion that parks were an unqualified good, pointing out that if not woven into the city's fabric, they would cause blight as fast as a superblock. The Rainbow Center plan, embracing the parkway that divided the parkland from the city, created a giant landscaped dead zone at the edge of the gorge. Jacobs's list of planning disasters reads like a synopsis of Niagara's plan: traffic arteries, parking lots, massive single elements out of scale with the streetscape. "To approach a city, or even a city neighborhood, as if it were a larger architectural problem," Jacobs wrote, "capable of being given order by converting it into a disciplined work of art, is to make the mistake of attempting to substitute art for life. The results of such profound confusion between art and life are neither life nor art. They are taxidermy."

Jacobs's book provided a rallying point, but many city planners already had the same idea. In New York City, the tide had turned against modernist planning's slash-and-burn approach to the urban jungle. Theorists like Lewis Mumford and Charles

Abrams had begun to advocate the kinds of community values Jacobs espoused, turning against Robert Moses and his meat axe. The six-year fight over Moses's plan to ram a highway through Washington Square Park, in which Jacobs played a key role, had ended with defeat for Big Bob the Builder. Congressional hearings were held in 1959, and in 1960 the reign of Robert Moses began to crumble as he was forced to resign from the Mayor's Committee on Slum Clearance. But it was too late for Niagara Falls.

On a snowy November morning in 1968, Niagara Falls proceeded to mount and stuff itself. Bells were rung, Mayor Lackey arrived by helicopter, speeches were made, the color guard stood at attention, and the first building was loudly brought down. The demolition proceeded apace. By 1971, the *Washington Post* reported that "great gaps punctuate the five- and six-story skyline, vacant lots are scattered all over the place, and bulldozers and earth movers are banging and thrashing around wherever you look." Journalists compared the appearance of Niagara Falls to Berlin after the bombings.

Dan Wiest, the retired Union Carbide worker, came to Niagara Falls in 1950, when the town was at its peak. In the heady years after World War II, when patriotism, progress, prosperity and sex all came together at the Falls, no one could imagine that a mere two decades later the city center would be a ghost town.

"I lived downtown on Prospect Street, at the Cascade Hotel," Dan tells me. "You'd walk up Falls Street during the day, and it was just full of people. There were souvenir shops, two big theaters; the place was hustling. The urban renewal project killed all that." I ask him if he can remember some of the businesses from downtown.

"Oh sure. On Main Street, there was a bowling alley, DiFazio's, a small place. They set the pins by hand. There was a big Sears and Roebuck. There were the two theaters: the Cataract and the Strand." Falls Street, he says, was always crowded with both cars and people before they closed it off to traffic. Somehow, taking cars away took the pedestrians away too.

"It just died, that's all," he says simply.

Dan's take is not unusual. Niagara locals who lived through urban renewal see it as a case of municipal citycide. A recent article in the *Niagara Falls Reporter* listing causes for the city's woes put E. Dent Lackey and Niagara Falls Urban Renewal at number one. The *Niagara Gazette* agreed, declaring in 1999 that urban renewal was the second most important story of the century (the collapse of the Schoellkopf Power Plant was number one). Residents who lived in pre-urban-renewal downtown, the paper declared, "speak as if it were the Emerald City."

The Rainbow Center plan was supposed to spark a firestorm of private development, and at first it seemed like it might work. The city opened its convention center, designed by Philip Johnson's firm, in 1974, amid a wave of excitement about other projects. The Black American Museum and Cultural Center was announced in 1973. The Wintergarden, an indoor arboretum hailed as an architectural triumph and featured in *Life* magazine, opened in 1977. The Native American Center for the Living Arts completed its nifty turtle-shaped building in 1978. There was a $10.5 million Niagara Hilton, a $1 million addition to the local Holiday Inn, and plans for a twenty-five-story rotating hotel, called the "rotel." The Carborundum Company even built its new corporate headquarters downtown, with a Carborundum Center and Crafts Museum on two of its floors.

The problem was, the new downtown was no longer a downtown. The past's small-time shops and restaurants had made for a lively street life. Residents headed for Sears mingled with tourists browsing through souvenir shops. Restaurants served both visitors heading for the Falls and residents coming out of a movie. The new downtown, in contrast, was nothing more than a conventioneer's extended lobby, a collection of superblocks appended awkwardly to a waterfall. More attention had been paid to architectural showmanship than pedestrian practicalities. Hotels turned their backs on the park. The giant convention center was not knit into the streetscape. Even the admired Wintergarden was badly sited, creating a barricade across Falls Street, the main thoroughfare to the Niagara Reservation. Visitors had a hard time finding the Falls.

And there was no one to point the way: residents had been moved to the outskirts. Office space, Carborundum notwithstanding, was scarce. Locals had no reason now to go to the city center, and they didn't. Vast stretches of downtown remained vacant, adding to the deadness and creating a vicious circle of neglect. With a shrinking tax base, city finances floundered; at several points in the seventies, Niagara Falls came close to default.

It was easy to blame the parkway: by 1974, Mayor Lackey was calling it "that damned Chinese wall." But the parkway was part of a larger vision of urban renewal that was harder to kill than the famous Moses momentum. Even in New York City, the top-down, super-block approach lived on post-Moses. The year the Rainbow Center plan was released, 1965, a plan for Lower Manhattan was presented that cleared away acres of housing and markets and piers and small shops to expand on the massive superblocks of the planned World Trade Center. In the wake of renewed interest in Lower Manhattan development, that plan was recently reissued. I bought a copy and was amazed to see that the neighborhood where I live—west of City Hall and north of the Trade Center—was assumed unsalvageable by sixties planners. Had the city not run out of cash in the seventies, no doubt the now-landmarked streetscape of low-rise lofts, restaurants and shops called Tribeca would be gone, bulldozed and replaced by lifeless, cookie-cutter towers.

After urban renewal, things went from bad to worse. Niagara's two biggest advantages had always been that everyone wanted to go there and everyone *could* go there; it was within a day's drive of the majority of the American population. In the late seventies, both things changed. First there was the energy crisis: as the OPEC oil embargo of 1973 was followed by the Iranian Revolution and a second energy crisis in 1979, skyrocketing gas prices took a huge bite out of the tourism market. And then there was Love Canal. The ecological disaster brought the eyes of the nation to the region in exactly the wrong way. Now, even if folks had the money to drive to Niagara Falls, they might think twice about doing so.

What happened next has a desperate feel to it. With manufac-turing all but gone, and its reputation for natural beauty tarnished, the city's development plan devolved into luring shoppers to town. It's as if the city planners could only focus on one thing: the clang of a cash register. "Tourist destination" came to mean "mall."

In the early eighties, the city poured massive amounts of development money into converting a parking ramp less than a block from the Falls into the Rainbow Centre Mall. It opened in 1982, with great fanfare, and did well at first, as droves of Canadians came across the border to get low-tax deals. A new development group called Niagara Venture was made the city's master builder in 1982, announcing plans for another mall along with a hotel, an indoor amusement park and a water park. Four years later, Canadian developers announced plans for a Niagara Falls megamall like the famous one in Edmonton, the largest mall in North America. The Niagara mall was to be called Fantasyland.

The name was appropriate. One by one, the mall schemes collapsed. The Fantasyland developers backed off when the state withdrew its offer of $400 million in financial incentives. They built their 4.2-million-square-foot Mall of America in Bloomington, Minnesota, instead, where household incomes were higher; it's now the world's most-visited mall. Master developer Niagara Venture faced charges of unpaid lease payments and water bills, and the city foreclosed on its malls and water park in 1992. By the nineties, even the Rainbow Centre Mall was struggling, and the last retail businesses there were shuttered in 2000. An Off-Track Betting shop limped on until 2005. Today the building sits empty, a looming cement pile between the Niagara Reservation and downtown.

In the meantime, the city continued to decline. The Black American Museum and Cultural Center evaporated. Niagara Falls mayor James Galie, citing rising energy costs that made it expensive to heat, began to talk about demolishing the Wintergarden. The Turtle struggled with insolvency for years, closing its doors in 1996, after IRS agents confiscated some of its artifacts and auctioned them off to recoup back taxes. Wampum belts, prehistoric stone tools, pottery, beadwork and art went on the block. Elwood Green, the center's executive director, told reporters "I guess people have to get their information about Indians from *Pocahontas* and

The Indian in the Cupboard." The city foreclosed on the building shortly thereafter. Since then, it has sat there, an empty shell.

Bob Baxter suggests I meet him at the Power Vista, the Power Authority's visitor center. It's an odd choice: although it's a public space, the Power Vista has a hushed, authoritarian feel. Soaring ceilings and gleaming floors give it an aura of despotic grandeur. Besides, Bob has a reputation here. Several administrators pass us in the lobby, and they give Bob stiff smiles, their greetings crackling with icy pleasantness. He stops to chat with each one, seeming to savor their discomfort.

Bob is conservation chairman of the Niagara Heritage Partnership, a group of locals with a different plan for Niagara redevelopment. They want the natural landscape of the Niagara Gorge restored as much as possible. The way to make that happen, they claim, is to remove the Robert Moses Parkway from the gorge rim.

The Robert Moses Parkway is still a sore spot in Niagara County. Planners all agree that putting the parkway along the riverfront downtown was a lousy idea. Local rumor has it that even Robert Moses admitted as much in private, when he came back years later and saw what it had done. Another rumor claims that Moses built the parkway in the first place because he was trying to punish Niagara Falls for the endless obstructions they threw up to his power project. It wasn't a mistake; it was revenge.

In the late seventies, urged on by Mayor Lackey, State Parks removed the small stretch of parkway that ran through the Niagara Reservation, demolishing the pedestrian bridge that had connected the parking lots and the riverfront. When you drive into Niagara Falls on the Robert Moses Parkway now, it takes you right by the upper rapids, but as it curves around the river's elbow at the Falls, it turns into the slower, two-way Prospect Street. Prospect Street ends at the entrance to the Rainbow Bridge. Fifty feet beyond the bridge, you pick up the parkway again, to be swept north along the gorge rim past Devil's Hole State Park, over the top of the Robert Moses Niagara Power Plant, and on to the Niagara Escarpment, where it jogs inland to descend the escarpment's steep face. It passes between Lewiston and Model City as it heads north, toward Lake Ontario and Fort Niagara.

The Niagara Heritage Partnership wants the state to remove all four lanes of the parkway from the Rainbow Bridge to Lewiston—the part that hugs the gorge rim below the Falls. They want the 6.5 miles of roadway replaced with a network of hiking paths and bike trails. Wildflowers and native scrub could bloom on spots now covered by mown grass. Ground-nesting birds and toads would come back. People could bike along the gorge at the top or hike along it at river level and enjoy its natural beauty.

Bob Baxter and I cross the glassed-in pedestrian bridge over the parkway and ride an escalator down to the Power Vista. He leads me outside, onto the deck, and waves a hand at the gorge.

"It's an untapped tourist resource," he declares, fumbling for his cigarettes and fixing me with watery, intense eyes.

I haven't known Bob for ten minutes, and already I'm worried about his health. Bob chain-smokes, and he's older than I expected. He has a single gray curl in the middle of his forehead, a perfect tube where he could stick a cigarette for safekeeping, and he seems like the kind of person who might do that. His outspoken, occasionally impudent writing style has given the Niagara Heritage Partnership a distinct voice for their crusade. In one magazine article, he declared that to see nature in Niagara's current landscape, "you'd have to be a one-eyed contortionist with a good imagination." When a group protesting high-powered boats on the Niagara River unfurled a banner that said Jet Boats Suck at a media event, the Niagara Heritage Partnership trotted Bob out to deny involvement. He did, but he began his official statement by saying "Jet boats DO suck." His campaign to remove a big hunk of parkway has earned him a lively batch of enemies. One surly local reporter pilloried him in print for getting food stuck in his beard when he eats.

In person, he's just as sardonic, with a speaking style you might call "salty." "There goes the goddamn jet boat," he growls when a craft full of screaming tourists roars by on the river. "What a piece of crap."

Bob has lived his whole life in the Niagara region. He ran wild in the countryside as a kid and worked construction on the power plant project as a youth. He held assorted jobs in local factories, often quitting if they wouldn't give him the first day of hunting season off. In those days, there was always another job. Sometimes he worked in tourism.

"Oh, we all used to drive tour buses for summer jobs," he tells me when I ask him about it, "me and all the losers that were my friends. Niagara Falls Boulevard was where all the information booths were set up, the ones taking kickbacks for sending tourists to certain businesses. They had big signs and arrows to lure the tourists inside. There was one guy who got a police cap and a little whistle—he would jump out in front of cars and direct them into his parking lot. We called Niagara Falls Boulevard the Boulevard of Broken Dreams." He laughs his raspy laugh.

The Niagara Heritage Partnership plan for parkway removal is controversial, although at first blush it's hard to see why. No one denies the stupidity of a four-lane, high-speed arterial that cuts off private real estate and public parks from their best natural asset. Communities to the north of Niagara Falls are well served by alternate routes, and the parkway itself is underutilized. But the off chance that the parkway might bring a couple more tourists to Fort Niagara, or shave a few minutes off a Lewiston resident's morning commute seems to torment local politicos. A group of politicians and residents north of the Falls even formed what they call the Parkway Preservation Committee, aimed at keeping the road open.

The problem is, parkway removal is not, at heart, an economic strategy; it's an environmental one. What the Niagara Heritage Partnership wants is a return to nature. What the state wants is a return on investment. The question is whether the two are compatible.

Ernest Sternberg thinks not. "I'm not sure this is the place where you try to have an indigenous natural environment," he tells me. "As an environmentalist, I'd rather see ten times the acreage preserved somewhere more remote, and see this place—not necessarily taken advantage of—but given a little freer hand in what they do there."

Sternberg is a professor of urban and regional planning in the architecture school at SUNY Buffalo. In 1997, he published a paper called "The Iconography of the Tourism Experience" that uses Niagara Falls as an example of failed planning. Good tourism planning, he argues, must understand the themes inherent in its destination, and must "stage" those themes in a coherent narrative. In other words, it has to figure out what the story of a place is, and tell that story through the experience of going there. Not only has Niagara Falls failed to come to terms with its themes—Sternberg proposes "ecosystem," "terror" and "freak" as themes that might be used—but it tells its story wrong. Because of the abundance of parking, its climax, the close-up view of the Falls, is reached too quickly. In the days of the Porters, you arrived at your hotel, walked across the bridge to Goat Island and wound your way through wooded paths to get your first glimpse of the Falls. Today you drive into the parking lot, cross the street, and there it is. Or you drive around, lost in the confusing streetscape of the drab little town. Experiencing Niagara today is like hearing a story retold by a four-year-old: it either distracts you with seemingly irrelevant tangents, or it blurts out its conclusion with no buildup.

As an example of tourism planning that successfully lays out a cohesive narrative experience, Sternberg cites Disney. Disney's park environments are famously "imagineered," in company parlance, to move people expeditiously through a prepackaged experience, extracting money from them at every narrative pause. What Disney codified is a tour not unlike that developed by the Porters and other early entrepreneurs, the commercial approach to tourism that Olmsted & Vaux's plan was meant to replace.

Sternberg brings out a dilemma that always rears its head in thinking about Niagara and about tourism. People come to Niagara to experience nature, a form of contemplation that's considered an uplifting experience. But on vacation they also expect to be entertained. A waterfall, however beautiful or sublime, is not inherently entertaining, especially if you can't ride it. It's hard to imagine that removing parking lots and restaging the pedestrian experience will make the Falls more entertaining. After all, the Canadians did this. But they also added something else: a carnivalesque entertainment district. For many, this sideshow has become the main attraction.

Canadian Niagara is constantly held up as an example of successful development, a shame stick used to smack Americans into better planning. "The Land of Oz!" a developer told *USA Today* in 2003, pointing to Canada's skyline. The Canadian development plan, articulated in a 1998 report by consultants Urban Strategies, divided Niagara Falls, Ontario, into distinct areas serving specific functions and markets, and established land-use regulations for preserving those distinctions. It proposed ways of connecting park areas to the rest of the city, recommended introducing a people-mover, established built-form controls for the skyline, and urged unified approaches to city entry points, landscaping, circulation systems, streetscapes, parking and signage.

Ontario's plan brings a feeling of consistency to the chaotic jumble of tourist development. High-end hotels are grouped in the Fallsview area, mid-range family hotels cluster around Clifton Hill, and budget hotels hang out at the edge of town. The riverfront downstream is lined with upscale bed and breakfasts. Parks Commission attractions are clearly designated with the tagline "the Authentic Falls Experience."

But the most important part of the plan was the near-abolition of parking anywhere near the Falls. Cars are banished to a giant parking lot upstream; people-movers shuttle tourists between their cars and the various commercial areas. Once this change was effected, the cluster of franchise restaurants, souvenir shops and attractions perched above Queen Victoria Park took off. Today this streetscape of flashing signs, themed buildings, wax figures and brand names is thick with pedestrians. The sideshow has moved to center stage. In fact, 47 percent of the tourists coming to Canadian Niagara, according to a 1998 visitor study, never visit a Falls attraction.

If, as Jane Jacobs argued, life follows life, Ontario proves that tourist development follows tourist development. This was confirmed in 1996, when a five-firm consortium called Falls Management opened the 100,000-square-foot Casino Niagara. With the arrival of high-stakes gambling, Canadian Niagara's conversion from natural wonder to Vegas-style fun park was complete.

The opening was huge. Seven thousand people crammed themselves into the casino, located in a former mall, while the Americans looked on with horror. They had spent more than twenty years trying to get gambling in their own town: Niagara Falls state senator Earl Brydges first proposed a state constitutional amendment to legalize gambling in 1972. Such an amendment requires ratification by two successive legislatures to go to a public vote. This had repeatedly failed to happen. And now Niagara Falls, New York, had to stand idly by as the Canadians began raking in $40 million a month. It was briefly proposed that the Americans could benefit too—by building a giant parking lot for gamblers headed to Canada.

A year after the Canadians opened their casino, Niagara Falls, New York, signed a memorandum of agreement with its latest developer-savior. In exchange for guaranteeing to attract $140 million of private investment, a group called Niagara Falls Redevelopment Corporation was given control of 200 acres of downtown, including the rights to manage the Convention Center, the Wintergarden, the Splash Park, parking ramps and the Rainbow Centre Mall, all operations on which the city was losing cash. Local newspapers were abuzz. They gave extensive coverage to the man behind the consortium, Eddy Cogan. Cogan (who died in 2003) was a Toronto real estate dealmaker known as "Fast Eddy," or "Canada's Donald Trump." A roguish, handsome man famous for throwing lavish parties in the eighties, Cogan was credited with having transformed Toronto in the boom period that began in the fifties. He lost nearly everything when Toronto's real estate market collapsed in 1989, and spent the nineties rebuilding his fortune. Niagara Falls was his last big dream.

After running ads inviting the public "to view Niagara's future," Niagara Falls Redevelopment presented its plan in January 1998. Over 1,000 people packed the Convention Center theater and adjoining pub, where the meeting was shown on closed-circuit television. The crowds were so heavy police had to close off the area. The slide show met with spontaneous rounds of applause. And no wonder; it looked great. The plan—this one was named "the Big Idea"—called for removing the entire downtown section of the Robert Moses Parkway and reconnecting Niagara Falls to its waterfalls. It set aside a stretch of Buffalo Avenue for low-rise, high-end resort development along the river above the Falls. It doomed the Observation Tower at the *Maid of the Mist* landing, but proposed preserving and renovating the Art Deco United Office Building, the Rainbow Centre Mall and the Flashcube formerly known as Occidental. In the area around the Convention Center, the plan laid out an entertainment district with movie theaters, live music venues, restaurants, shops, attractions, a high-rise hotel and a casino.

There, of course, was the rub. Casino gambling had yet to make it to a statewide referendum, and even if it did, there was no guarantee it would pass. The plan, Cogan assured the city, was "not dependent" on the casino. But it would be a whole lot better if it had one. Three months later, he told the *Niagara Gazette* that the casino element was "critical." "We're not dealing with purity," he declared. "We're dealing with reality." By June, he was announcing that if the state would not agree to gaming, "I'll build a box mall, I'll cry and I'll leave town." If that happened, he told the *Gazette*, "Niagara Falls will be Mexico North, instead of a world class tourist destination."

The casino had gone from being the icing on the cake to being cake, icing and plate. At a planning meeting where local residents were allowed to ask questions, a little girl approached the mic and asked developers what impact their plans would have on the children of Niagara Falls.

"Do you play blackjack?" one of them quipped.

At first it looked like "the Big Idea" might succeed in spurring further development. In 1999, a private company announced plans to build an underground aquarium called AquaFalls at the Flashcube. New York governor George Pataki hailed the $35 million project as "the most significant private-sector investment" in Niagara Falls in the last fifty years. Inspired by the successes of cities such as Baltimore and Chattanooga, where aquariums were the centerpieces for themed urban renewal plans, the city and county provided tax abatements and direct assistance. Never mind that Niagara Falls already had an aquarium that was struggling to meet its visitorship goals.

AquaFalls was scheduled to open in the summer of 2000. It didn't. Developers dug a two-story-deep hole next to the Flashcube in 1999 and promptly ran out of money. An initial bond offering failed. Investors grew even more skittish when Ripley's revealed plans to build a giant aquarium on the Canadian side of Niagara Falls, as part of its Great Wolf Lodge and Indoor Waterpark. AquaFalls developers bailed. The hole sat empty, a conspicuous gap in the main tourist area, collecting water when it rained.

Plans for theme parks, convention centers, aquariums and malls all have one main goal: drawing visitors to the region and getting them to leave some money behind when they go. They are not about life—the life of the city, the life of the environment, even really, the lives of tourists, outside of that magic moment where they take out their wallets. Nowhere is this urge more obvious than in a casino, a machine literally guaranteed to make more than it spends. As Niagara Falls Redevelopment reneged on promise after promise—backing out of a millennium New Year's party, snarling itself in legal arguments over asbestos removal in the United Office Building, wrangling control of the Convention Center from the city then refusing to market it, and finally suing the city over its failure to hand over the shuttered Splash Park—Eddy Cogan obsessed about two things: the airport, which he wanted to redevelop for commercial traffic, and the casino. In an interview with the *Niagara Gazette* in January 2000, he harped on them again and again. "No area turns around with local money," he declared. Niagara's future depended on getting tourists into town quickly, and just as quickly getting their quarters into the slots. Every other aspect of a vision that had caused locals to burst out in applause had slipped over the brink and vanished.

In 2000, fed up with the lack of results, Mayor Irene Elia told Niagara Falls Redevelopment to "put a shovel in the ground" by

July or be sued by the city. The group announced it would reno-
vate the Turtle. As of this writing, it has not.

One afternoon at the Niagara Falls Public Library, I'm photocopy-
ing a picture of Niagaraphile Paul Gromosiak, and the man himself
strolls in. In real life, he's smiling, just as he smiles up from the
Buffalo News story, where he lofts a model he made himself. The
article is part of a little packet I've assembled from the library's clippings file. It starts with "Historian Envisions Grand Museum," and
ends with "Historian Throws in Towel on Museum." The pages in
between trace the rise and fall of Gromosiak's vision for the Niagara
Historical Center, a world-class Falls interpretive museum.

The real Gromosiak, a little balder than his 2-D counterpart,
is wearing shorts and walking with a jaunty bounce. The Niagara
Historical Center couldn't be further from his mind. He has a new
idea now: the Niagara Experience Center. It's a world-class Falls
interpretive museum, this time centered on geology.

"I'm all excited, like it's Christmas Eve," he cries in his slightly
high-pitched voice. "I just got a letter from Warren Buffett! Well,
not Warren Buffett, but his representative." Paul pulls a folded
piece of paper out of his shirt pocket and hands it to me. Buffett's
representative is writing to say that the Niagara Experience Center
sounds like a noble thing, but Mr. Buffett is unlikely to make a
significant contribution to it.

"What do you think?" Paul asks me eagerly.

"It doesn't look like they're handing you a big chunk of money,"
I say cautiously, not wanting to burst his bubble. Apparently, this
is not possible.

"I know, but they think it's a good idea!" he cries.

An older lady sitting at one of the library tables compliments
Paul on his recent appearance in a PBS documentary. In it, he
gives a tour of his home, a minishrine to Niagara filled with educational diptychs and models of unbuilt projects from previous
big dreams.

"I have a disease called Niagara Falls," he tells her, beaming
like an Oscar-winner.

• • •

The Niagara Experience Center has made it a little further down the path toward reality than Paul's last project.

"We all felt that ultimately it's about the Falls," Nick Winslow tells me on the phone. "You can talk about the history, the industry, all those things, but people really do want to get close to it. It's no accident that all the top attractions are things where people are trying to get as close as they can. Also, that is something we felt the Canadian side did *not* do particularly well."

Winslow is working with BRC Imagination Arts, the company brought in to design the Niagara Experience Center.

"You have the foundation of this incredible park—the first state park in America—and there ought to be a seamless transition from that into the city itself, and the capstone should be the Niagara Experience Center. It celebrates the history, the drama, the natural wonder, the industrial past and the present of this place."

Nick talks fast, unfolding a clear vision: a gleaming interpretive center, with displays telling stories about the Falls: the geology, the power development, the Underground Railroad. There are indoor and outdoor gardens, a tourist information center, an artificial lake with nighttime illumination, and—the star attraction—a combination 3-D movie and thrill ride on which tourists soar over an Omnimax projection of the Falls with their legs hanging free: Niagara Falls, the roller coaster.

"In Canada it's all glitz and neon," Nick says. "We thought we ought to be the antithesis of that."

Planners on the American side of Niagara have consistently imagined using authenticity—cultural, historic, environmental—to differentiate themselves from Canada's middlebrow mall of attractions. There's a smattering of carnival on the American side—a dusty, outmoded wax museum, a poorly attended 4-D theater, the new balloon ride—but New York's planners have always shown more excitement for the highbrow: history museums, cultural centers, geology museums, interpretive trails and parks. It makes sense from a market perspective: differentiate New York's attractions from what you get in Canada. But there's something emotional behind it too: a desire to reclaim what's been lost. Nostalgia for the lost city and its landscape are at the heart of every plan that has captured the town's imagination. Focus groups with residents frequently yield persistent terms like "gaslight district" and "Village of Niagara." Planners may consider Canadian Niagara the Land of Oz, but the residents of New York's Niagara just want to get back to Kansas.

The past is what's really at stake in the struggle over the Robert Moses Parkway too. It's not just about six miles of asphalt. It's about what part of America you want restored. Parkway advocates still cling to the vision of Robert Moses: a strong, industry-based economy with solid infrastructure—highways and parks—all in service of the hardworking taxpayer. Main Street crowded with commerce, kids playing on well-kept playgrounds, a new car every three years.

The Niagara Heritage Partnership, on the other hand, wants the return of the American wilderness. They claim their parkway removal plan is compatible with emerging trends toward heritage and cultural tourism. They insist new visitors would be drawn to a renatured gorge: not track-suited slot junkies but affluent ecotourists and Boomers who might spend big for some organic salmon and a nice local wine instead of swinging through McDonald's on their way out of town. But they can't promise those ecotourists—there's not enough data—and to their minds, even without them, parkway removal would be a success. It would bring back the grasses, the trees and the birds.

One day, Bob Baxter drives me to a flat mesa north of the power plant, where unusable rubble from its construction was dumped. We stand on top of a blunt, artificial hill, and he describes what the area beneath looked like when he wandered its woods as a boy. He tells me how he used to hunt for rabbits here, how the leaves would flicker with sunlight and his dogs' barking would echo off the escarpment. Now the trees and streams he loved are buried under twenty feet of spoil. As he talks, his eyes grow pink.

Usually, I listen to painful stories with blank concentration. Looking at Bob's watery eyes and long, disappointed face, suddenly it's all too much. He glances off, struggling, and I surprise myself by abruptly turning away. I walk to the edge of the dirt square and stare at its grassy shoulder. There's a wood-shaving path here, winding its way through Queen Anne's lace and over the edge of the spoil pile. A green sign planted at a rakish angle says Wildlife Habitat Area: Please Stay on the Trail.

In 1993, Baxter published a book of poems called *Looking for Niagara*. The title poem is a dreamlike boat ride through Falls history. In one stanza, he lists famous writers who came to the Falls:

and Dickens broke off a piece of its rock
thinking he could take it home with him.

Well Charlie, I want that rock back.

Chris Schoepflin stops his car in front of a red sandstone church near Main Street: Sacred Heart. He tells me it was his childhood church.

"This church will probably be closed by the time your book comes out," he says. There's a chink in the armor of his voice, the slightly false note you hear in a kid trying to be tough.

Chris has a boyish face, but he's no kid. He's the president of USA Niagara Development, the latest group convened to revive Niagara's downtown. He seems to have his finger on the pulse of every project in town. "Is that sod?" he murmurs to himself as we pass a crew working along Rainbow Boulevard. "It's a little late for them to be putting in sod."

He wears a slate-gray suit with a tie the exact same color. We start off our meeting with excellent steak subs on fresh-baked rolls at a local place called Viola's. "I don't take people to Como's," he told me when I arrived at his office, a bright windowed room in the former headquarters of the Carborundum Company. The Como is the most famous restaurant in Niagara Falls, and Chris likes introducing people to Niagara's lesser-known treasures. He was born here, and after lunch he takes me for a drive around the Falls, starting with a cruise down Willow Avenue, where he grew up. His parents still live in the same neat clapboard house with a brick front porch, not far from the Italian-American restaurants of Pine Avenue. He shows me where you used to get really good pizza, and the park where he hung out in high school. Then we cruise through the Main Street neighborhood, the sorry spectacle of a boomtown gone bust. Main Street, Niagara Falls is a strip of boarded-up storefronts and foreclosure notices, signposted with the fading names of defunct stores: Kresge; the Gaslight Lounge; Hart to Hart Furniture; Slipko's Food King. Two businesses are visibly open: the Center City Neighborhood Development Corporation and, across the street, an establishment that appears to be known only as Adult Videos.

"This is a viable crack neighborhood," Chris says, that edge in his voice again.

USA Niagara was created in 2001 as a special subsidiary of New York's Empire State Development Corporation, dedicated to "promoting economic development and tourism and leveraging private investment in Niagara Falls." It issued the latest entrant in the cavalcade of city plans in 2002. Phase 1 called for developing the usual suspects downtown: the Flashcube, the Wintergarden, the Turtle, the Rainbow Mall, the pedestrian mall, the United Office Building. It called for repurposing the Falls Street Faire, an abandoned mall and indoor amusement park, and building a new casino.

USA Niagara bought the Falls Street Faire and turned it into a convention center. Expected to break even at best, it's a loss leader, meant to spur greater private development. So far, it has worked: a Phoenix-based real estate development company has upgraded the run-down Holiday Inn next door into a 3.5-star Crowne Plaza. The $34 million project was the town's biggest nongaming private investment in decades. There's even a Starbucks on the ground floor. But the renovation of the hotel was not spurred just by the convention center; it also had to do with the building that looms right across the street from it: the Seneca Niagara Casino.

The casino is thus far the most-realized part of the USA Niagara plan. It has sailed through Phase 1 and right into Phase 2, even though the machinations to get it going were complex. In an almost comic inversion of history, New York State seized prime real estate downtown by right of eminent domain and sold it to the Senecas, including the much-vaunted previous convention center, for which the Senecas paid $1. The Senecas who made the deal were the Seneca Nation of Indians, located on the Cattaraugus and Allegheny Reservations, about 80 miles from the Falls. The two closer Indian nations, the Tonawanda Band of Senecas and the Tuscaroras, are traditionalists, and unfriendly toward casinos. They sent representatives to Washington to try to convince the Department of the Interior to block the Seneca Nation's gaming compact, on the grounds that it would "undermine the cultural and religious values" of their own nations. Even for the less traditional Seneca Nation, who replaced their clan mothers and chiefs in 1838 with a democratically elected president, entering into a gaming compact was controversial. When a May 1998 referendum of tribal members produced results in favor of opening negotiations with the state, antigaming activists with scissors broke into president Michael Schindler's office and threatened to cut his hair. He promptly nullified the vote and resigned his office, but changed his mind the next day.

The road was rocky and strewn with lawsuits, but the gaming compact was finally signed in August of 2002. The federal government approved both the compact and the land transfer, and the Senecas opened their temporary casino in the old conference center less than four months later, on New Year's Eve. By the end of 2005, they had built a shiny new twenty-six-story hotel and spa to go with it. The Seneca Niagara offers both traditional table games like poker and blackjack, and slot machines. And it lures Canadians across the border with craps, free drinks, and smoking, none of which can be enjoyed in Canada's casinos.

Chris doesn't point out the casino as we tour downtown, but he doesn't have to: the gleaming rectangular box, glowing at night with a multicolored geyser of lights, is the biggest thing on Niagara's American skyline. Besides, Chris is a pragmatist: his job is to bring economic development to Niagara Falls, not to question the one financially successful venture to date. The Senecas now own 50 acres in downtown Niagara Falls, including the old Carborundum building where Chris works. The casino brings 5 million visitors a year to town. Even if 1 or 2 percent of them spent some money outside its walls, the difference would show.

Beyond the casino, the USA Niagara plan takes into account the city planning learning that followed in the wake of Jane Jacobs's critique. Road projects are aimed at widening sidewalks and decreasing road width, creating greater coexistence of pedestrians and cars. Traffic circles are being built to calm traffic, and barriers are being removed where possible, including the berms that separate the downtown from the river along the rapids above the Falls. The new convention center has been designed to spur usage at different times of day. There's a ballroom for nighttime functions, conference rooms for weekday events, and a convention hall expected to fill up on weekends. The pedestrian mall outside, which has been decrepit and unused for years, is being renovated and geared for street-level commerce. As for the Robert Moses Parkway, its downtown stretch is slated for removal.

"Nobody spends money driving forty-five miles per hour," Chris says.

He's noncommittal about the section north of town, the part the Niagara Heritage Partnership especially wants removed to enable the return of nature. "All of this gets figured out by the public in the public scoping process," he tells me. "Hopefully a compromise solution will be figured out." I can't get him to express an opinion. Chris is a political appointee; he speaks with meticulous diplomacy at all times.

Like any development planner, he thinks in terms of product. He praises the Canadians for having "created a lot of product" on their side of Niagara. But rather than copy their strategy, he wants to "differentiate the product."

"I almost look at it like a mall," he says as we sit on soft chairs in the new convention center, its maze of empty meeting rooms set up and ready, as if hosting a convention of ghosts. Chris gets out a pen and turns over a piece of paper, drawing two squares on it. "This is the Niagara Falls State Park, and this is the Seneca Gaming Corporation fifty acres. And this is Falls Street." He draws a line between them. "You have somewhere between eight and fourteen million people coming here"—he circles the Falls—"and five or six million going to the casino. It's almost like having Lord

& Taylor and Sears and Roebuck on each end, and our charge is in the middle."

I like Chris Schoepflin. I like his suit and tie the exact same shade of gray, as if he's making neutrality a vocation. I like the way he chats with the steak sandwich lady, and the catch in his voice when he tells me his childhood church is dying. I like what he says when I ask him how he keeps the faith in the midst of so much cynicism: "For me," he says of Niagara Falls, "accepting its decline is not an option."

But I walk away from him with an odd question bouncing around my head. Is tourism a business, like any other, a packaging of commodities to meet the market's needs, real or perceived? Is Niagara Falls an anchor tenant in a mall—Sears to the casino's swanker Lord & Taylor? Come see the softer side of the sublime? Nineteenth-century planners like Olmsted saw travel as a means of intellectual and moral enrichment. The Free Niagara movement that created the Niagara Reservation in 1885 won the public to its side by arguing that sublime landscapes were not simply places to be exploited, but sites of spiritual uplift, the pride of a nation and the birthright of its citizens. Such idealism would no doubt be laughed out of town today. But are we really ready to dispense with the notion that our connection to a place is somehow important beyond economic impact? Or that travel—in spite of many tourism theorists' claims to the contrary—can ever be anything other than a commodity, a manufactured experience sold at whatever price the market will bear?

In city planning too, it seems the notion of public good has faded from view. Niebuhr derided the "doctrine of salvation by bricks," but where is salvation meant to come from today? When I ask Chris to sum up USA Niagara's vision, he puts it in straightforward economic terms: "The ultimate vision is to attract private development and to generate jobs and to create and rebuild the tax base based on the tourism industry, which is the second-largest industry in the great state of New York."

In a way, he's simply putting it in terms people might be able to believe. No one's buying salvation here anymore. Everyone who talks about the difficulty of fixing Niagara Falls eventually mentions the cynicism of the town's residents. Niagara's long history of utopian dreamers works against it. Too many wizards have put on too many shows. The locals have had their fill of broken dreams. They've got their eye on the man behind the curtain.

"Many people have lost hope," Bob Baxter tells me. "They don't want to hear any more promises." The sentiment echoes what Paul Gromosiak told *The New York Times* in 2001. "I think even if Christ would come here and say 'I have come to save you,'" he said, "people would say, 'Yeah, I heard that before.'"

At the time, Niagara's mayor was a former nun.

Late one afternoon, I drive out Buffalo Avenue to its intersection with Hyde Park Boulevard. Three corners here contain industrial buildings. The fourth is Echota, the utopian workers' town. The sky overhead is scored with power lines. A couple of smokestacks hang out like hoodlums just down the street. And there, incongruously, sit Stanford White's houses, still remarkable, even in their dilapidated state, bankrupted turn-of-the-century gentlemen uneasily regarding their new neighbors, the featureless boxes the Power Authority built to replace the houses they moved in the sixties.

The original stone curbs and sidewalks are still here, grown over but largely intact. Some of White's homes have been re-sided. Others, boarded up, look abandoned. Some lots among them are empty: in the late eighties, when residents complained that trees in the neighborhood were dying from air pollution, DuPont, whose plant is nearest, began buying homes and demolishing them to create a "buffer zone." A few preservationists roused themselves to make a fuss, and DuPont desisted.

I park on D Street, near a post-White home with a detached garage on which someone has spray-painted the directive Fuck You. I get out and walk along Gill Creek. Seven and a half miles long, Gill Creek begins in the Tuscarora nation, swings around the Power Authority reservoir in a rerouting channel, passes through agricultural lands, a railyard and a golf course, glides through Hyde Park in Niagara Falls, where it's impounded to form a recreational lake, then slips over a small dam to flow through the factory district and into the Niagara River. On the opposite bank here, the scrubby trees occasionally part to offer glimpses of Echota's new next-door neighbor: the grassy Olin Industrial Welding hazardous waste landfill, capped after the soil and groundwater were contaminated with mercury and PCBs.

At A Street, I keep going, whacking into the brushy area between Echota and Buffalo Avenue. There, in the scrub, I come to a manhole cover stamped with the letters NFPC. Niagara Falls Power Company, the folks who built Echota. Just beyond is a stretch of what must be the old 1891 Gill Creek retaining wall, pride of its engineers.

How fortunate is the dweller in this charming corner of the earth! I sit down on the wall, feet dangling toward the creek. Someone has left a banana lying here.

The sun is moving toward the horizon. Crickets chirp; a seagull circles above. Framed inside a row of high-voltage transmission towers is the Seneca Niagara's glass tower. Reeds line the creek banks; a beer bottle nestles in some cattails. A shopping cart lies on its side, half-submerged in the sludgy water. A squirrel with two racing stripes of mange down its back climbs onto the wall and walks by, glancing at me with passing interest. A minute later, I hear a plop and look up to see the squirrel dog-paddling across the creek. It crashes through the underbrush on the other bank and heads for the landfill. In its wake, an orangish fin breaks the water and ripples. The body of a largemouth bass hoves into view, lingering lazily just below the surface, as if aware the state has declared this stretch of Gill Creek off-limits for fish consumption. A heron the color of bluestone sails in and alights in the creek shallows, standing still as a hunk of garden statuary. There's something peaceful about the scene. Eliminate the casino, the power lines, the landfill, the shopping cart and the mange on the squirrel, and it might be a vision of Niagara's lost natural landscape. It might be the sylvan woods below the escarpment where Bob Baxter once whistled for his dogs, a brace of rabbits at his belt.

The Niagara Heritage Partnership vision is radical: it imagines a Niagara that's better all around, pleasanter for residents, more interesting to tourists, and most importantly, thriving for its own sake, the way the Tuscaroras wanted their land simply to *be*, a desire that flummoxed Robert Moses. But of course it seems downright utopian to ask private developers to consider something other than profit. The casino, rising higher than anything else on the skyline and gleaming like a colossal one-eyed bandit, seems designed to refute the very idea. In spite of its 70-foot lobby waterfall, the Seneca Niagara has nothing to do with the Falls, and not much to do with Indians, whose culture turns up there as café theme and architectural motif. Presenting a blank cement wall to the seedy streetscape that flanks it, the casino turns inward to count its cash while, outside, the city and the state bicker over the spoils of the gaming compact.

Inside, on the gaming floor, winners pad across the carpeting to a sign that says Redemption. And so it was sold to the public: as Niagara's last chance to save itself from the dirty shame of being what developer Eddy Cogan called "Mexico North." "Casino May be Last Hope for Honeymoon Capital," declared *USA Today*, reporting on its 2002 opening. Even Mayor Irene Elia, the former nun, had to support it. "As long as it is family oriented," she told *The New York Times* resignedly, "with day care and other things."

A *Buffalo News* article six months after the casino's opening tabulated its effects good and bad. The casino had brought 2,000 new jobs and was on target to deliver $9 million to Niagara Falls, the city's negotiated share of the slots revenue. Home sales were up around the casino, and city revenues from parking tickets had jumped by 400 percent. But the promised construction boom had not happened. And since 65 percent of the casino's patrons came from Erie and Niagara counties, it wasn't so much an influx of outside cash as a new means of taxing locals. Today some in the community suggest that even the rise in home sales has been detrimental to development: a flurry of land speculation around the casino's opening drove prices up, setting the entry bar too high for the small entrepreneurs who might otherwise revitalize the district. So the blocks around the casino—with the exception of the Crowne Plaza—are still squalid.

The casino now competes with two Ontario enterprises: the second Canadian casino, the Fallsview, opened in 2004, featuring a 200,000-square-foot gaming floor, 368 hotel rooms, 10 dining and food facilities, and a 1,500-seat theater. In the lobby of that casino is a giant fountain made partly from architectural salvage from old power plants: it rears up like a time machine from an H. G. Wells novel, ready to zap passengers into the utopian future, or perhaps backward, to the moment when the harnessing of the Falls spawned visions of a gleaming, perfect world. The casino visitors, hurrying by on their way to the blackjack table or the slots, barely give it a glance.

THE VOICE OF THE LANDSCAPE

AT ONE TIME OR another, I have tried to convince every one of my friends to drop everything and come to Niagara Falls with me. *I'll show you around!* I tell them. *I know where to get good steak sandwiches!* I never cease to be amazed at their spoilsport resistance. One of the few who takes me up on the offer is my friend Pawel, a video artist. He has a new project that he thinks could use some Niagara footage. So early one morning, I pick him up in front of Gourmet Garage on Broadway. He has a bag of really superior whole wheat rolls and another bag of apples. We drive straight through to the Falls, leaving a trail of apple cores strewn in a jagged westward diagonal across New York State, as if marking out a trail to lead us home.

When we get to Niagara, it's still light, so I drive right to the spot where I think you get the best view.

"Oh my God," Pawel intones in his level baritone. He's originally Polish, but his way of talking is less an accent than a disposition. He hits every consonant precisely but draws out and savors the vowels. "It's *bea-oootiful.*" We slow to a crawl, ignoring the frustration of drivers behind us. Pawel presses his face to the window.

"Look at the lines," he says rapturously. "They're so *artiiiiiistic*. What's that carved-out part?"

"They must still be working on that bit," I say.

"It's a work of art," he declares. "Can we get closer?"

"I don't know," I say. "We'd have to call CECOS."

CECOS is the company that operates the landfill Pawel is admiring with such rapture. Pawel's current video is about landfills, which is why I insisted he come up and see Niagara. Niagara's landfills are *amazing*, I told him, with a hint of pride. Plus, I know by heart the location of every Superfund site in Niagara County, and have even located some that aren't in the Environmental Protection Agency's perkily named Web database, the EnviroMapper. Now, as we cruise along in the shadow of the CECOS mountain, I can't help but take a proprietary pleasure in Pawel's immediate enthusiasm. Also I'm hoping to make up for a political argument we had in the car that lasted for at least 250 miles.

The CECOS landfill is owned by Phoenix-based Allied Waste Industries, the second-largest waste disposal company in the nation. (The largest is Waste Management, owners of Chemical Waste Management and their hazardous waste landfill in Model City; anybody who's anybody in dumps has an outpost in Niagara County.) But while Model City may be able to boast of PCBs and anthrax desks, the CECOS landfill is visually far more awe-inspiring. It takes twenty minutes just to circumnavigate this beast. According to the EPA, dumping began at CECOS in 1897 and has gone on merrily ever since. Today it covers 385 acres and includes 1 operating landfill, 10 closed landfills, a wastewater treatment facility, and container storage. Coming off the Grand Island Bridge into Niagara Falls, you see it looming in the distance, a giant man-made land mass. There are always bulldozers chewing on some part of it, but the vast majority of it hulks there, green and gargantuan—in winter, white as a ski slope—as if humans had tried to outdo the Falls in reshaping the landscape: *You think that puny gorge is impressive? Well, check out this monster mountain!*

Pawel has borrowed a friend's high-definition camera, and I can see him planning his shots. I whip out a map I always carry in my door caddy, the one made by the Power Authority showing the county's groundwater contamination plumes in angry black topographical lines. A toxic rose blooms outward from CECOS and infiltrates the surrounding neighborhoods. Pawel's eyes widen and I know the whole highway squabble is forgotten. What are politics to garbage? He can't wait to get out his camera and start capturing it all in supersharp digital splendor.

The Falls entered the world of ideas less as a place than as a picture. They have appeared in books and magazines, on maps, railway timetables, postcards and china, on T-shirts and pens, on Shredded Wheat boxes, cracker tins and cans of spray starch, worked into Indian beadwork, lit from behind and mounted on the walls of Chinese restaurants. New York State license plates have two pictures on them: in one corner, the New York City skyline, in the other, Niagara Falls, as if the two—skyline and waterfall, cityscape and landscape—are squaring off. George Washington and Niagara Falls were the two most frequent subjects of early American art: America's complementary wonders, robust, unspoiled emblems of the world's new empire.

  Today the sight of Niagara is so familiar, it's almost hard to see. People point their cameras at it, but what are they trying to capture? Not an image of the Falls: those are everywhere. What people want to capture is the feeling, the experience of being there. But that experience is best when it matches up with the representations of it. From the *Maid of the Mist* ("Ladies and gentlemen, *this* is Niagara Falls!") or in a helicopter swooping low over the brink, what you see looks just like the images of it, and that's why it feels real. "Venice is a folding picture-postcard of itself," Mary McCarthy once wrote. Niagara is no picture-postcard; it's a great big IMAX film of itself.

Pawel decides he doesn't even want to see the waterfall. This is in spite of the fact that we end up staying walking distance from the Niagara Reservation, after checking the rates at a long list of hotels. Pawel is a practicing Buddhist, which means he has infinite patience for questioning hotel desk clerks. Finally, we settle on a hotel we call the "Bujay," French style, because the *d* in the word

"Budget" has fallen off the sign. The "Bu get" is an L-shaped red brick motor lodge owned, like several hotels in Niagara Falls, New York, by "Smokin Joe" Anderson, the Tuscarora cigarette impresario. Smokin Joe is the son of Wallace "Mad Bear" Anderson, scourge of surveyors. The registration office of the Bu get is plastered with huge, brightly lettered signs: T-Shirts! Tours! Walk to Casino! Inside, its shelves are stocked with shotglasses, pencil cases and plates depicting the Falls, each stamped with the warning "Not for food consumption: Plate may poison food."

It doesn't surprise me that Pawel doesn't want to join in the tradition of picturing the Falls. His films are all about seeing things in new ways. But what new way could there possibly be to see Niagara? Instead, we go to find some dinner at Niagara's other anchor tenant: the Seneca Niagara Casino.

The gaming floor at the Seneca Niagara is huge and hangarlike, with the colored lights of the slots flickering through a miasma of cigarette smoke. But what's most otherworldly is the sound. The audio experience of moving through the casino is like being underwater: an onslaught of bells, rumbles and burbles merging into a dense, immersive soundscape. I want Pawel to experience this, so I tell him to close his eyes as we walk in, which he promptly does. I take his arm and lead him blindly through the room.

"This is like the first time I saw the Sistine Chapel. Only then I was blindfolded," he tells me.

Pawel wants the complete casino experience, so we stand in line for the Thunder Falls Buffet. For $20.99 you get all you can eat from a series of buffet tables that hit every highlight of America's hybrid cuisine: an assortment of sushi, a multitude of southern specialties, a profusion of Chinese dishes, a glut of pizzas, a bevy of roasts and a veritable cornucopia of seafood. A giant bowl of platter-sized stone crabs is so popular that attendants are perpetually restocking it from a giant vat. Claws and jointed legs clatter onto the pile as we arrive. It makes me think of the stories of Niagara's abundance, the stunned fish, broken waterfowl and dismembered deer the Indians and the French garrison supposedly feasted on below the Falls.

Pawel is a vegetarian, so I'm surprised when he joins me in

heaping a plate with crabs. When we sit down, he calls a waitress over and asks her to explain how to open them. She goes away and comes back with a little plastic tool called a zipper for each of us. Pawel saws away at a crab leg and returns to the subject of the CECOS landfill.

"It is the most beautiful earthwork I have ever seen," he declares. "It's better than Michael Heizer." Earth artist Michael Heizer is known for carving huge trenches in the desert, which he called "un-sculpture." Pawel rhapsodizes some more about the landfill as he works his way up the crab. Droplets of crab juice mist our table and flecks of shell strafe diners nearby.

"You should go get a pork chop," the guy at the table next to us tells Pawel, flicking some crab off his shirt.

But Pawel continues happily assailing his prize, eviscerating the claws and sucking the meat out of the legs with palpable carnivorous glee. Then he goes back and heaps his plate with prime rib.

You never know what effect Niagara will have on a person, even without being seen.

The first published picture of Niagara Falls got it all wrong. The print in *A New Discovery of a Vast Country in America*, Father Louis Hennepin's embellished account of his trip with La Salle, illustrates the priest's fabrications perfectly: the Falls are 600 feet tall and far narrower than in reality. The Niagara Gorge looms with ominous jagged rocks. Above Goat Island, the Niagara River takes a sharp dogleg east—which is correct—but then it quickly joins what looks like Lake Erie, editing out at least ten miles of upper river. Where the river enters the lake, there are mountains: the peaks of Buffalo, of course!

Hennepin's inaccuracies would be repeated for a hundred years, as illustrators all based their images on the Hennepin print. It may have been geographically in error, but the picture published in *A New Discovery*, like the Maid of the Mist legend, was also somehow right on: it captured the feeling you still get standing at the brink of Niagara. The drop is huge, the gorge impassable. As for the waterfall—well, that's a lot of water. We can quantify it now (signs at the various American prospects recount the number of gallons per second), but when you stand there and look at it, you think exactly what Hennepin thought: *Whoa.* For the French priest, it wasn't just about falling water. It was how he and everyone else felt about the New World. This new place was stupendously huge, completely unlike Europe, and packed end-to-end with marvels.

Pictures are about feelings as much as they are about place. "Before it can ever be a repose for the sense," writes Simon Schama, "landscape is the work of the mind." Or as painter Frank Moore once put it more cynically, "There should be a German six-word compound that says, I-go-into-a-virgin-ecosystem-and-as-soon-as-I-set-foot-in-it-I-turn-it-into-my-own-inner-likeness."

Moore's own painting *Niagara,* from 1994–95, depicts a Niagara where what you see is completely familiar, and what you don't see is huge with mystery. Hanging at the Albright-Knox Gallery in Buffalo, *Niagara* is based on Church's 1857 painting *The Great Fall, Niagara.* Both are painted from the vantage point of the Canadian rapids just above the Horseshoe Falls, and both artists fill the lower halves of their pictures with water boiling over the brink. But Moore puts the *Maid of the Mist* boat in the picture; there's no painting humans out of the landscape now. You see the row of chemical factories and smokestacks on the American shore, and, in the left foreground, a person is largely obscured by the Panasonic video camera on his shoulder. The camera is pointed at the writhing mist, in which float the symbols of chemical skeleton structures: benzene, toluene, methyl hydrazine, nitropropane. Look closer, and they can be seen shimmering beneath the emerald green water of the rapids as well, menacing, yet full of mysterious promise. As the tagline for Niagara Falls, Ontario, tells us, there's magic in the mist.

On an almost unbearably beautiful autumn day, Pawel and I visit the landfills of Niagara County. The sky is brilliant blue, and the whole town is lit by the clear fall light that makes you wonder if your eyesight has just improved. The old Shredded Wheat grain elevator rises like a Charles Sheeler painting; the factories along

Buffalo Avenue gleam. Even the landfills are gorgeous. Love Canal, fenced off and landscaped, rustles its grass for the benefit of the new Vincent Morello Senior Housing complex next door. Across the LaSalle Expressway, Hooker 102nd Street turns its broad face to the sun while kids scramble over the jungle gym at its edge. We glide by Hooker's more obscure Hyde Park dump on a New York Power Authority private road, cruise by Olin Industrial Welding's disposal site across Gill Creek from Echota, and develop a special affection for a nearby unnamed landfill between the Robert Moses Parkway and Buffalo Avenue: it has a perfect landfill shape, but it's only a couple of acres—like CECOS in miniature.

"The other landfills *teeeeease* this one, because it hasn't grown up yet," Pawel says.

Pawel films Love Canal and Hooker while I lie in the back-seat of the car, dozing. We drive back to CECOS and circle it a few more times, and then I take him to a landfill I discovered on Lockport Road. I'm especially proud of this one because it's not in the EPA database. Across from a huge stack of junked cars, the low landfill gently swells the earth behind a chain-link fence with three rows of razor wire at the top. Methane vents dot its grassy expanse. A sign on the fence says Town of Niagara Wildlife Refuge.

Can looking make us better people? Throughout its history, the sight of Niagara Falls has been said to have moral meaning. It's not just a view; it's a message. As the report of the Free Niagara movement put it, scenes of natural beauty "are instruments of education. They conduce to the order of society. They address sentiments which are universal. They draw together men of all races, and thus contribute to the union and peace of nations." It's a lot to expect from a land-scape. Such high-minded notions may be why, even though everyone agrees capturing the Falls is impossible, people have never stopped trying. Every time there was an advance in picture-making, folks raced to the Falls to try it out. Niagara guidebooks are a chronicle of print technology: woodcuts, engravings, aquatints, chromolitho-graphs, photographs. When panoramas were first made, Niagara was immediately a popular subject. As soon as the camera obscura was invented, one sprang up at the Falls. More stereoviews were made of Niagara than of any other place. The Lumière brothers patented their Cinématographe in 1895, and less than two years later they produced a film called *Les Chutes*, aka *Niagara Falls*. In the first decade of film, no fewer than eighteen shorts were made of the Falls. The 1952 newsreel *This Is Cinerama* illustrated the new widescreen format with shots of Niagara. IMAX technology brought *Niagara: Miracles, Myths and Magic*, and when high-definition television arrived on the scene, that too quickly resulted in a documentary about America's waterfall.

The irony is that, even though Niagara is the most-recognized landscape in the world, we don't really see it. We don't see the water diversions because they've been disguised. We don't see the PCBs leaching out of the landfills or uranium molecules slipping invisibly over the brink. Nor do we see the hybrid histories of its myths, the stories of its Indians, the hidden histories of its freedom-seekers—unless we go looking for them in darker places. We can't see the lost landscapes that live on in the memories of residents. Even in this landscape marked by the urge to see and record, the real story remains invisible.

Pawel likes to meditate in the morning. For a *long* time. I on the other hand, wake up antsy to get going. On our third day at Niagara, I decide to take a walk while Pawel meditates, instead of doing what I want to do, which is bang on his door in a totally unenlightened and non-Zen way. I get a silo-sized cup of coffee at the gas station across the street and head down the dilapidated sidewalk of Second Street to the old aquarium.

The Aquarium of Niagara is a smallish, circular building built in the sixties, before the trend for spectacular mega-aquariums like the ones in Baltimore, Atlanta and Monterey began. Outside the front entrance, it has a small teardrop-shaped cement pool occupied by four harbor seals. The aquarium isn't open yet when I arrive, but the seals are enjoying their pool. I hang over the railing with my coffee and watch. Sandy, the plumpest, is resting on the bottom, a wavery dark blob, but Cady, Lucy and Clarisse circle incessantly. Clarisse and Cady both have cloudy white eyes, and reading the exhibit placards, I learn they're both blind. Cady was

born that way, but Clarisse was rescued on Cape Cod after someone found her injured by a gunshot.

The seal pool reminds me of the swimming pools in the parking
lots of the low-budget mid-century motor lodges that line Niagara Falls Boulevard. You pass them coming into town, dilapidated
throwbacks with names like the Algiers, the Bel-Air, the Sands and
my favorite, the Bit o' Paris. Their signs trumpet their little luxuries:
Color TV! Air Conditioning! At some of them I've seen rates as low
as $29. When there's a pool, it's a tiny cement hole parked in the
asphalt out front and framed by a chain-link fence.

Clarisse circles the aquarium pool methodically, pausing frequently to poke her humanlike head out of the water and blink
her cloudy, sightless eyes. Fat Sandy floats up, blimplike, now and
then to snuff a breath of air. She can see, but she has cataracts.
Lucy, the only seal with good vision, pauses occasionally to look
up at me. Her nostrils flare between her whiskers. *Why?* her gaze
seems to ask. *Why are you here?*

I'm reminded of something Neil Patterson said when I visited
him at the Tuscarora Environment Program. He was telling me
about "habitat restoration" attempts the Power Authority had been
funding upstream of Niagara Falls. They were creating what he
called "little island paradises" for birds, with platforms for osprey
nests. They were doing this instead of focusing, as he thought they
should, on cleaning the water so the fish the birds eat would be
healthy. The whole thing, he said in a phrase I found instantly
memorable, was just an example of environmental voyeurism.

"Bird-watching is seen as a great ecotourist activity," he said.
"What could be more voyeuristic? Bird-hunting is a more ecological activity. You get much more intimate contact with the resource
and interact with it; you recognize you're part of the environment.
We want to put the natural world in a terrarium and say 'let's look
at it from out here,' then go back to our cars and our homes. It's
not natural." He paused while I took this on board.

"It's so funny," he said after a moment, "that people think we
were born to walk around in the natural world and stare."

I think of this as I stare at the seals. Cady and Clarisse bump
into each other occasionally and adjust their orbits. *Why would*

someone shoot a harbor seal? I wonder, and suddenly, even with a tankard of hot coffee in my hand, I'm overwhelmed by sadness. Not for the seals, or not just for them, but for the whole small, underfunded aquarium, for the fish in it and the fish in the Niagara River, for the Indians who still eat the fish, for the Falls, for Love Canal and the landscape that was once so beautiful. For the odd human desire to make our mark on the world and then deny having done it. We shoot a harbor seal, then we rescue her and bring her to live in a fake sea.

I feel sad for Jeff, the sea lion at Marineland on the Canadian side, who in 1963 escaped and went over the Falls (what a ride!) then spent three glorious days swimming free in the Niagara River. Two local guys found him sunning himself on a Lake Ontario beach and pinned him down. Marineland officials, summoned to retrieve their errant animal, assured the public that Jeff was better off in captivity: left in the polluted Niagara River, he would have quickly gone blind.

At exactly 9 A.M., the aquarium's music comes on. Soft, New-Agey arpeggios trill over the pool, and suddenly the seals are no longer pathetic, blinded animals on display in a crummy small pool, but ballerinas, whirling through a gorgeous and perfectly calibrated dance of joy.

The history of the environment, as Richard White says of Indian-white relations, has rarely produced complex stories. When it can be written at all, it's often written as a tale of human violation of a passive natural world. The landscape is a rock, and Robert Moses the bulldozer. The riverbank is a disfigured body, and Frederick Law Olmsted its surgeon. The water is a powerful horse, and Nikola Tesla its harness.

But a waterfall doesn't fit that story so well, because it doesn't seem passive, the way other things in the natural world appear to be. Grass grows silently, mountains stand frozen in time, a cow munches its cud and waits to be milked. A waterfall, on the other hand, is active—it grinds out a gorge and throws down anyone hapless enough to enter its rapids. It hurries down waterfowl and slaps tourists with salmon. Go near it, and it gets you wet.

The distinction is imagined, of course. Grass is active, mountains are on the move, and a cow is certainly conscious in some sense of the word. But as a feeling, the idea remains, deep within us, and it accounts for an emotional response to the outside world. Why is a thunderstorm more fun to watch than a flock of grazing sheep? Thorstein Veblen, the turn-of-the-century political economist who invented the phrase "conspicuous consumption," proposed in his famous *Theory of the Leisure Class* that "barbaric" early cultures divided the world not into animal and nonanimal, but into animate and nonanimate. Some animals—worms or sheep, say—were not animate, whereas some natural phenomena—waterfalls and thunderstorms—were. Man couldn't help but match himself with the latter. Animate things—wolves, bears, other humans, waterfalls—sparked in humans a desire for mastery.

Veblen was writing in 1902, right after Niagara was harnessed and Annie Taylor slipped over the Horseshoe in her barrel. His conspectus of primitive cultures is dated, but there's something in the idea that the animate compels us to dominate. Could this be at the heart of our tortured relationship with Niagara Falls? Even as waterfalls go, it's especially animate: not a glittering, Alpine curtain, but a loud, violent actor on the landscape, a chewer of rocks and demolisher of outlooks, a breaker of boats and hazard to humans almost eager to tempt you to your doom. It's hard not to see early explorers' fascination with the animals killed by Niagara as a startled acknowledgment that here was a thing that competes with us in its ability to make changes in the land. It reshapes the landscape, dominates wildlife, fills the air with noise and kills those who don't respect it, and in all those things, it acts like us. Is it any wonder we want to prove we can top it? It steals our thunder.

And yet this is what Niagara should teach us. Throughout its history, it has been cited as proof that nature is stronger than humanity, or conversely that humans have mastered nature. Both are simplifications, simplifications reflected in the standoff between a fringe of deep ecologists who see humans as a cancer on the earth, and the so-called wise-use movement, who see the land as a limitless resource for exploitation, little more than a human pantry. These opposing worldviews share the bizarre urge to see humans as separate from everything else in the world.

Environmentalism is a way of seeing. It's time to look the world squarely in the face and try to understand our role in it. There's no painting ourselves out of the picture. This is not to say we must always make something of nature, never leaving it alone. It's to say that we are it, and it is us, and until we stop trying to separate the two, we'll never get beyond seeing the natural world as either virgin or whore, something to be put on a pedestal and admired, or else used up with little regard for its own potential. It is to say that in order to find balance, we must consider the natural world not as merely waiting to be of service or to be saved, but must respect it as equal partner in shaping the future of our planet. To do so surely starts with opening our eyes to what we have done to it, and what we are doing to it now.

On Pawel's and my last morning in Niagara Falls, a silver fog rolls in and curls itself around streets and buildings. Everything is in glistening soft focus. The Falls, I realize, will be spectacular. Pawel is meditating, but I bang on his door. He appears, blinking like someone who has just been dragged from the brink of Nirvana.

"Get your stuff," I command. "We're seeing the Falls."

We head for Goat Island on foot. In the thick mist, the town looks magical. The Twist o' the Mist ice-cream stand hovers like a movie set, and the Flashcube glows translucent green. Even the putt-putt course, the balloon-on-a-string ride and the souvenir shops of Falls Street loom up through the fog like visions.

Goat Island is gorgeous. The rapids swirl and crash, and the trees in their brilliant autumn colors have a hallucinatory three-dimensionality. The little glades along the riverbank look like habitations for sprites and dryads, and the burbling river glints like crystal. When we get to Luna Island, we see that the mist has obscured the Canadian Niagara skyline, so that across the river we see just water and brown bank, as Hennepin would have seen it, or Augustus Porter on that first surveying trip. A shimmer of droplets fills the air, just as it was filled with mist before water diversion began. It's as if Niagara has re-created itself as it was before the

Porters began building on it and Olmsted landscaped it and the factories polluted it and the power plant sucked up its water.

"Oh wow," I keep saying. "It's like a picture."

Pawel sets himself up on the Luna Island bridge with a tripod and begins ecstatically filming falling water. I find myself getting out my camera, even though Niagara photos have already clogged up my computer and made iPhoto impossible to use.

Luna Island isn't crowded; maybe ten or twenty other tourists are milling about. I go to its prow and lean over the railing. A funny thing happens when I do—the waterfall grows louder. Moving my head back and forth a mere 8 inches changes the volume dramatically. I stand at the railing, leaning out, leaning back, for a long time. When I stand up straight, I hear the roar of the waterfall like something nearby; it's over there, I'm here. But if I put my ears forward of the railing and cliff face, the roar encompasses me. I'm inhabiting a dense soundscape, hollow and continuous and full of subtle variations. I realize this is why I'm fascinated by the soundscape of the casino; it too is an immersive world of noise. It's the one thing in the Seneca Niagara that truly references the Falls.

What does the waterfall say? The world stands for nothing. The waterfall says just that: water, falling. Water, falling. And again, and more. The voice of the landscape says change. It says movement, time. And at the same time it says *right here.*

Pawel is filming away like a man who's been told this twenty minutes of battery are his last ever. His fancy camera has droplets of water on the lens. He keeps picking up his tripod and filming from a slightly different angle. He looks happy. There's not a single angle he can find that won't have been woodcut or watercolored or daguerreotyped or posted online, but who can resist? Not me, not the Chinese tourists crowding next to me, not the Lumière brothers or Frederick Church or Captain Basil Hall, who set up a camera obscura and made precise, mechanical sketches of every view. When we finish here, we will eat some surprisingly good Indian food from a pushcart and then hop in the car and drive east, toward home. We'll listen to music. We'll argue. Somewhere in the Catskills, not far from New York City's water supply, we'll

run out of apples. We will stop at a Citgo station near an over-
pass to get Cortlands and gas. And as we're standing at the cash
register, and Pawel's asking the clerk if he can wash our apples in
their sink, I will look up and there, at the back of the grubby little
Citgo store, hanging over a fridge full of Snapple, I'll see it: the
image that lights up from behind to give the effect of falling water:
Niagara Falls.

But that's later. Right now, we're here, our clothes soaking
through in the cold mist. The waterfall is the voice of the landscape. I go over to Pawel. I have to lean in to yell over the sound
of the Falls.

"Close your eyes," I tell him.

"Listen."

Sources and Acknowledgments

ALL HAIL LIBRARIANS! WITHOUT them, all of civilization—excepting those *I Love Lucy* episodes still zinging around space and the increasingly bloated compendium of fact, factoids and fakery known as Google's main index—would surely vanish down the memory hole. I am grateful to a phalanx of librarians, but to no one more so than Maureen Fennie and Linda Reinumagi in the Local History section at the Niagara Falls Public Library, who with wry, crackling wit, kept me good company as I rifled through the *Wunderkammer* of history. I am extremely grateful to the American Antiquarian Society for a grant to draw on their amazing collection and their even more amazing staff; special thanks to Georgia Barnhill, Joanne Chaison, Thomas Knoles, Marie Lamoureax, Laura Wasowicz and S. J. Wolfe in the library, and to James Moran, Cheryl McRell, John Hench and John Keenum for helping make it all happen. I am also deeply grateful to the MacDowell Colony for a residency fellowship during which a trunkful of notes began to look something like a book.

I have benefited from Niagara's long—and occasionally daunting—literary legacy. The most widely read popular history is Pierre Berton's bestseller *Niagara* (Kodansha, 1992), which I found useful as a map of the standard story. Linda Revie offers a survey of artists' and writers' responses to the Falls in *The Niagara Companion* (Wilfred Laurier University Press, 2003). Charles Mason Dow's giant compendium, *Anthology and Bibliography of Niagara Falls* (State of New York, 1921), is a necessary desk reference for any Niagaraphile, as are the souvenir volumes *Notes on Niagara* (R. Lespinasse, 1883) and *The Niagara Book* (Underhill & Nichols, 1893).

Many folks have written well about tourism and its relationship to national identity; books I found illuminating were John Sears, *Sacred Places: American Tourist Attractions in the Nineteenth Century* (Oxford University Press, 1989); Hal Rothman, *Devil's Bargains: Tourism in the Twentieth-Century American West* (University Press of Kansas, 1998); Claudia Bell and John Lyall, *The Accelerated Sublime: Landscape, Tourism and Identity* (Praeger, 2002); Dean MacCannell, *The Tourist: A New Theory of the Leisure Class* (Schocken, 1976); and the essay collection *So Glorious a Landscape: Nature and the Environment in American History and Culture*, ed. Chris Magoc (Scholarly Resources, 2002).

I relied heavily on old histories and especially old guidebooks in the collections of the American Antiquarian Society, the New York Public Library, the Niagara Falls Public Library, by which I mean the one in New York, and the Niagara Falls (Ontario) Public Library: between their collections, I got to read every Niagara tour guide printed in the nineteenth century, and many of the following century's as well. I will not list them here, but Walter McCausland compiled a list of every guidebook printed prior to 1850 and read it as a paper to the Literary Clinic of Buffalo on January 8, 1945; and Douglas McMurtrie privately printed 200 copies of his *American Book Collector* article "The First Guides to Niagara Falls" in 1934. The New York Public Library, to their infinite credit, has both bibliographies as well as many of the items in them: send them a donation at once.

ONE: WHITE MAN'S FANCY, RED MAN'S FACT

"If you want to learn about our history, let us tell it," Neil Patterson, Jr., told me, and I held his words in mind as I tried to tell a story about native and European histories entwining to create a truly new world. In particular, I took myths told to me in person as authoritative, because that's how the Haudenosaunee see them. I am grateful to Neil, to Joseph Bruchac and to Darwin John for spending generous amounts of time telling me stories, and hope I heard them a little better than the nineteenth-century ethnologists did. Neil Patterson directed me to the Web site sixnations.org, where the Haudenosaunee discuss their own history. Also helpful was his book with Bryan Printup, *Tuscarora Nation* (Arcadia, 2007).

Daniel K. Richter's *The Ordeal of the Longhouse: The Peoples of the Iroquois League in the Era of European Colonization* (University of North Carolina Press, 1992) was indispensable, not least for its Haudenosaunee-centric approach. My thanks to folks at Ganondagan for bringing it to my attention. Laurence M. Hauptman's *Conspiracy of Interests: Iroquois Dispossession and the Rise of New York State* (Syracuse University Press, 1999) was especially helpful on transportation technology, land use and the Iroquois. A good summary of Haudenosaunee relations in the region is Alan Taylor's "The Divided Ground: Upper Canada, New York and the Iroquois Six Nations, 1783–1815," *Journal of the Early Republic* 22:1 (Spring 2002). Richard White's brilliant book *The Middle Ground: Indians, Empires and Republics in the Great Lakes Region 1650–1815* (Cambridge University Press, 1991) changed my way of thinking about native history, colonial history and the interactions between them. William Cronon's *Changes in the Land: Indians, Colonists and the Ecology of New England* (Hill & Wang, 1983) was also worldview-shifting.

Antiquated ethnographic studies of the Iroquois may not tell us much about the Indians, but they say a lot about their times; I used Henry Rowe Schoolcraft, *Notes on the Iroquois* (Bartlett & Welford, 1846) and of course Lewis Henry Morgan, *League of the Ho-de-no-sau-nee* (Sage & Brother, 1851) and *The Indian Journals*, ed. Leslie A. White (University of Michigan Press, 1959). Information on Haudenosaunee marriage traditions I found in Judith K. Brown, "Economic Organization and the Position of Women Among the Iroquois," *Ethnohistory* 17:3–4 (Summer 1970).

"Iroquois myths" turn up in all sorts of places; some more reliable ones are *Legends, Traditions and Laws of the Iroquois, or Six Nations,* by Tuscarora headman Elias Johnson (Union Printing & Publishing, 1881); "Myths and Legends of the New York State Iroquois" by Harriet Maxwell Converse (Ya-ie-wa-noh), published in the New York State Museum's *Education Department Bulletin* 437 (December 15, 1908); *Iroquois Folklore* by Reverend William Beauchamp (Deiler Press, 1922); *Legends of the Longhouse* by Jesse Cornplanter (J. B. Lippincott, 1938); and *Iroquois Stories: Heroes and Heroines, Monsters and Magic* by Joseph Bruchac (Crossing Press, 1985). A version of the Canandaigua serpent story also appears in an afterword to James Seaver's *The Life of Mary Jemison* (1824), where it is said to be recounted by Horatio Jones, like Jemison a white captive who chose to live out his life as an adopted Seneca.

I am grateful to Robert Emerson of Old Fort Niagara (which I call simply Fort Niagara throughout this text) for sharing his scholarship, as well as discussing the fur trade with me at length while standing in the hot sun in eighteenth-century regimental gear and armed with musket, sword, bayonet and tomahawk. Indian dramas are discussed at length by Priscilla Sears, *A Pillar of Fire to Follow: American Indian Dramas 1808–1859* (Bowling Green University Press, 1982) and Eugene Jones, *Native Americans as Shown on the Stage 1753–1916* (Scarecrow Press, 1988).

For La Salle, one turns first to the great and fascinating liar Louis Hennepin, *A New Discovery of a Vast Country in America, Extending Above Four Thousand Miles Between New France & New Mexico; with a Description of the Great Lakes, Cataracts, Rivers, Plants and Animals* (Printed for Henry Bonwicke, at the Red Lion in St. Paul's Church-Yard: 1699). My La Salle biographies include Anka Muhlstein, *La Salle: Explorer of the North American Frontier*, trans. Willard Wood (Arcade, 1994); Donald S. Johnson, *La Salle: A Perilous Odyssey from Canada to the Gulf of Mexico* (Cooper Square, 2002); and the more antiquated *La Salle: The Life and Times of an Explorer* by John Upton Terrell (Weybright and Talley, 1968). All three authors are pro–La Salle, and none attempts to move beyond the Eurocentric point of view bequeathed by the explorers. Fergus Fleming, *Off the Map: Tales of Endurance and Exploration* (Atlantic Monthly Press, 2005), includes a chapter on La Salle.

Although I adore the supercilious style of Francis Parkman in *The Conspiracy of Pontiac* (Boston, 1870), I learned most about Pontiac's Rebellion from William Nestor's *Haughty Conquerors: Amherst and the Great Indian Uprising of 1763* (Praeger, 2000). For William Johnson, I was delighted to find the intelligent and fascinating biography by Fintan O'Toole, *White Savage: William Johnson and the Invention of America* (Farrar, Straus & Giroux, 2005), a great read for lovers of biography or history. I also utilized Milton Hamilton's *Sir William Johnson: Colonial American* (Kennikat, 1976).

Toward the end of my researches, I was fortunate to meet scholar Susan Berry Brill de Ramirez, whose book *Native American Life-History Narratives* (University of New Mexico Press, 2007) brings out many of the problems inherent in reading native ethnographic texts, and whose perceptive comments on this chapter helped me to be more alert to those problems in my own interpretations. What I get wrong is due to my own intransigence and not to her advice.

TWO: THE EIGHTH WONDER OF THE WORLD

The history of landscape alterations at the Falls has to be pieced together from newspapers, old guidebooks, local histories and visual records such as postcards and stereoscopic views, all of which I found at both the American Antiquarian Society and the Niagara Falls Public Library. An excellent overview of Niagara Falls prints is Christopher Lane's *Impressions of Niagara: The Charles Rand Penney Collection of Prints of Niagara Falls and the Niagara River* (Philadelphia Print Shop, 1993). This print collection was recently acquired by the Castellani Art Museum. A comprehensive history of Canadian parks is George A. Seibel, *Ontario's Niagara Parks: A History* (Niagara Falls, Ontario: Niagara Parks Commission, 1985), which I discovered at the Weir Collection in Queenston, Ontario, thanks to curator Gary Essar. If you love hydroinfrastructure as I do, you will enjoy Carol Sheriff's rattlingly good read, *The Artificial River: The Erie Canal and the*

Paradox of Progress (Hill & Wang, 1997). Also gripping for the waterworks fan is Peter Bernstein's *Wedding of the Waters: The Erie Canal and the Making of a Great Nation* (W. W. Norton, 2005). A good discussion of the Porters' role in the Erie Canal debates is in Dan Murphy's *The Erie Canal: The Ditch That Opened a Nation* (Western New York Wares, 2001).

For Porter history, I utilized Hauptman's *Conspiracy of Interests,* as well as Merton Wilner, *Niagara Frontier: A Narrative and Documentary History* (S. J. Clarke, 1931); J. C. A. Stagg, "Between Black Rock and a Hard Place: Peter B. Porter's Plan for an American Invasion of Canada in 1812," *Journal of the Early Republic* 19:3 (Autumn 1999); John C. Fitzpatrick, ed., *The Autobiography of Martin Van Buren* (U.S. Government Printing Office, 1920); Charles Mulford Robinson, "The Life of Judge Augustus Porter," *Proceedings of the Buffalo and Erie County Historical Society* 7 (1904); and Daniel C. Roland's Ph.D. dissertation, "Peter B. Porter and Self-Interest in American Politics" (Claremont Graduate School, 1990). Best of all, the Peter and Augustus Porter Papers at the Buffalo and Erie County Historical Society provided deeds, legal documents and letters that make you feel you're eavesdropping on the men themselves. I am grateful to librarian Patricia Vergil for helping me navigate that treasure trove.

The story of the pirate *Michigan* appears in Berton and all of the early tourist literature; I found it most interesting to go back to contemporary newspaper reports. Janet Larkin interprets the event in "Schooner *Michigan:* a Symbolic Voyage," *Western New York Heritage* (Spring 1999).

The opening section quotes are from early guidebooks: "How awful is the scene!" is from C. D. Ferris, *Pictorial Guide to the Falls of Niagara: A Manual for Visiters* (Salisbury & Clapp, 1842): 128; "Where may the ambitious . . . this sacred shrine?" is from *Burke's Descriptive Guide; or, The Visitors' Companion to Niagara Falls* (Andrew Burke, 1850): 78. Anna Jameson's quote is from *Winter Studies and Summer Rambles in Canada* (Wiley & Putnam, 1839): 262.

Three: Skipper the Two-Legged Dog

The grim façade of the Archives of Ontario belies the historical joy to be found within: I spent many delightful hours there reading old letters, journals and bills. (And when I say many hours, I mean *many:* to the Canadians' credit, their libraries stay open *late.*) All quotes from Sidney Barnett's journal are from the Archives of Ontario, F 684, Sidney Barnett fonds, which include his sketches as well as many Barnett papers and letters. The fascinating Doctor Douglas can be heard from in *Journals and Reminiscences of James Douglas, M.D., Edited by his Son* (privately printed in New York, 1910). The history of the fake Poyais colony can be found in David Sinclair, *The Land That Never Was: Sir Gregor MacGregor and the Most Audacious Fraud in History* (Da Capo, 2004). L. P. Gratacap's screed "Natural History Museums" appeared in *Science* 8:184 (July 8, 1898).

British crank George Drought Warburton pronounces on Niagara in *Hochelega; or, England in the New World* (London, 1847): 129. William Dean Howells is quoted on the five-legged calf in Ronald L. Way, *Ontario's Niagara Parks: A History* (Niagara Parks Commission, 1960). Snippets of the history of the Niagara Falls Museum appear in that institution's publications, but its story is best pieced together from period newspapers. The ones I used most were the *Welland Tribune*, the *Welland Telegraph*, the *Niagara Falls Review*, the *Niagara Courier*, the *Niagara-on-the-Lake Gleaner*, and the *Kingston Chronicle*.

Museum history is discussed in Tony Bennett, *The Birth of the Museum: History, Theory, Politics* (Routledge, 1995); Edward Alexander, *Museums in Motion: An Introduction to the History and Functions of Museums* (American Association for State and Local History, 1979); Ken Arnold, *Cabinets for the Curious: Looking Back at Early English Museums* (Ashgate, 2006); and the essays in Oliver Impey and Arthur MacGregor, eds., *The Origins of Museums* (Oxford University Press, 1985); and Susan Crane, ed., *Museums and Memory* (Stanford University Press, 2000). Patrick Mauries unpacks the *Wunderkammer* in *Cabinets of Curiosity* (Thames & Hudson, 2002). And I was much influenced by

Lawrence Weschler's sparkling gem of a book, *Mr. Wilson's Cabinet of Wonder* (Vintage, 1996).

I want to thank Jacob Sherman for graciously sharing his family's story, Mark DeMarco for giving me a splendid tour of his curiosity cabinet, S. J. Wolfe at the Antiquarian Society for getting me started on Niagara's mummies, and Harry Mueller, former proprietor of the Houdini Museum, for talking with me about the history of Falls attractions and for feeding me a lovely dinner. And I am extremely grateful to the overgenerous Billy Jamieson for granting me interviews, sharing his papers, giving me access to his collection, making me Bloody Caesars and letting me sit in the electric chair.

FOUR: THE OTHER SIDE OF JORDAN

Blondin and other daredevils at the Falls tend to be ignored by serious historians and scholars, relegated to lighthearted tourist books such as Paul Gromosiak's *Daring Niagara* (Western New York Wares, 1998), or salacious accounts of deaths and daring rescues, such as T. W. Kriner's *Journeys to the Brink of Doom* (J & J, 1997) and *In the Mad Water: Two Centuries of Adventure and Lunacy at Niagara Falls* (J & J, 1999). I found all of these fascinating, as well as Dean Shapiro's biography *Blondin* (Vanwall, 1989) and Shane Peacock's *The Great Farini* (Viking, 1995). Blondin's contemporary biographer was George Linnaeus Banks, who interviewed both Blondin and Colcord to write *Blondin: His Life and Performances* (Routledge, 1862), which helped me reimagine Colcord's trip. Here too, contemporary newspaper accounts were essential, especially the *Buffalo Republic*, the *Buffalo Morning Express*, the *Eastern Argus*, the *Essex Register*, the *Rochester Journal*, the *Farmer's Cabinet*, *The New York Times*, the *Niagara Falls Gazette* and the African-American newspapers the *National Era* and the *Provincial Freeman*. Lincoln's rebuke to his critics was recalled by Frank Carpenter in Henry J. Raymond, *The Life and Public Services of Abraham Lincoln* (Derby & Miller, 1865): 752.

For Annie Edson Taylor, there is her autobiography, *Over the Falls* (privately printed, 1902) and a biography, *Queen of the Mist:*

The Story of Annie Edson Taylor, by Charles Carlin Parish (Empire State Books, 1987).

The history of the Underground Railroad is beginning to be explored in more depth. A recent readable account is Fergus Bordewich's *Bound for Canaan* (Amistad, 2005), following on Jane and William Pease, *They Who Would Be Free: Blacks' Search for Freedom, 1830–1861* (University of Illinois Press, 1990). Early accounts include Benjamin Drew's *The Refugee; or, The Narratives of Fugitive Slaves in Canada* (Boston, 1856) and William Still's *The Underground Railroad* (1871; reprinted by Johnson Publishing, 1970). For Harriet Tubman's story, I went back to her earliest biographer Sarah H. Bradford, who wrote *Scenes in the Life of Harriet Tubman* (W. J. Moses, 1869), though I should note that in quoting, I dispensed with Bradford's annoying "negro dialect." The significance of shackles is discussed by Charmaine Nelson in "Hiram Powers's America: Shackles, Slaves and the Racial Limits of Nineteenth-Century National Identity," *Canadian Review of American Studies* 34:2 (2004). My understanding of blackface minstrelsy as a complex interplay between domination and liberation is shaped by Eric Lott's brilliant *Love and Theft: Blackface Minstrelsy and the American Working Class* (Oxford University Press, 1993). I want to thank the curators of the Castellani Art Museum, and especially Kate Koperski, for sharing their time and knowledge with me.

Solomon Moseby's story has garnered a lot of interest. Anna Jameson's account is in *Winter Studies and Summer Rambles in Canada*. It is also recounted, along with many other stories of Canadian fugitives, in Robin Winks, *The Blacks in Canada: A History* (McGill-Queens University Press, 1997) and Byron Prince's *I Came as a Stranger: The Underground Railroad* (Tundra, 2004). In addition to the Porter papers at the Buffalo and Erie County Historical Society, I used David Murray, "Hands Across the Border: The Abortive Extradition of Solomon Moseby," *Canadian Review of American Studies* 30:2 (2000), and Adrienne Shadd, "The Lord Seemed to Say 'Go': Women and the Underground Railroad Movement" in Peggy Bristow, ed., *We're Rooted Here and They Can't Pull Us Up: Essays in African Canadian Women's History* (University of Toronto Press, 1994).

"You can't dig up a hole, but history is full of them." I flagrantly stole that delectable line from my friend Mac Wellman, who gives it to Josephine Herbst in his brilliant play *Two September*. Thanks, Mac.

FIVE: FREE NIAGARA

Charles Mason Dow, an early commissioner, wrote a useful if boosterish history of the park's early years, *The State Reservation at Niagara: A History* (J. B. Lyon, 1914). The *Niagara Falls Gazette* is essential in tracing changes made in the park. My understanding of landscape's relationship to power was profoundly influenced by Raymond Williams's classic study, *The Country and the City* (Oxford University Press, 1973), from which I lifted the phrase "pleasing prospects."

Frederick Law Olmsted has been written about fairly frequently of late. I used the biographies *FLO: A Biography of Frederick Law Olmsted* by Laura Wood Roper (Johns Hopkins University Press, 1973) and *Park Maker: A Life of Frederick Law Olmsted* by Elizabeth Stevenson (Macmillan, 1977), as well as the beautiful *Frederick Law Olmsted: Designing the American Landscape* by Charles Beveridge and Paul Rocheleau (Rizzoli, 1995). George Scheper summarizes the traditional view of Olmsted in "The Reformist Vision of FLO and the Poetics of Park Design," *New England Quarterly* 62:3 (September 1989), as does Witold Rybczynski in his speculative *A Clearing in the Distance: Frederick Law Olmsted and America in the Nineteenth Century* (Scribner, 1999). Elizabeth Blackmar and Roy Rosenzweig take issue with Olmsted's elitism in *The Park and the People: A History of Central Park* (Cornell University Press, 1992), as do Geoffrey Blodgett, "Frederick Law Olmsted: Landscape Architecture as Conservative Reform," *Journal of American History* 62:4 (March 1976); and Ross Miller, "The Landscaper's Utopia Versus the City: A Mismatch," *New England Quarterly* 49:2 (June 1976); also useful were the essays in the exhibition catalog *The Distinctive Charms of the Niagara Scenery: Frederick Law Olmsted and the Niagara Reservation* (Niagara University, 1985). Landscape architect Anne Whiston Spirn argues for a middle ground in "Constructing Nature: The Legacy of Frederick Law Olmsted," in *Uncommon Ground: Rethinking the Human Place in Nature*, William Cronon, ed. (W. W. Norton, 1995).

Olmsted's first pronouncement on Niagara is the *Special Report of the New York State Survey on the Preservation of the Scenery at Niagara Falls* (Charles Van Benthuysen & Sons, 1880). His final report is the *General Plan for the Improvement of the Niagara Reservation* (Martin B. Brown, 1887). His essay "Public Parks and the Enlargement of Towns" appears in *Civilizing American Cities*, S. B. Sutton, ed. (MIT Press, 1971). Jonathan Baxter Harrison's newspaper essays were collected in *The Condition of Niagara Falls, and the Measures Needed to Preserve Them* (J. Wilson & Son, 1882).

I used the Frederick Law Olmsted Papers at the Library of Congress, Manuscripts Division. Thanks are due Jeffrey M. Flannery for guiding me through the massive collection. I am grateful to Christine Beauregard at the New York State Library for helping me find Evershed's map. Special thanks to Louise and Tom Yots for hospitality and conversation. And thanks also to Russell Flinchum, archivist at the Century Club, for digging up materials from their library and letting me use their billiards table as a desk.

SIX: KING OF POWER, QUEEN OF BEAUTY

Power development at Niagara is one of the best-documented parts of its history, having been immediately recounted in the popular and scientific press. Especially useful for the turbine buff is the special "Niagara Power" number of *Cassier's*, published as *The Harnessing of Niagara* in 1895. The Edward Dean Adams two-volume history, *Niagara Power* (Niagara Falls Power Company, 1927) is also essential. William Irwin's *The New Niagara: Tourism, Technology and the Landscape of Niagara Falls, 1776–1917* (Pennsylvania State University Press, 1996) tells the story of Niagara's harnessing in its cultural context. David Nye's sweeping *Electrifying America: Social Meanings of a New Technology* (MIT Press, 1990) helped me understand the paradigm shift electrification sparked. Also useful was a Ph.D. dissertation by Gail Edith Evans, "Storm over Niagara: A Study of the Interplay of Cultural Values, Resource Politics and Environmental Policy in an International Setting, 1670s to 1950" (UC Santa Barbara, 1991).

The real estate brochure I quote from is *Buffalo and her Wonderful Prospects: A Treatise on Niagara Falls Power as a City Builder*, A. E. Richmond, ed. (Niagara Printing Co., 1895). The Buffalo, Niagara and Eastern Power Corporation's pamphlet is called *The Lengthening of Niagara Falls* (Buffalo, 1927). H. G. Wells wrote about Niagara in *Harper's Weekly* (July 21, 1906).

The Rivers and Harbors bills, treaties and various reports to Congress and the International Joint Commission on preservation of the Falls are all in the public record. The 1931 report I discuss is the Special International Niagara Board's report *Preservation and Improvement of the Scenic Beauty of the Niagara Falls and Rapids* (71st Cong. 2nd sess., Sen. Doc. 128). Post-treaty alterations are laid out and discussed—along with excellent diagrams and photos of the working Niagara models—in the International Joint Commission's 1953 *Report on the Preservation and Enhancement of Niagara Falls*. Post-treaty power redevelopment and waterfall remediation are outlined in Wallace McIntyre's "Niagara Falls Power Redevelopment," *Economic Geography* 28:3 (July 1952). The waterfall remediations made by the Army Corps of Engineers are described in part in Nuala Drescher's *Engineers for the Public Good: A History of the Buffalo District U.S. Army Corps of Engineers* (U.S. Army Corps of Engineers, 1982). For an opposing point of view, see Gene Marine, *America the Raped: The Engineering Mentality and the Devastation of a Continent* (Simon & Schuster, 1969).

For the history of Robert Moses and the Tuscaroras, in addition to talking to Neil Patterson, Jr., about the Tuscarora oral history project, I used the Robert Moses Papers in the Rare Book and Manuscripts Division at the New York Public Library. Edmund Wilson discusses the case with his usual insight in *Apologies to the Iroquois*, first published as a series of *New Yorker* essays in 1959 and later as a book (Syracuse University Press, 1992). And no one can discuss Robert Moses outside the shadow cast by Robert Caro's monumental biography *The Power Broker: Robert Moses and the Fall of New York* (Knopf, 1974). Caro wrote without benefit of the papers now held by the NYPL, and the biography has its blind spots—most notably Moses's work outside New York City. While I am skeptical about recent attempts to cast Moses in a rosy light, it may be time for a new biography that grapples with the many contradictions of this complex man—though Caro's will always be a brilliant character study and a great read.

The pages dedicated to illumining Love Canal would fill the canal itself many times over. The Niagara Falls Public Library in New York has a section dedicated to clippings files, legal documents, information pamphlets, and government studies. In addition, my main resources were Lois Gibbs, *Love Canal: My Story* (State University of New York Press, 1982) and *Love Canal: The Story Continues* (New Society, 1998); and Thomas Fletcher, *From Love Canal to Environmental Justice: The Politics of Hazardous Waste on the Canada-U.S. Border* (Broadview Press, 2003). Fire chief Edwin Foster's 1964 letter is quoted in Russell Mokhiber's and Leonard Shen's essay "Love Canal" in *Who's Poisoning America: Corporate Polluters and their Victims in the Chemical Age*, eds. Ralph Nader, Ronald Brownstein and John Richard (Sierra Club, 1981): 273. The Environmental Protection Agency Site Description, Reviews and Records of Decision are available through the EPA's CERCLIS database at http://cfpub.epa.gov/supercpad/cursites/srchsites.cfm. Perhaps the most gripping document is the official New York State report written by Michael Zweig and Gordon Boyd, *The Federal Connection: A History of U.S. Military Involvement in the Toxic Contamination of Love Canal and the Niagara Falls Region* (Report to the New York State Assembly Speaker, 1981). I am grateful to Ralph Krieger for making me a copy of this report, and to Michael Zweig for talking to me by phone about it.

Many thanks to Paul Gromosiak for his help here and elsewhere. I owe a special debt to Norm Stessing for making sure I understood exactly how his power plant works, though I wish he had agreed to turn the Falls off for me, just for a minute.

SEVEN: SENTIMENT IN LIQUID FORM

There's one scholarly study of honeymoons at Niagara, Karen Dubinsky's fun book *The Second Greatest Disappointment* (Between the Lines, 1999). In the cataract of Marilyn exposés and hagiographies, Sarah Churchwell's *The Many Lives of Marilyn Monroe* is a beacon of intelligence (Henry Holt, 2004). I also used Ernest Cunningham, *The Ultimate Marilyn* (Renaissance Books, 1998). Photographer Jock Carroll's *Falling for Marilyn* (Friedman/Fairfax, 1996) is an indispensable photographic essay about Marilyn's trip to the Falls.

The text that launched the idea of femininity as a performance is Joan Riviere's "Womanliness as a Masquerade," published in the *International Journal of Psychoanalysis* 10 (1929); central to thinking today is Judith Butler's *Gender Trouble: Feminism and the Subversion of Identity* (Routledge, 1990).

For the history of honeymoons, I consulted Chrys Ingraham, *White Weddings: Romancing Heterosexuality in Popular Culture* (Routledge, 1999); Kris Bulcroft, Linda Smeins and Richard Bulcroft, *Romancing the Honeymoon: Consummating Marriage in Modern Society* (SAGE Publications, 1999); Martha Saxton, "The Bliss Business: Institutionalizing the American Honeymoon," *American Heritage* 29:4 (June-July 1978); and Elizabeth McKinsey, "The Honeymoon Trail to Niagara Falls," *Prospects* 9 (1984). Rebecca Mead's incisive *One Perfect Day: The Selling of the American Wedding* (Penguin, 2007) came out as I was editing the book; it deepened my feelings about the commodified nature of the American wedding and honeymoon.

Special thanks to Carol Castelli at the Red Hat Society for making my conference attendance possible, to Sue Ellen Cooper and Linda Murphy for generously granting interviews, and to Constable Allen A. Rodgers, who gave me new respect for the many talents of the Royal Canadian Mounted Police. O Canada!

EIGHT: THE BOMB AND TOM BROKAW'S DESK

For the toxic histories of Niagara County sites, I used the Environmental Protection Agency's very handy online CERCLIS database, which allows you to access site documents about any EPA-listed site. Although as a rule I distrust online research, this resource is fantastic and should be a regular part of your life.

For the history of the Manhattan Project, I used Jeff Hughes, *The Manhattan Project: Big Science and the Atom Bomb* (Columbia

University Press, 2002); and Robert S. Norris, *Racing for the Bomb: General Leslie R. Groves, the Manhattan Project's Indispensable Man* (Steerforth Press, 2002). The history of private contractors in the Manhattan Project was detailed in Peter Eisler's multipart report "Poisoned Workers, Poisoned Places" in *USA Today*, which began on June 24, 2001. James Maroncelli and Timothy Karpin's CD-ROM book *The Traveler's Guide to Nuclear Weapons* (Historical Odysseys, 2002) was a great resource, as were the authors, to whom I offer many thanks for answering endless queries about atomic history and the workings of nuclear bombs.

The history of the Rochester medical experiments was covered in the media and is surveyed in Eileen Welsome, *The Plutonium Files* (Delacorte, 1999). For the history and ongoing remediation of the Lake Ontario Ordnance Works and the Niagara Falls Storage Site, I utilized the wall of documents deposited at the Lewiston Public Library by the Army Corps of Engineers. Linde's letter explaining their decision to dump effluent in shallow wells appears as exhibit 3 in the appendix to *The Federal Connection*.

Most of all, I want to extend real gratitude to the people who so generously shared their stories, some of whom appear in the chapter and some of whom, for space reasons, do not: thanks to Ralph Krieger for spending an entire day showing me around, to Dan and Harry Wiest for finding time in their busy lives to tell me about themselves, to Reverend Charles Lamb and Lou Ricciuti for discussing environmental issues, to Professor Joseph Gardella at SUNY Buffalo for explaining chemistry to me—or at least trying to—and Professor Joseph Bieron at Canisius College for helping me understand the region's industrial legacy. I am grateful to Amy Witryol and Vince Agnello, activists, and Bill Kowalewski, Judy Leithner, Joan Morrissey and Bruce Sanders of the Corps of Engineers for discussing the LOOW site with me.

NINE: BOULEVARD OF BROKEN DREAMS

Patrick McGreevy's *Imagining Niagara* (University of Massachusetts Press, 1994) looks at themes of death and the future at Niagara. Echota is discussed in Leland M. Roth, "Three Industrial

Towns by McKim, Mead & White," *Journal of the Society of Architectural Historians* 38:4 (December 1979), and in an article by John Bogart in *Cassier's* "Niagara Power" issue. For discussion of the transformation of urban planning mid-century, I am indebted to the essays in *Robert Moses and the Modern City: The Transformation of New York*, eds. Hilary Ballon and Kenneth T. Jackson (W. W. Norton, 2007).

Canadian development of the Niagara Peninsula is surveyed in *Niagara's Changing Landscapes*, ed. Hugh Gayler (Carleton University Press, 1994). The Niagara Falls (Ontario) Public Library has a copy of the Urban Strategies, Inc., final report, *Niagara Falls Tourist Area Development Strategy.* The visitor survey I quote from is the *Niagara Falls Visitor Study Final Report* by Research Resolutions (1998). Ernest Sternberg's illuminating paper, "The Iconography of the Tourism Experience" appears in *Annals of Tourism Research* 24:4 (1997).

The Niagara Falls Public Library is the source for most of the New York side's master plans; USA Niagara's plan and updates on its progress can be found at their Web site: www.usaniagara.com.

David Lempert at the Bureau of Labor Statistics provided essential numbers. Chris Schoepflin managed to be both honest and diplomatic. The acerbic yet kind E. R. (Bob) Baxter III offered me a window to the Niagara I never had the chance to see, and kept me apprised of developments on the parkway issue. For the record, I have eaten donuts with him and he did not get crumbs in his beard.

EPILOGUE: THE VOICE OF THE LANDSCAPE

One of the most respected Niagara scholars is Elizabeth McKinsey, whose *Niagara Falls: Icon of the American Sublime* (Cambridge, 1985) traces the development of an American artistic sublime through representations of the Falls. It was useful to me here and elsewhere in the book when considering the waterfall's history as iconic image. Other books I consulted on Niagara and its images are Anthony Bannon's *The Taking of Niagara: A History of the Falls in Photography* (Media Studio, 1982); and

Jeremy Ellwell Adamson, *Niagara: Two Centuries of Changing Attitudes* (Corcoran Gallery of Art, 1985). Simon Schama's quote about landscape comes from his magisterial study *Landscape and Memory* (Knopf, 1995): 6.

Archives, manuscripts, museums, books and articles in obscure scholarly journals are all essential to understanding a subject as big as Niagara, but they will only get you so far. I could not have written this book without the help and forbearance of countless people. Mark Crispin Miller started me along the road to a book. Richard Fox gave me excellent feedback on an early outline. My agent, Nat Sobel, believed in the book before it was a book. Hal Clifford, friend and editor extraordinaire, helped me figure out what I was saying and why. Heidi Julavits went at one chapter hammer and tongs. At Simon & Schuster, Sydny Miner tirelessly shepherded the manuscript through the publishing process and patiently put up with my angst.

Sarah Zimmerman provided research advice, long conversations about landscape, and moral support, usually straight up with an olive. Anne-Lise François taught me to think harder about nature. Robin Haueter, Lisa Lerner and James Wallenstein generously offered comments. Pawel Wojtasik was both accomplice and muse. Darcy Haylor and Miranda Strand provided first-rate research assistance along with a never-ending stream of salt and vinegar chips and Cadbury bars. And Robert Brown let himself be marched around the Niagara Gorge, lectured at the Power Vista, misted at the Whirlpool Rapids, splattered on the *Maid of the Mist*, and drenched at the Cave of the Winds. He also bought me a car. Thanks, Bob, and I'm sorry about the gash on the side. But that mural—you've really got to see it with me one day.

Index

New York State:
  anti-slavery societies in, 115–16
  casino gambling in, 276, 282–83
  and Indian lands, 54
  murder penalty in, 163
  and Treaty of Utrecht, 25
New York State Department of Environmental Protection, 224
New York State Office of Parks, Recreation, and Historic Preservation, 98, 146, 147, 181, 191, 270
New York State Parks Council, 176
New York State Scenic Trails Association, 209
New York State Survey, 142–43, 148
New York Sun, 66
New York Times, The, 131
New York Tribune, 154–55
Niagara (Berton), 73, 112, 133, 199
Niagara (film), 198–99, 214–15
Niagara (Moore), 295
Niagara Book, The, 71–72
Niagara County Anti-Slavery Society, 115
Niagara Diversion Treaty (1950), 159, 162, 165, 176, 180, 190
Niagara Escarpment, 270
Niagara Experience Center, 278–79
Niagara Falls, 3
  American Falls, *see* American Falls
  bird-nesting habitats, 170, 298
  Bridal Veil Falls, 47, 69, 169
  bypass routes around, 18
  and control of trade, 21–22, 172–73
  and erosion, 173–74, 193
  evolving image of, 8, 247, 255–56, 296–97
  first published picture of, 294–95
  fish-spawning areas, 170, 298
  going behind, 69, 80, 85, 93
  going over, 65–69, 74, 108–10, 130, 131, 133–34, 300
  going to, 45–50, 60–61

guidebooks to, 5, 6, 10, 17, 27, 28, 34, 35, 38, 48, 49, 52–53, 65, 69, 72, 79, 98, 112, 144, 167, 178–79, 296
height of, 4, 294
Hermit's Cascade, 158, 166
as honeymoon spot, 203–4, 206–7, 210, 213–15, 219–21
Horseshoe Falls, *see* Horseshoe Falls
maps, x, xi
as natural wonder, 5, 52, 172, 175–76, 178, 195–97, 241, 254, 259, 268, 273, 292, 296–97, 301–2
observation deck, 49
reshaping of, 5–6, 7, 47, 48, 49–50, 135, 170, 178, 191–92, 193–94, 195, 198, 255
as sacred place, 49
and tourism, 50, 52, 63, 64–71, 80, 95, 98–99, 141, 144, 159, 167–68, 178, 192, 203, 258, 259–60, 262, 263–64, 272–75, 277, 280, 284, 285
turning them down or off, 166, 168–70, 171, 175, 177, 193, 197, 255
turning them on, turning them up, 158–59, 164–67
volume of water over, 4, 60, 158–59, 170, 175, 190–91, 194, 255, 294–95
water diversions from, 48, 69, 155, 159, 161, 173, 175, 178, 180, 195
and water power, *see* water power
Niagara Falls (film), 209, 210
"Niagara Falls" (song), 203
Niagara Falls, New York:
  Chamber of Commerce, 209–10
  commercial development of, 60, 71, 80, 140, 141, 143, 155–57, 175, 178–79, 258, 262–64, 267–70